The Hat in the Ring Gang

The Combat History of the 94th Aero Squadron in World War I

Also by Charles Woolley

FIRST TO THE FRONT: THE 95TH AERO SQUADRON 1917-1918

UNIFORMS & EQUIPMENT OF THE IMPERIAL GERMAN ARMY 1900-1918 (*two volumes*)

THE KAISER'S ARMY IN COLOR: UNIFORMS OF THE IMPERIAL GERMAN ARMY AS ILLUSTRATED BY CARL BECKER • 1890-1910

The Hat in the Ring Gang

The Combat History of the 94th Aero Squadron in World War I

Charles Woolley

Schiffer Military History
Atglen, PA

Dust jacket and aircraft profile artwork by S.W. Ferguson, Colorado Springs, CO.

THE WORTH OF WENTWORTH

On May 27, 1918, 1st Lts. Douglas Campbell and John Wentworth were on a voluntary patrol at 3000 meters over the lines near Montsec, France. Campbell spotted three single-seaters below them and leaving Wentworth as cover he dove on the Germans, firing some eighty rounds – he fired thirty rounds at the closest and then turned on the other two. One enemy aircraft did a reinversement to escape allowing Campbell to fire fifty rounds into the other which was diving away. A moment later Campbell turned and saw a machine falling in two or three pieces. Thanks to Wentworth's protection, Campbell scored his fourth victory. More on the mission can be found at the end of chapter three.

Dedication

To NNW, who during the writing of this book not only did all the word processing and editing, but also unselfishly took on the responsibility for making sure we got over some rather serious bumps in the road. All my love and thanks. C.W.

Book design by Robert Biondi.

Copyright © 2001 by Charles Woolley.
Library of Congress Catalog Number: 2001089020.

All rights reserved. No part of this work may be reproduced or used in any forms or by any means – graphic, electronic or mechanical, including photocopying or information storage and retrieval systems – without written permission from the copyright holder.

"Schiffer," "Schiffer Publishing Ltd. & Design," and the "Design of pen and ink well" are registered trademarks of Schiffer Publishing, Ltd.

Printed in China.
ISBN: 0-7643-1427-0

We are always looking for people to write books on new and related subjects. If you have an idea for a book, please contact us at the address below.

Published by Schiffer Publishing Ltd.
4880 Lower Valley Road
Atglen, PA 19310
Phone: (610) 593-1777
FAX: (610) 593-2002
E-mail: Schifferbk@aol.com.
Visit our web site at: www.schifferbooks.com
Please write for a free catalog.
This book may be purchased from the publisher.
Please include $3.95 postage.
Try your bookstore first.

In Europe, Schiffer books are distributed by:
Bushwood Books
6 Marksbury Ave.
Kew Gardens
Surrey TW9 4JF
England
Phone: 44 (0)208 392-8585
FAX: 44 (0)208 392-9876
E-mail: Bushwd@aol.com.
Free postage in the UK. Europe: air mail at cost.
Try your bookstore first.

Contents

Acknowledgments

To write this history of an American Aero Squadron which existed some eighty-two years ago is a challenging task. Today there are no survivors, little previously written material of any degree of accuracy, but there are pockets of priceless material to be found if one has a notion of where to search. The United States Archives holds the *History of the American Air Service, A.E.F.*, known to researchers as the Gorrell Report; the United States Air Force Museum in Ohio has become a repository and treasure trove for much material from the participants themselves, photos, letters, and memorabilia; the Hoover Institute, the Smithsonian, and the Airman's Museum all have bits and pieces of the mosaic which makes the job of putting the picture together somewhat easier and my thanks to them for their past assistance.

Another real and important source of information which gives a deeper richness to the story are those fellow World War I Aero historians who over the years have unselfishly shared with me much of the fruits of their research. To mention a few: Alan Toelle with whom I have been swapping information for 30 years is a world authority on World War I aircraft camouflage, markings, serial numbers, and what pilot flew what plane. He has been most helpful and generous to a fault. Ted Hamady, who knows more about Nieuport 28s than Nieuport design engineers, has contributed to the cause. Greg Van Wyngarden has provided information from the German perspective. Nancy Graham, who from her vast aeronautical library, loaned me a copy of the rare volume containing Ham Coolidge's war letters. Ray McGuire, who 34 years ago rekindled my boyhood interest, is still a military history bookseller in Maine. To all of the other World War I aviation affecianados whom I have known over the years, I offer my utmost thanks. Lastly, my gratitude to Bob Biondi, friend and editor, who encourages me to write books on military matters, and allows me to incorporate the artistic skills of guys like Steve Ferguson to paint dust jackets and color profiles.

The subject of photographs and, more importantly their credit, should be addressed at this point, the author taking the following position. Photos which were taken by the original participants in 1917 and 1918 were widely shared among squadron mates, as well as interested friends and members of other squadrons. We must remember the United States Air Service was a very small group and most of those who made it to the front knew one another from training and other pre-front duties.

When one studies the various pilots albums held privately and in museums, the same pictures are duplicated in many of them. This is a question of "the chicken and the egg" as to who actually took the pictures, and then by either largess or request shared them with others. Occasionally one finds a few pictures in a given period album which are unique to it and therefore might be assumed to be credited to the album creator.

Early pre-World War II collectors of photos like Charles Donald and others found their sources, including the United States Archives and the Signal Corps pictures. They had them copied or printed by the Archives and then signed, when applicable, by the surviving pilots. Later many of these photos were bought, sold, and traded, and in so doing the seller often took credit for some and lost the identity of the original source on others. Therefore, photo credits should be given to all those who originally took the pictures and thought enough of the originals to share them with others at the time, and thanks of appreciation should go to all the many public and private institutions who continue to share their holdings of these treasures with today's researchers.

Many of the pictures seen here I copied in the 1960s and early 1970s from albums located at the United States Air Force Museum, United States Archives, National Air & Space Museum, Smithsonian, and some that were still in the hands of the original owners like Doug Campbell, Joe Dawson, Sumner Sewall, Jim Knowles, Bill Casgrain and from my own father's album.

H. Hugh Wynne in California was more than generous in sharing with me his vast collection which was amassed from many sources, as did Peter Kilduff, Alan Toelle, the late Tim Miller, and Bob Cavanaugh, and so many other World War I aero historians. My thanks to you all.

1

Forming Up - Texas to Toul

The 94th Aero Squadron, like many of the other early American Air Service squadrons, had its humble beginnings at Kelly Field, Texas being officially formed on August 20, 1917. At the end of September, after their basic training finished, the enlisted men began the long journey to the front, first to Mineola, Long Island, then to the troop ship *Adriatic* that took them to Liverpool. By train they traveled to Southampton, across the Channel to Le Havre, arriving on November 13, 1917. The Squadron at this point in time was without any pilots, some of whom by chance had traveled, untrained and unassigned, on the same ship on their way to the French flying school at Tours, and later to the American aviation complex at Issoudun.

Upon arrival in France, the enlisted men were broken up into seven detachments and then assigned to various engine or airframe factories to learn their basic trade firsthand. After completion of this training, they were sent to the mud, mire and confusion of the embryonic American training center at Issoudun where, among other duties, they were pressed into the lowly construction work of hangars and barracks.

Most of the pilots-to-be were sent to the French basic flight school at Tours where they learned to master the docile and usually forgiving Caudron G3s and the clipped wing Bleriot *Penguins*. Learning to fly with instructors speaking only French, which was incomprehensible to most, and being directed in the air with a short slap on the right shoulder to turn right; the same on the left shoulder for a left turn; a pull on the exterior side of the coat while turning meant "redress the machine and put yourself in normal flying position" was not easy at first. One command sure to get the student's attention was "a knock on the helmet means 'Let go all commands and turn around so as to look at the instructor.'" Further, light pressure in the middle of the back meant the machine was climbing too much, so push forward on the stick; and finally a pull backwards on the coat meant "the machine was inclined too much toward the ground 'so pull slightly on the stick'." These quaint instructions appeared in a booklet entitled *Military Aviation, Flying School of Tours, Instruction for the American Pupils."*

Also printed on the first page of the booklet was the daily schedule, from dawn to dusk, for the students to follow:

"Morning Call	4 o'clock, A.M.
Morning Work	4h.30[1]
Lunch	10h.30
Rest	from 12 heures until 4:30 P.M.
Dinner	4:30 P.M.
Conference	5:15 P.M. until 6:00 P.M.
Afternoon Work	from 6:00 P.M. until night"

The students were awarded their French wings upon completing the conditions of the *Military Brevet of Aviation* which were to include the following:

"(a) spiral glide from 500 meters with the motor stopped;

(b) two journeys of 60 kilometers; (minimum) go and return with landings on different grounds to be made each of both between the sun rise and the sunset;

(c) two different triangular journeys of 200 kilometers to be effectuated each in two consecutive days for the utmost *with focaltatif* intermediary landing during one of the two triangles. One of these two triangles can be replaced by a straight line of 150 kilometers to be made without any intermediary landing.

(d) A test of height, consisting in "one hour flight" at 2,000 meters (this test can be made during one of the trips of 200 or 150 kilometers); or: two ascents of two thousand meters independently executed of the above tests with the obligation to remain a minimum of 10 minutes at a minimal height of 2,000 meters;

(e) To have a proved minimum of 50 landings flying alone;

(f) To have a proved minimum of 25 hours of flight time (time of the trials for the military brevet included)."

These conditions are included here in the exact wording as they appeared in the *Instructions for the American Pupils* and upon completion of these requirements, the student was awarded his wings and a brevet as a "Pilote-Aviateur" by the "Fédération Aéronautique International-France." At the time the first Americans were receiving these brevets, which was confirmed by a small pocket-sized blue leather bound folder, the sequential numbering of the document was around 8900-9000, so only that number had been awarded totally since the beginning of licensed flight in France.

Once graduated from the basic school at Tours, the advanced training for the American "Pilote-Aviateurs" was conducted at the various fields at Issoudun and at each field the level of difficulty increased, finally graduating as a "Chasse", or pursuit pilot.

There were two future 94th pilots, Douglas Campbell and Hamilton Coolidge, who sailed over on the *Ordina* with many of the other men who went to Toul, but who ended up doing administrative duties as well as their basic and advanced training at Issoudun. Interestingly, the positive futures of Campbell and Coolidge was predicted by fellow *Ordina* passenger, Waldo Heinrichs, in his diary entry at sea Wednesday, August 8. He wrote "Ham Coolidge and Doug Campbell, the two best aviators to be, as far as I can size them up, and I spent some time polishing up our boots and puttees and indulging in the two subjects of speculation that are occupying us: (1) where we are going and all about our flying experience; (2) when we are to land and how we are to proceed from there." Heinrichs went on to train at Tours, then to Issoudun, and was a member of the first flyers of the 95th Aero Squadron to hit the front.

1st Lt. Douglas Campbell writes of his training experiences which were well beyond the norm in a series of letters home, from September 30 to December 4:[2]

"Sunday, Sept. 30, 1917

Things are looking brighter! We expect to leave here Friday for that place you guessed in your last letter, and we expect to start about 10 days after that. It is to be an advanced school with pretty fast equipment, so Capt. Miller[3] says he will try to arrange for me to get my elementary work at a French school about 20 miles southwest of there, on slower apparatus. If all goes well I ought to be hopping every day within ten days.

Also, the Chief of our department is reported to have said yesterday that he didn't want us to be tied up in administrative jobs any longer than necessary, for it was important that we get out training and get to the front as soon as possible. That is certainly good news to us!

Yesterday I saw some splendid flying. Two machines of new types were racing each other, looping, tail-spinning, and trying to see how close they could come to roofs of hangars without hitting them.

This morning we had to get up and down to the office by 8 o'clock to be mustered for payroll. On the way back to the hotel, we ran across a man who was carrying small baskets and yelling "Petits fraises!" at the top of his voice. We immediately piled on him and each bought a basket of his wild strawberries. Then Ham and Bill Ely and I discovered a butter-eggs-and-cheese store and bought some thick cream and some sugar. We certainly had *some* breakfast at the hotel.

Our commissions are still almost here, as they have been for almost two weeks. Last week they were sent to this office for the third time when only twice was necessary, and Lord knows what has happened to them now. The system is fearfully and wonderfully made. Apparently the examining board, which is the only body which ever sees the candidates, has less to say about it than anyone else. I hope they'll arrive before next Friday, because if we are to be on the administrative staff at the school, it wouldn't be very effective to arrive at the school as a private and not become an officer until after everyone had got used to seeing you as an enlisted man. But I'm not kicking, for it won't do any good, and if I can get my training I'd just as leave be a water-carrier if necessary.

Must stop and do a little work. Sunday isn't always a day of no work.

France, Sunday, Oct. 7, 1917

We didn't start south on Friday as planned, for there were various matters that could not be finished to our satisfaction until last night. The Captain is leaving today, and Ham and I will go tomorrow; Eddie Bates is to remain here for a few days to see that our supplies get shipped. We are not going to trust to railroad service, but are having everything urgent sent down on trucks. If we open the 15th, we have a hard week ahead of us.

All of us received our commissions as First Lieutenants on Wednesday the 3rd, were sworn in that evening and appeared all dressed up on Thursday morning. It really was very pleasant to be considered a gentleman and to feel like one again after having been more or less of a tramp and office boy for many weeks; although we had been treated splendidly by most of the officers here, as an enlisted man you feel decidedly inferior to any officer. I think our having been enlisted, however, makes us appreciate better the privileges *and* duties of an officer.

Five of our number leave this morning to take charge of detachments and get their own training in a well-known island which I traveled across 8 weeks ago. I am hoping to make arrangements to start training this week at the place I spoke of in my last letter (Ch——x).

I received your draft for Fr. 577, for which I am much obliged. I have plenty of money now, and since I can't spend much at camp and will be closer to the French people, I hope to carry out your instructions as to charity, which I have been unable to do here. My pay will be about $185 per month for the present, and about $220 monthly when I have officially become what I came over here to be, so I should have no trouble in doing it, unless it arises from being too busy to spend enough time on it.

Conditions at camp will probably not be too pleasant at first, as it will be quite cold and extremely muddy when it rains. But we have some nice barracks ready, and I have spent quite a lot on high trench boots, coats, and other things, so don't worry about my taking care of myself. The government will furnish us with flying suits that have fur linings, electric heaters, hot and cold running water, elevators, fireless cookers, and all sorts of things.

No letters this week; the boat they are on must be spending a week or two in Halifax.

October 21, 1917

Last Monday I began my flying instruction on a double-controlled Nieuport, 23 sq. meters wing surface, 80 H.P. Le Rhone motor. Sgt. Billiet, an excellent instructor, has been training me, and I have been up every day since Monday except Thursday, when it was raining. We go up for three circuits in the morning and three in the afternoon, totaling about _ hour per day in the air. It is the most fascinating and absorbing game I have ever tackled; it is a real problem which involves eyes, ears, nerves, delicate touch, a lot of brain, and a sixth sense which is called "air sense," which consists in knowing, by feeling the machine, whether it is in the right position or not. I am now going through the stage of discouragement which every student experiences at various times. Day before yesterday I thought I was pretty good, but yesterday I discovered that I wasn't. All the men who are flyers tell me it is a good sign, for when you get so you know something is wrong, you are well on the road toward doing it right. Billiet is a corking moniteur: when the air is calm, he takes his hands off the stick and lets me see that they are off, and since I can feel the pressure of the rudder on my right foot, I know I am doing it all. Then if I am doing something wrong which does not need instant correction, he signals with his hands so I can do it myself. I am still unable to do very well with the landings, but hope to learn soon. Capt. Pellissier says I am doing very well, particularly as I am learning on the machine on which French pilots are perfected *after* they have flown for some time alone on slower avions.

On Friday I fooled them all. One of the difficult things with piloting a Nieuport is getting off the ground. They have a long, rather heavy fuselage (or body), and when you are starting off the tail tries to swing to one side or the other, and if you don't stop it by using your rudder, the machine will swing around. This is called a "cheval de bois", and will sometimes tip you over and smash the machine before you leave the ground. The rudder movements must sort of anticipate the swing, for if you correct a swing to the right and leave the rudder hard over, you will have a cheval de bois to the left. In order to train pilots against cheval de bois, they have "rouleurs", or "penguins", little monoplanes with wings clipped short, so they can't leave the ground. These rouleurs are much more touchy than a regular airplane, and generally go around in circles, turn over, smash up, or do most anything the first time you try to run one. Well, on Friday they decided to let me smash the first rouleur, so I got in one, had the motor started, received last instructions, and started off. The other fellows and the French pilots expected to see me spin around and do everything else, and were expecting at least a good laugh if not an accident. To their great, and my even greater, surprise, I found the rudder work easy and the elevator manipulation nearly so, and ran the fool thing in almost a straight line. The next time, I tried it faster, and that went well too. When I stopped, I was informed that I had "roule comme un as." If I can only improve my air work and landing now, I may fly in a little while.

This morning's mist seems to be starting to burn off a bit, so I'll have to stop and "aller chercher" my air togs.

Well, I feel happier today than I have for some time. On Thursday afternoon my moniteur in the double control pronounced me ready for solo work; but Friday we had bad weather, so I didn't try it that day. Yesterday about noon the fog lifted to about 300 meters, and flying began at 1:30. The French chief pilot, who was worried about me, insisted on my taking one more ride in double control, and as luck would have it, I made a perfect landing. After waiting around for half an hour or so while the single control machines were brought out, I heard my name called, and was told to take machine No. 15. I climbed in, fastened the strap securely, received last instructions from the chief pilot (he was pretty scared by this time, for, according to him, it is the first time in France that anyone has done his first flying in a machine of that speed), and told the mechanic to start the motor. About six other students held the wings while I tested the motor, which turned up beautifully; then I throttled it down, and they left the machine free. The chief pilot signaled me to start, I pulled back on the throttle lever, and off I went. The machine felt surprisingly lighter, with only one person in it, and left the ground very quickly. When I got into the air, I felt as if I had been there all my life. It didn't seem very difficult, for the air was reasonably calm, and the avion practically flew itself. I made a tour of the field just under the "ceiling" (clouds), making turns to the left. It was a most exhilarating feeling to be in absolute control of the machine, and is the best fun I ever had. I didn't really know whether I would judge the field just right on landing or not, but managed to land within three or four hundred feet of the place I tried to hit. The landing was nothing to write home about, as it was rather bumpy, but I didn't break anything. I took another ride for a few minutes later, but the landing wasn't much better.

The chief pilot had a grin on from one ear to the other, and said he felt very much relieved. I'm not a flyer yet by any means, you understand, but at least I have passed the first test on a fairly difficult machine.

Thursday, Nov. 22, 1917

Rather funny, my writing in the middle of the week, isn't it? I am in charge of flying records, and there hasn't been any flying for two days on account of fog, so I'm not very busy.

I have had all kinds of luck. On Monday, I had three trips in the large machine I learned on, and all the starts and landings were perfect, so I was pronounced ready for the next class. Tuesday morning I started on a machine having about 45 sq. ft. less wing surface, and which goes considerably faster. I found it really a lot easier to fly and land, although I had myself pretty well scared once. The first machine I took up was badly adjusted, so that it tried to tip to the right all the time, and when I made a right turn I felt a violent wind in the side of my face, and discovered that I was side slipping. A wood of evergreens seemed to be jumping up to meet me, so that altogether it was a bit annoying. But I caught myself before I had fallen more than 50 or 75 feet, and after that it went fine, except that when I was gliding down my goggles were too loose, and were flapping all over my face. The landing was perfect, however, and I borrowed some better ones before going up again.

In the afternoon I had 7 trips, and all the landings were perfect. I tried some vertical turns, that is, sharp turns with the machine banked up so that the wings were vertical rather than horizontal; but it was really a bit dangerous, as the clouds prevented my going higher than 1000 feet, so I contented myself with only 2 or 3. After my 6th landing, I was pronounced ready to take up the scout the next day. I am crazy to fly it, for it is said to handle very delicately, and it lands quite rapidly, but the last two days have been foggy, so I haven't had my chance yet. Imagine flying a 110 miles per hour machine after having had only 2 hours experience alone in the air! It sounds absurd, but the monitors say I am ready for it, and I am perfectly confident that I can fly it.

Ken's packages of shredded wheat and chocolate are arriving regularly, and are certainly appreciated. I would object to using shipping space for luxuries, but I think anything edible has a right to come over here if it wants to.

In my last letter I was so wild on the subject of flying, that I forgot to tell you of the party we had a week ago last Sunday. Capt. Miller, Cord Meyer, Ham Coolidge, and I had Sunday dinner at the chateau of General Exelman, about 30 miles from here. It was a chateau built in the late 1400s, fitted up and improved in splendid taste. The General and his wife set us up to a perfectly wonderful meal, with all kinds of hors d'oeuvres and three meat courses, not to mention about four kinds of wine, including champagne and most delicious burgundy. These French people certainly are sensible in their method of drinking. They give you small amounts of different kinds of wines that they have had in the cellar for about 50 years, and they drink it just as one would eat a particularly rare dish of some sort.

There were 3 or 4 very attractive young ladies present, one of whom made a tremendous hit with Ham. Our French was really quite adequate for the occasion, and also improved a great deal in the process of the afternoon. We discovered a landing field near the place, so we are expecting Ham to have a "panne de chateau" when he makes a cross-country flight. "(Panne = breakdown or motor failure)."

The General's grandfather was one of Napoleon's Marechals and the General took great pride in showing us many interesting relics, among which was an epaulet worn by Nap. at Waterloo.

Hooray! Clouds are breaking up. Hope they'll be all gone in the morning.

Friday: Flew the scout 3 times this morning. It surely is a bird! Climbs like thunder, goes to beat h—l, and is tricky to land. (*Note: Campbell is referring to the Nieuport 24, 15 sq. meters wing surface.)*

Dec. 1, 1917

Can't remember when I last wrote; about Tuesday, I guess. Thanksgiving was a holiday at this post, which was a crime, because the weather was flyable. Yesterday it was punk again, except late in the p.m., and there was a monthly muster going on, so there was no flying then. This morning it cleared up at about 10, and we flew for an hour and a half. I was the first man up in the scout class and it sure was pretty. There was still a slight mist up to 100 meters, so that below that point you could see the ground but couldn't see out to the sides; but it only took a few seconds to roar up through that, and above that the air was perfectly clear as far as the ceiling, which was at about 1200 meters. I had 4 rides, the last one fairly long, and 3 of the landings were pretty good. The scout is hard to land, it is so light and so delicate on the elevator control.

This afternoon we didn't fly, because some big gun came down from Paris to inspect this post (I wish we didn't have so many military interruptions, but I think that was the last for awhile); but I am still a good grafter even in this line of activity, and am as keen after flights as I used to be after auto rides when I was a kid. This morning when flying stopped, I noticed that one of the little scouts was laid up with a broken shock absorber, and as it was on a field quite distant from the hangars, I immediately chased up the engineering office *(Note: Probably Eddie Rickenbacker)* and asked if I could fly it back when it was fixed. He said O.K., so this p.m. at 3 I went out, found three mechanics who had fixed it, inspected the wires, planes, landing gear, etc., climbed in, and started off. The sky was entirely overcast, but the air below the ceiling was clear as crystal, and I could see for miles. This is the first time I had been free from the restrictions necessarily placed on one when flying in classes, so I decided to have some good fun. I climbed until I hit the clouds (1300 meters by the altimeter), and then did a couple of "vrilles." To do this you cut the motor, stall the machine by pointing it up, and then throw the rudder and ailerons to the same side. The machine hovers a moment, then falls nose down, turning rapidly on the wing tip as a pivot. After it has turned a few times, you put all controls in neutral and wait. In a very short time the whirling ceases, and you find yourself diving down vertically; then all you have to do is pull back on the stick gradually so as not to wreck the wings by subjecting them to too great a strain, and turn on the motor, and the machine is flying level again. It sure is fun, but it would be dangerous under 600 meters, for you lose altitude very rapidly. I also tried some vertical turns, but find I need much more practice on them, for they are very difficult to do without losing altitude by slipping sidewise.

The end of my flight was quite dramatic and decidedly satisfactory. I cut the motor at 700 meters and took a straight glide to the landing T (a white canvas T with the cross-bar against the wind). By rare good luck I made a perfect landing within 25 yards of the T, and then discovered that the Chief Pilot, the post commander, several French pilots, and a visiting officer from the French War Office were watching me. Capt. Pellissier (Chief Pilot) had been wondering who the pilot was, and was simply tickled to death when said person crawled out of his helmet and goggles and proved to be the most inexperienced flyer in the school.

I don't entirely approve of talking about myself and my flying, particularly as an aviator who does most of his flying with his mouth is more or less of a sin to be avoided; but probably you don't mind it, and I must say that I have never been so satisfied with myself as I am after flying. I have for some months considered this particular machine I'm flying as something I could never reach, and to be able to fly it passably well is a great satisfaction. Fortunately for me, I am at the same time able to realize that I still have a long way to go to become an expert, but to have got this far is something.

When I write you, I wish I had Wad's[4] ability to describe events and sensations accurately so I could let you know something about the joys of flying. As soon as you get into the machine, every single worry you ever had – and we've had some here – simply vanishes. When you open the throttle, and the tremendous power sets you in motion, you can't think about anything else, because while you are ripping along the ground you have to be on the alert so as not to swing sidewise or get your tail too high and turn over. Then when you are in the air, the panorama of this beautiful world, which looks better every time you go up, unfolds itself under you and gives you a thrill of delight which lasts for a long time. Coming down seems more like one's preconceived notion of flying than anything else, because the motor is silent, and you are simply floating down. But you don't have much time to enjoy that part of it, for you are busy picking that landing field, judging your height and distance, keeping the nose straight into the wind and, later, leveling off before the ground hits you, and keeping the wheels just off the ground while you lower the tail and make the angle of incidence greater and greater as you lose speed, until you can't stay in the air longer, and touch the ground as lightly as a feather – sometimes.

Poor old Ham tried to come home Thursday from his cross-country trip, had a forced landing, and hit a small tree with one wing tip. Didn't get a scratch himself, but the machine was all smashed up, and he has been badly kidded ever since.

Same Place, Dec. 4, 1917.

Just a short one to let you know what a lot of fun I am having. Yesterday I took an altitude test, going up to 4000 meters and remaining there 15 minutes. Started up at 7:30 a.m., when there was frost on the ground. My fingers haven't entirely recovered from the cold yet. It was great up there, though. The horizon was just the same height as ever, but gosh what an area it included!

Today, started out on my first cross-country flight, leaving at 7:40 a.m. for Tour, the place I was to have gone if I hadn't been kept in Paris. Perfectly wonderful ride; sailed along at 1000 meters, over woods, winding rivers, chateaux, and little towns, and didn't lose my way for a moment. I covered the 80-odd miles in 50 minutes, then came down in a vrille and steep spirals, making a landing 75 feet from a hangar (closer than I had intended, I must admit). The other 4 men who went over arrived a little later, and a couple of them broke tail skids or tires on landing, so I had to stay a couple of hours to make arrangements for repairs. Had the steed fed and lubricated, started back at 11, arrived here at 12:10, just in time for lunch, making perfect landing. It's surely the way to travel, – the auto is passé.

Start acrobatics tomorrow, in machines specially strengthened to avoid accident if overstrained."

December and January saw the continuation of the flight training of the pilots, both from the Tours to Issoudun group as well as those totally prepared at Issoudun. This flight training ended at the advance Field Number 5, also known as St. Valentin, and around the 25th of January they began receiving orders to the aerial gunnery school at Lake Cazeaux near Arcachon. Campbell's letter of February 3 describes the school in part:

"Grand Hotel de France

Arcachon, Feb. 3, 1918

About 8 days ago, six of us received orders to proceed to the French School of Aerial Fire to learn how to shoot from an airplane. We had a day in Paris to do a little shopping, and arrived here last Tuesday. We are living at this very comfortable but reasonable hotel, and take a truck at 6:30 each morning to the school, which is about 10 miles away on the shore of Lake C———. (Note: Etaing de Cazeaux. The other five men in the group were Thorne Taylor, John Wentworth, Bill Thompson, Bob Moore, and (perhaps) Monk Hunter). After eating French breakfast there, we are met by our special instructor, who conducts us to whatever lectures or practical work may be on the schedule. We have done some flying, but will not do any shooting until tomorrow. C——— is a beautiful place to fly. As soon as you have climbed a couple of hundred meters, you can see two lakes, the estuary at Arcachon, and several miles of Atlantic coast. The only trouble is that there is no landing field in sight except the aerodrome itself, so if you have a "panne de moteur" when you are out of gliding distance, there is nothing to land on except pine trees. This would not be very pleasant, although it has been done many times without injury to the pilot. But this condition of the terrain keeps pilots from wandering away and having "pannes de chateau", a form of diversion which consists in conveniently having a "forced" (?) landing near a prosperous looking chateau in time for lunch or just before sunset. A "pilote" is always welcome at a chateau, but I have never tried it out.

The machines we have been using are pretty punk, for they have seen a lot of service. It's good practice, though, for they are plenty strong enough, but the wings are warped a little, and they do all sorts of peculiar things. When we start shooting tomorrow, we'll get really good one.

Note: the landing field was of smooth sandy-clay soil, no grass, and in order to keep the airplanes' 'tail skids from chewing it up, they had been fitted with broad metal runners instead of the usual sharp points. This made the run-out after landing somewhat longer and more difficult to control; however, we thought we were getting to be pros, so anyone who made a cheval de bois was stuck for a bottle of champagne the next non-flying day'.)"

On March 4, the 94th pilots who had been assembled at the 3rd Aviation Instruction Center at Issoudun departed and headed by slow train to the front and Villeneuve-les-Vertus which was located some 20 miles south of Rheims, where the 95th Aero Squadron had preceded them and had arrived on February 18. The eager 94th pilots then had to wait to receive the first of their new Nieuport Type 28s. Those first officers who actually received Special Orders No. 58, March 1, 1918 assigning them to the 94th Aero Squadron, S.C., were 1st Lts. Douglas Campbell, John Wentworth, Thorne Taylor, Reed Chambers, Oscar J. Gude, William E. Loomis, C. A. Rankin, and 2nd Lts. Arthur L. Cunningham, Linn P. Cookson, Alan F. Winslow, Philip W. Davis and Charles W. Chapman.[5] This group was met at Villeneuve-les-Vertus by Major Raoul Lufbery, veteran of the Lafayette Escadrille, the leading American ace, and Lt. Henry L. Lyster who was a non-flying officer acting C. O., Lt. Charles A. Rankin, Engineering Officer, and Captain Paul H. Walters, Squadron Surgeon.

Major Gervais Raoul Lufbery was born in France, March 14, 1885. His mother, sadly, died a year after his birth; his father re-married in 1891 and immigrated to the United States. Raoul stayed in France, working in a chocolate factory and sending most of his earnings to help his father establish himself in America. In 1904, Lufbery, with a young man's eagerness to travel, left France and set off for Algiers. From there he traveled to Tunis, Egypt, Turkey, the Balkan States, Germany, South America, and finally, in 1906, to Wallingford, Connecticut to visit his father, where he remained for two years. Raoul was then off again to Cuba, New Orleans and San Francisco, where he enlisted in the United States Army. He was stationed in the Philippines for two years, and after his discharge, wandered on to China, Japan, and finally to India. There he met Marc Pourpe, a French aviator who was making a series of exhibition flights with a Blériot monoplane, which finally culminated with Pourpe's famous flight from Cairo to Khartoum and return. Lufbery became Pourpe's mechanic and traveled with him throughout the old civilizations of the East, and in 1914 returned with him to France in order to obtain a new Morane Parasol. While during this visit, war was declared. Pourpe, with no hesitation, enlisted in the French Air Service; Lufbery enlisted in the French Foreign Legion and within days somehow affected a transfer to the Air Service, joining Pourpe as his mechanic. Together they went immediately to the front.

Pourpe was killed December 4, 1914, and to avenge his friend's death which deeply affected him, Lufbery applied for and was accepted for flight training, being sent to the Aviation School at Chartres. After training, he was sent to the front with Voisin Bombardment Squadron 106. In the early spring of 1916 he was able to enroll in the school for "pilote de chasse", learning to fly Nieuports. He proved to be clumsy in his early attempts at flying the swifter single-seaters, but he prevailed and on May 24, 1916 he was sent to N. 124, the Lafayette Escadrille. His first victory was in the skies over Verdun on July 30 that beginning his long string of seventeen in total. In January 1918 he received his commission as Major, United States Air Service, and was sent to Issoudun where he restlessly waited to get to the action again. In February he was sent to Villeneuve-les-Vertus where he began his all too short association with the 94th and 1st Pursuit Group, U.S.A.A.S.

March 7 saw the arrival of Major John W. F. M. Huffer who had flown with the French, replacing Lt. Lyster as Commanding Officer, and, 1st Lts. Edward V. Rickenbacker, James A. Meissner, Seth Low, Hobart A. H. Baker, Edwin Green, Edgar G. Tobin, and Joseph H. Eastman.

Major Jean Huffer, born of French and American parents and living in Paris, enlisted in the French Foreign Legion on

September 28, 1915. He was immediately sent to the basic school at Pau, then to Cazeaux and Avord. His first assignment at the front was with Escadrille N. 95 in April, 1916, then with Escadrilles N. 62, F. 36, and back to Escadrille 62, now equipped with Spads and designated Spa. 62. His service with the French earned him the Médaille Militaire and the Croix-de-Guerre with three palms and two stars. He served in both pursuit and reconnaissance squadrons on the Western and Italian fronts. He was commissioned Major, U.S.A.A.S. on November 7, 1917; made C. O. of the 94th March 17 to June 7, 1918; Assistant Operations Officer First Pursuit Group June 7 to July 25; and then back to the front as C. O. of the 93rd Aero Squadron until the Armistice.

Lts. Low and Baker were soon re-assigned and on April 8, Major Lufbery, Capts. Kenneth Marr, David McK. Peterson and James Norman Hall, all old Lafayette hands, were formally assigned to the Squadron.

Captain Kenneth Marr was from San Francisco and had originally come to France to drive ambulances for the American Field Service in 1915-16. On July 20, 1916, he enlisted in the French Air Service and trained at Buc, Avord, Cazeaux, and Pau. He was assigned to the Lafayette Escadrille on March 29, 1917, and remained attached to Spa. 124 until February 18, 1918. Marr later was promoted to Major and served both as a flight commander and the C. O. of the 94th, finally being transferred to the United States Air Service on September 25, 1918. While with the Lafayette, Marr was awarded the Croix-de-Guerre with palm and star, attaining the final rank of *Sergent.*

David McKelvy Peterson came from Honesdale, Pennsylvania, enlisting in French Aviation October 9, 1916. He learned his early flying skills at Buc, Avord, and Pau, being brevetted on April 16, 1917. He immediately joined the Lafayette Escadrille, serving with them until February, 1918. With the French he scored three victories for which he was awarded the Croix-de-Guerre with palms and attained the rank of *Sergent*. He was a patrol leader with the Lafayette and was particularly known for his totally unflappable nature and uncanny ability to see the enemy in the air.

James Norman Hall was a native of Colfax, Iowa and was not only a soldier of fortune, but also a writer of considerable skill.[6] On August 18, 1914, he joined the 9th Volunteer Battalion, the Royal Fusiliers of the British Army. From the Royal Fusiliers he was honorably discharged on December 1, 1915; then on October 11, 1916 he enlisted in French Aviation attending schools at Buc and Avord. Winning his brevet in April, he was assigned to the Lafayette on June 16, 1917. Ten days later he was wounded in combat, not returning to action until October 3, 1917. He was assigned to Spa. 124 until February 18, 1918, attaining a final rank of *Sergent* and through his dash and bravery was awarded the Légion d'Honneur, Médaille Militaire, plus the Croix-de-Guerre with five palms.

The 94th Aero Squadron was extremely fortunate to receive this proven talent which gave them seasoned flyers at the top four jobs of Commanding Officer and the three flight leaders. Without doubt, much of the later success of the Squadron came from the experience and guidance of these men which brought to fruition the natural talents of the green pilots fresh from Issoudun.

The 94th was soon to be equipped with two batches of Nieuport 28s, the first ferried in sometime around the 11th-12th of March when Major Lufbery and Lts. Loomis, Wentworth, Taylor, Davis, Cookson, Cunningham, Chapman and Winslow were granted leave of two days to visit Paris for the purpose of "securing equipment."[7] The second batch was in the form of a gift. The 95th Aero Squadron, it was discovered, had not gone through the aerial gunnery course at Cazeaux, so they were pulled unceremoniously from the front to attend that school and their precious Nieuports were given to the gleeful 94th. This took place around March 25 much to the disgust of the 95th pilots who felt they were above such additional training, having been at the front for 38 days.

The pilots and crews of the 94th were eager to decorate their planes with some sort of specific squadron insignia in the same manner as the French squadrons had done. The squadron's medical officer, Captain Paul H. Walters, who had joined the 94th on March 1, suggested some design which would show America's entry to the war vis-à-vis Uncle Sam throwing his hat into the ring. The final design task fell to Lt. John Wentworth of Chicago, a descendent of "Long John" Wentworth, the 6 foot 6 inch first Republican mayor of that city. Wentworth was a graduate of Harvard and had studied architecture at M.I.T., so with his flair for composition the final result was the famous insignia borne by the squadron through its history, even into the 1960s when it was designated the 94th Fighter-Interceptor Squadron, part of the 1st Fighter Wing.

From Villeneuve-les-Vertus the 1st Pursuit Center moved to Epiez on March 31; the 94th moved a day later due to a hangar fire which destroyed two of their Nieuports. On April 9 they moved again to Gengoult Aerodrome located near the city of Toul, and not too distant from Nancy, from which they began operations assigned to the 8th French Army.

Doug Campbell described being assigned and equipping his new Nieuport 28, which in all likelihood, was S/N 6164 in which three days later he experienced his first trip over the lines:

"Air Service, A.E.F.
March 25, 1918

Up to day before yesterday, I was thoroughly disgusted with the outlook of things, for I had been "setting" for 2 weeks and had nothing to do. But on Saturday, I was assigned to a plane, and since then I have spent most of my waking hours in the hangar. My three mechanics have put a compass, a clock, and an altimeter in the machine under my direction, and they spent most of yesterday fitting on some sights and timing the mitrailleuse to shoot thru the propellor. In an hour or two I expect to test the sights and take the machine up for a few minutes to see whether it is properly aligned. Then it will be ready for business, unless something else turns up. This is a slow game; everything requires such careful attention, and all sorts of things to be done keep showing up from time to time.

Towns in our vicinity have been severely bombed, but so far the Boche hasn't come after us. I can't remember whether I told you that a French plane bumped its wheels against the roof six feet over my head and smashed itself all to pieces, without hurting anyone in the building or doing more to the pilot than break his nose.

These Boches are certainly a clever bunch in military matters. Who would have thought, when all the world was yelling about their cutting down fruit trees a year ago, that they did it so as to prevent the Allied troops from hiding when they made their big shove last week? I hope I can help to lick them when they make their expected drive in this sector.

Air Service, A.E.F.
March 28, 1918

At last I have started the job. Last night after supper, Major Lufbery told Eddie Rickenbacker and myself that he would take us over the lines this morning if the weather permitted. The morning was beautifully clear, and after a leisurely breakfast we crawled into our warm duds and took to the air, at about 9 o'clock.

Major Lufbery led, with Rick and myself above and behind him on the right and left respectively. With these fast and powerful little machines it didn't take us long to reach the lines at an altitude of 4000 meters. Then we turned to the left and patrolled up and down two times on a front of about 30 kilometers. Our planes were scarcely ever flying in a straight line; we were continually banking and turning from one side to the other in order to see at all angles and to make it harder for the anti-aircraft battery which shot at us occasionally. The sector was so calm it was almost dead. I could see no artillery activity at all; merely two intricate systems of trenches with a pockmarked area of variable width between them. I didn't spend much time looking at the ground, but now and then I would glance at a spot where a few marks on the ground indicated the site of a village blown to atoms.

The Major saw one Boche flying very low, but my untrained eye didn't even observe that. Once I saw two black specks out of the corner of my eye, and glanced back quickly, thinking they were planes, but they widened out into large clouds of black smoke, and I knew that they were only two A.A. shells which had exploded about 600 meters away from me. I'm sorry we didn't see any Boches, but I guess we will next time, and anyway, it is something to have been one of the first two American-trained chasse pilots over the lines.

I am pretty sleepy this afternoon. We stayed between 4500 and 5000 meters for an hour, and I'm not used to it yet."

---

[1] The French usually quoted time in this manner and in most of the reports used by the U. S. Air Service, the same applied.

[2] *Let's Go Where the Action Is!* Letters of Douglas Campbell to his parents July 22, 1917 to July 12, 1918. Privately printed 1968 by Campbell.

[3] Capt. James E. Miller, who was in charge of getting Issoudun up and running and who became the first C. O. of the 95th, sadly killed in action, March 8, 1918.

[4] "Wad" was Campbell's brother who was serving overseas as an officer in the U. S. Engineers.

[5] For some unexplained reason, some of the pilots were commissioned First Lieutenants and some Second Lieutenants. This was grossly unfair, but was remedied fairly quickly.

[6] Hall wrote *Kitchener's Mob*, a book of his experiences in the British Army, *Falcons of France*, as well as *The Bounty Trilogy*. All but the first were written with Charles Nordhoff, another American who flew with the French.

[7] Headquarters 1st Pursuit Organization Special Orders, Number 15, March 9, 1918.

July 1917, aviation cadets gather at the Kissel Home in Morristown, New Jersey prior to sailing for France. Front: R. L. Moore, E. E. Bates, H. Coolidge, D. Campbell. Rear: W. S. Ely, W. B. Baron, G. H. Kissel. *Campbell Album*.

94th Aero Squadron enlisted men during basic training limber up at Kelly Field, Texas, September 1917.

Hamilton Coolidge as a Sergeant, 1917.

Sgt. Eddie Rickenbacker when serving as a driver for General Pershing.

Right: Alden (nicknamed "Madame") Sherry served with the American Field Service driving ambulances prior to attending the French Flying School at Tours.

Opposite
Left: Prior to America's entry into the War, Alan Winslow flew with the Lafayette Flying Corps and is seen here in his French uniform.

Right: Cedric Fault Le Roy, seen here in a dark blue French uniform, trained and flew with the French prior to American involvement. He joined the 94th late in the War.

Below: The steady and forgiving Caudron G3, which was used for training, prepares to land at a large French field. *Credit Musée de l'Air, No. 797.*

Eddie Rickenbacker seen with a G-3 at Tours during his initial flight training.

A French instructor stands awaiting another terror-filled lesson with his American students. The G-3 has school number 7. Tours, 1917.

94th mechanics during ten-week training at Brasier Motor Co., Paris. *R. E. Hartz album.*

Right: Doug Campbell poses by a trench dug for latrine use at Issoudun during the early days of creating the American Flying School complex. *Campbell album.*

Any landing is a good landing if you can walk away from it. This poor G-3 received some real punishment from its American student pilot. Tours, 1917.

Ham Coolidge who honed his flying skills while on administrative duty at Issoudun, looks pleased with himself in a Nieuport bearing the initials "H.C." on the fuselage.

Thorne Taylor looks as if he shot a good score with the camera gun mounted on his 23-meter Nieuport.

The drafty barracks constructed in part by the Air Service enlisted men form a somber row at Issoudun. *1st Lt. Sumner Sewall album.*

Doug Campbell is suited up for cold weather flying, standing by a Nieuport 27, of which the Air Service purchased 287 for training. Nieuport 24s and 27s looked very much alike, but with the serial number of 6083, this plane would be in the type 27 production series. *Doug Campbell album.*

The flight line forms up at the advanced field, St. Valentin. *Doug Campbell album.*

Doug Campbell dressed for flying in more temperate weather. Note the early style fiber-type crash helmet. Fall 1917. *Doug Campbell album.*

John Jeffers at Issoudun before he was granted his wings. The flying cadets were issued enlisted men's uniforms with no officer's cuff braid.

More of the mud of Issoudun. Doug Campbell holds a saucepan for his friend "Smitty" who is wearing an officer's overseas cap and a French rifle slung over his shoulder. *Doug Campbell album*.

Lt. Charles T. Crocker at Issoudun. K.P. duty? Joined the 94th September 14, 1918.

Right: Campbell again appearing to hold up the tail of a French A. R. at Issoudun. *Doug Campbell album*.

Eddie Rickenbacker, right, and a French instructor at Issoudun. Winter 1917-18.

Villeneuve-les-Vertus – 94th pilots arriving early in March 1918.

Below: Doug Campbell seated in a Nieuport 27 trainer, Issoudun, 1917-18.

Nieuport 27, manufacturer's number 6083 in U. S. service as a trainer. Note the French cocardes and the Issoudun school number 126; Campbell in the cockpit. *Doug Campbell album.*

Harvey Weir Cook relaxing on a sailboat while at the aerial gunnery school at Cazeaux, February 1918.

Lt. Eddie Green, all smiles by the barracks at Villeneuve-les-Vertus.

John Wentworth, the designer of the "Hat in the Ring." Issoudun, Fall 1917.

A warm day at Villeneuve-les-Vertus. A mix of 94th and 95th personnel. L/R Seth Low, Eddie Rickenbacker, Edgar Tobin, Doug Campbell. From the 95th, Ned Buford, Alex McLanahan, and Harold Buckley.

Ken Marr stands by a pile of bombs on the airfield at Villeneuve-les-Vertus. March 1918.

The Red Cross hut at Villeneuve-les-Vertus was a meeting place for both the 94th and 95th pilots. Gene Jones, 95th, with his back to the camera, Doug Campbell, 94th, Harold Buckley, 95th, John Mitchell, 95th, and two unidentified pilots make up those in the photo. March 1918.

Left: Alan Winslow, sporting a garrison cap and Lafayette Flying Corps wings on his left breast. Villeneuve-les-Vertus. March 1918.

A sunny day in March. Villeneuve-les-Vertus. L/R Eddie Green, 94th, Eddie Rickenbacker, 94th, Russ Hall with pipe, 95th, Alex McLanahan, 95th, Louis Shultz, Ground Officer 95th, John Russell Adams, Lafayette Flying Corps, and Ned Buford, 95th.

Eddie again with a larger bomb. What he was trying to prove or demonstrate with his bomb lifting remains a mystery.

Eddie Rickenbacker poses with two light bombs at Villeneuve-les-Vertus at the same spot that Ken Marr stood in a previous photo. March 1918.

Right: Reed Chambers with a freshly delivered Nieuport 28. Note the camouflaged cowling, and single Vickers gun. Villeneuve-les-Vertus. March 1918.

Ken Marr, Jimmy Hall, John Huffer, Doug Campbell and Eddie Rickenbacker at the field, Villeneuve-les-Vertus. March 1918. *Doug Campbell album.*

Right: Eddie Green relaxes with a large cigar at Villeneuve-les-Vertus. *Eddie Green album.*

Below: Alex McLanahan, 95th, Russ Hall, 95th, Eddie Rickenbacker, 94th, and John Russell Adams, Lafayette Flying Corps, with SPA 81 pose by a Spad VII of Groupe d'Combat Maynard at Villeneuve-les-Vertus. March 1918. *USAF Museum Collection.*

Major Raoul Lufbery stands by one of the barracks at Villeneuve-les-Vertus, March 1918. *C. H. Woolley album.*

Above right: Major John Huffer by a barracks at Villeneuve-les-Vertus.

Right: Jimmy Meissner, John Huffer and an unidentified ground officer pose by a wrecked French A. R. 1 which hit one of the 94th barracks causing quite a stir on the field at Villeneuve-les-Vertus, March 1918.

More views of the crashed A. R. 1. Note the barracks in the background which were hit and came close to extinction by the French 2-seater.

On the night of March 31, 1918, a spark from a barracks stove ignited a nearby hangar housing 94th Nieuports destroying two of them and burning holes in the wings of several others. Here are the smoldering remains of the hangar. March 31, 1918. *Doug Campbell album.*

Another view of the hangar fire on the night of March 31, 1918.

Typical wing damage caused by the hangar fire. Note the propeller and cowling covers and the French wing cocards. Villeneuve-les-Vertus. March 31, 1918.

General Pershing's Headquarters, Chaumont, France. March 1918. The staff car in the foreground was the type driven by Rickenbacker before his transfer to the Air Service. *Signal Corps 10939*.

2

April - Action at Gengoult

After the April 9 move from Epiez to Gengoult Aerodrome near Toul the Squadron was required to take several days to settle in and adapt to its new quarters with only a few flights being taken to get a feel of the field and the area in general. The first known Operations Report[1] was dated April 12, stating that four trial flights were made, six Nieuports were ready and one combat took place. "At 12.25 Major Lufbery attacked a group of three Albatroses in the vicinity of Xivray, about 40 cartridges were fired on one of these planes which appeared to be seriously damaged, and which fell nose diving into a vrille. Major Lufbery was prevented from following this plane down on account of the other two planes.

At this time a plane either English or French was above the combat and perhaps can confirm this combat if located. The other two enemy planes were seen to retire. Altitude of combat, 3500 meters." Confirmation of this action was never received.

German records show that Lufbery's fight was with three Albatros single-seaters of Jasta 64.

Doug Campbell's letter of April 13 refers to his arrival at Gengoult Airfield outside of Toul:

> "Air Service, A.E.F.
> France, April 13, 1918
>
> We have moved again, not far, just a few miles northeast. If you will look up the location of our walking trip in 1911 before father got sick, you will find a river which has its mouth at the point where our walk began. I am just outside of T—, which is on that river, not so very far from the lines. (Note: Gengoult airfield, on the outskirts of Toul.)
>
> At last we have equipment, machine guns, and good liaison with the French, and day after tomorrow we begin steady work. That means going over the lines every other day, and being ready for any "alertes" which may be telephoned in on the alternate days,– such as Boche planes coming over to take pictures, day-bombing raids, etc. We have 5 Lafayette veterans with us, including Major Lufbery (the owner and manipulator of the best pair of eyes in existence) and Capt. James Norman Hall, who Luf says to be a comer. He is a writer of no mean caliber, having written *Kitchener's Mob* and *High Adventure*; the latter are the best and truest air stories written, and have been published in the *Atlantic Monthly.* On his second trip over the lines,[2] Capt. Hall attacked a biplace from above, mistaking it for a monoplace, and got a bullet through his lungs. He fainted before reaching the ground, and was lucky enough to dive into a trench. The wings caught the sides of the trench, and broke his fall enough to save his life. He will fight anything, but Lufbery says he has developed an unerring judgment in picking and timing his attack. There isn't any pilot in this squadron that isn't just itching to get started.
>
> Incidentally we have wonderful quarters – cement buildings with rooms for two, and a building full of shower baths with a quick heating apparatus. No mud, good roads, fascinating country, and beaucoup Boches. Can't beat it."

April 13 saw fairly active enemy aerial presence with four alerts signaling six individual enemy aircraft, plus an entire squadron which was observed over Chateau Salins flying south at 14h 50. Major Lufbery answered one alert with nothing to report and Capts. Hall and Peterson answered the fourth, reporting they were shot at by enemy A. A. fire. Ten Nieuports were reported ready for duty.

On April 14 an early 6:00 a.m. patrol flown on a line from St. Mihiel to Arrocourt achieved no results and reported very bad visibility. At 8:44, 2nd Lt. Alan Winslow, who was French trained and had briefly flown with Spa. 152, and 1st Lt. Douglas Campbell were alerted to intercept two German single-seaters who were, as later stated in Lt. Winslow's combat report, "menacing Toul." They departed the field at 8:50 and 8:51 and by 8:53 two combats took place at an altitude of 800 meters. Lt. Winslow drove his opponent to the ground first, having riddled his victim with bullets, the German pilot landing his Albatros D. Va just 200 meters from Gengoult airdrome. The enemy aircraft was damaged in landing, but was basically intact. The pilot, Unteroffizier Simon of Jasta 64 (w), uninjured, was captured. Two minutes later, Lt. Campbell's adversary fell in flames, also a short distance from the field, but the Pfalz D.IIIa's pilot, Vizefeldwebel Wronieke, also of Jasta 64 (w), was not as fortunate, sustaining a fractured leg and severe burns. These were the first two confirmed victories by the American Air Service, with the official confirmation appearing in the April 14, 1918 *Compte-Rendu of the 8th French Army*, Paragraph 8. Doug Campbell's letter of the 15th gives his immediate recollection of the event:

"Air Service, A.E.F.
France, Apr. 15, 1918

It was a great war yesterday. On Saturday, Major Huffer informed the French Aviation, under whom this squadron is working, that we would be ready to start regular patrols and alerts on the 14th. Alan Winslow and I were on schedule to be on alert from 6 to 10 a.m. At 6 we had our planes wheeled out, and tested the motors to make sure they were running O.K.

The first 2 1/2 hours were slow, but then things began to happen so quickly that we could hardly keep track of them. At 8:45 the telephone rang, and the message was that 2 Boche planes had been sighted some 15 miles away, headed this way. At 8:50 I took off, and had made a round of the field at 500 meters altitude when Winslow got into the air. He was to lead, and when he reached 200 meters I was just getting into position behind him. It was quite misty. All at once he turned, and I saw him chase a plane which wasn't over 300 m. high. *It had black crosses on it!* I heard him shoot, and they both went out of sight under my wings. I banked up 90 degrees and turned to get a view below so as to go help Winslow if necessary, and it was lucky I did, for just as I turned I heard the pop-pop-pop of a machine gun behind me, and there was another Boche shooting at me. For some reason or other, I thought his tail was turned toward me as he shot, and the thought "Biplace, keep under him" flashed into my brain. He turned out afterwards to be an Albatros monoplace, but I had guessed wrong, and instead of getting above him, which would have been easier, I kept below him, maneuvering so as to try to get under his tail without letting him point toward me or get a shot at me from a broadside. In a biplace, you see, the gunner-passenger can shoot through a 180-degree arc behind the wings above the tail, and through large arcs down at the sides, while the pilot can shoot to the front by aiming his plane just as we do. It took over a minute to maneuver into a position behind and under his tail without exposing myself to his fire (I thought), but I finally found myself right under him. Then I pulled my nose straight up into the air and let him have the bullets, and I think he got some in his motor, for I saw some tracers hitting his nose. The next thing I knew, he was diving at about 45 degrees, and I was behind and above him, but behind his tail. Then I got a good aim, pulled the trigger, and held on to it. Two or three tracers hit him, and after about 50 rounds had been fired, a streak of flame came shooting out of his fuselage near the motor. I ceased firing, and watched him land and crash in a ploughed field, his plane a mass of flame and wreckage. The pilot had had sense enough to unfasten his belt, and was thrown clear of the machine, escaping with some bad burns and broken bones. Winslow had shot his Boche down; it landed and turned over in a ploughed field on the other side of the aerodrome. I was so excited that I was afraid to land until I had made a tour of the field. (Note: From takeoff to landing, the Winslow and Campbell flight lasted only 4 1/2 minutes.

When I rolled up to the hangar, everybody who hadn't run to the fallen Boches was on hand to haul us out of our planes and give us a slap on the back. (Note: the writer recalls that his mechanic Corporal Prince, forgetting military custom, shouted "That's the stuff, Lieutenant old kid!") I ran over to my victim (only 500 meters from the hangars), but they had already sent him to a hospital, and what was left of the plane was being rapidly torn into souvenirs by French and American soldiers. I got a few pieces, though. Winslow's plane wasn't badly damaged, and he got 2 Boche magnetos, the spark plugs, and a splendid altimeter and compass.

The remains of the two planes were taken to T— and exhibited in the main square yesterday. Al and I had to go down to be stared at while the band played yesterday afternoon. We were informed that a French General will be around in a day or two to pin on a Croix-de-Guerre with palm. Not bad luck, the whole thing. Our squadron will now be able to get anything it needs from either the French or the Americans."

Alan Winslow in his letter home described his joy of April 14:

"Dearest Mother and Father:

If anybody was ever more happy than I am right now, I doubt it very much. I tried to cable you the news, but found it practically impossible from here; so I wrote Paul immediately and asked him to do it for me. But I suppose you already know something about it, for in the last two days I have been interviewed by nine reporters.

Here is the story:

On Sunday morning, April 14th, I was "on alert" from 6:00 A.M. till 10:00 A.M., that is I, with Lt. Douglas Campbell of Harvard and California, were on emergency call duty. We were sitting in the little alert tent, playing cards, waiting for a call. Our machines were outside, ready at a moment's notice. I was patrol leader. At 8:45 I was called to the 'phone, told by the information officer, who is in direct touch with all batteries and observation posts, that two German aeroplanes were about two thousand meters above the city, which is only a mile or so from here. We were told that they were going east. We were rushed down to our machines in sidecars, and in another minute were off in the air. Doug started ahead of me, as I was to meet him above a certain point at five hundred meters, and then take the lead. I gave him about forty-five second's start, and then left myself, climbing steeply in a left-hand spiral, in order to save time. I had not made a complete half-turn, and was at about two hundred and fifty meters, when straight above and ahead of me in the mist of the early morning, and not more than a hundred yards away, I saw a plane coming toward me with huge black crosses on its wings and tail. I was so furious to see a Hun directly over our Aviation field that I swore out loud and violently opened fire. At the same time, to avoid my bullets, he slipped into a left-hand reversement, and came down, firing on me. I climbed, however, in a right-hand spiral, and slipped off, coming down directly behind him and "on his tail." Again I violently opened fire. I had him at a rare advantage, which was due to the greater speed and maneuverability of our wonderful machines. I fired twenty to thirty rounds at him and could see my tracers entering his machine. Then, in another moment, his plane went straight down in an uncontrolled nose-dive – I had put his engine out of commission. I followed in a straight dive, firing all the way. At about six feet above the ground he tried to regain control of his machine, but could not, and he crashed to earth. I darted down near him, made a sharp turn by the wreck, to make sure he was out of commission, then made a victorious swoop down over him, and climbed up again to see if Doug needed any help with the other Hun: for I had caught a glimpse of their combat out of the corner of my eye.

I rose to about three hundred again, to see Doug "on the tail" of his Boche, and his tracer bullets were passing throughout the enemy plane. I climbed a little higher, and was diving down on his second Hun, and about to fire, when I saw the German plane go up in flames and crash to earth. Doug had sent his Hun plane down one minute after I had shot down mine.

Mind you, mother, that the fight took place only three hundred meters up, in full view of all on the ground and in the nearby town; mine dropped about one hundred yards to the right, and Doug's one hundred yards to the left of our field. These are remarkable facts, for one of our Majors, who, with the French army since 1915, has shot down seventeen machines, never had one land in France – and here we go, right off the bat and stage a fight over our aerodrome and bring down two Huns right on it. It was an opportunity of a lifetime – a great chance.

When we landed, only our respective mechanics were left in the drome, to help us out of our flying clothes. The whole camp was pouring out, flying by on foot, bicycles, sidecars, automobiles; soldiers, women, children, majors, colonels, French and American – all poured out of the city; in ten minutes several thousand people must have gathered. Doug and I congratulated each other, and my mechanic, no longer military, jumping up and down, waving his hat, pounded me on the back instead of saluting, and yelled: "Damn it! That's the stuff, old kid!" Then Campbell and I rushed to our respective Hun wrecks.

On the way there – it was only half a mile – I ran into a huge crowd of soldiers – blue and khaki – pressing about one man. I pushed my way through the crowd, and I heard somebody triumphantly say to the surrounded man in French: "There he is; now you will believe he is an American." I looked at the man – a scrawny, poorly clad, little devil – dressed in a rotten German uniform. It was the Hun pilot of the machine I had shot down. Needless to say, I felt rather haughty to come face to face with my victim, now a prisoner, but did not know what to say. It seems he would not believe that an American brought him down. He looked me all over, and then asked me in good French if I was an American. When I answered, 'Yes', he had no more to say."

From the interrogation of the two captured pilots, it would appear they had lost their way and had dropped through the overcast to get their bearings. At this point in time there were two German squadrons based opposite the 94th, Jasta 64 (w) which was made of Württembergers and Jasta 65, which were both equipped with Albatros D. Va and Pfalz D. IIIa fighters. The Jagdstaffeln who were on the more active fronts were equipped with the more up-to-date Fokker D. VIIs which, by the fact they were operating in other areas, was to the advantage of the fledgling pilots of the 94th.

Jagdstaffel 64 was formed at the end of January and early February 1918 from the reserve unit FEA. 10. The commanding officer, Leutnant Hanko, an old hand from Jasta 28, brought his unit from Böblingen in Germany to Nercy le Haut on February 5 where they found extremely poor airfield conditions. This problem was remedied by a move to Mars la Tour on March 22 when the non-commissioned officer pilots, most just assigned from fighter training schools, began their daily patrols. On March 27, due to this lack of experience, Offizier Stellvertrater Schüschke and Unteroffizier Simon became lost while on patrol; Schüschke ran out of fuel and landed in French territory and was made a POW; Simon was able to find his way back to Mars la Tour, only to be brought down by Winslow 18 days later.

There are interesting comparisons between the 94th Aero Squadron and Jasta 64 (w) in that they both arrived at the front in March of 1918, and that for the most part pilots from both squadrons had just finished their respective flying schools. Their equipment was not the most up-to-date, but the 94th had more than a slight edge as Major Lufbery, with Captains Marr, Peterson and Hall, the flight commanders, all had combat experience flying with the Lafayette Escadrille.

The flight conditions from April 15 until the morning of April 19, consisted of very poor visibility and heavy rain. The usual patrols, Pont-à-Mousson to St. Mihiel, resumed on April 19 and 20 with no successes to report.

Poor weather returned until the morning of April 23, when at 9:52 Major Lufbery and 1st Lt. Campbell responded to an alert and attacked a biplace machine flying at 3500 meters between Bois de Mort Mare and St. Baussant. Major Lufbery fired five rounds, Lt. Campbell 50 rounds, both reporting smoke issuing from the enemy plane. The time of the fight was 10:10. Four minutes later, Captain Marr and Lt. Winslow answered an alert and encountered two fighters and an observation plane 5 kilometers west of Pont-à-Mousson at 3500 meters. Winslow's machine gun failed and there were no results. The crew of a two-seater from FA (A) 298 reported a fight with two single-seaters at 10:45 over Seicheprey which must have been Marr and Winslow.

Official German records show that many of the two-seater crews reported no fewer than five air battles with single-seaters. They said the enemy attacked even beyond their own lines with "great energy and endurance." One of the two-seaters was badly damaged, but the crew was not injured. This fight must have been the Lufbery/Campbell attack. Major Lufbery, with Lts. Campbell and Rickenbacker, answered two additional alerts without further results.

April 21, 1918 – Letter from Doug Campbell:

"Enclosed is a picture of what was left of the Boche plane. A study of the wreck proved it to be not an Albatros as was Winslow's, but a Pfalz, about which I enclose a clipping. Under separate cover I am sending an 8" x 10" enlargement of a better photo of the wreck.

The victory was largely due to good luck, but was very gratifying and has given me a great deal of confidence.

However, I still have to learn how to see things over the lines. Yesterday I went up with Capt. Peterson, and we saw two Boche observation planes just across the lines. Pete led me across thru a barrage of anti-aircraft shells, which sounded very loud even above the roar of the motor, and we caught up with them about 5 kilometers the other side of the lines. One of the principles drummed into young pilots is that they must never attack unless the patrol leader does, for he may see planes that they don't, so when he circled above the Boches, I stayed right with him and followed him home when he came. Didn't I kick myself when he told me, after landing, that he had hoped I would attack, but couldn't do it himself because his gun was jammed! (Note: At this time the squadron's planes were equipped with only one machine gun each; the second gun per plane was not received and installed until about June 7.) I surely would have done it if I had known, for the intoxication of danger had keyed me up for anything, and I was just itching for a scrap. I want to bring down a Hun on his own side of the lines, too; it is more of an achievement even if the victor doesn't get credit for it because of lack of witnesses. But don't think I mean to rush in blindly; the game isn't played that way. Nerve is necessary, but the head picks out the time to use it.

On Wednesday, a French Major appeared and decorated Winslow and myself with the Croix-de-Guerre with a palm (I'll buy an extra one and send it to you). The French pilots of this center lined up with the Americans and the French Major read the citation by the general commanding the 8th Army, as follows:

> *'Le Lieutenant Douglas Campbell: Remarquable pilote de chasse. (Bunk!) Le 14 Avril, a abbatu un avion ennemi dans nos lignes après un combat aussi rapide que brillant.'*

Then he stalked up, affixed the hardware to my heaving bosom, and wrung my hand off. He didn't kiss me on both cheeks; apparently they give so many C. de G.'s that they save the osculation for the higher medals. Thank God he didn't, for a movie man was there, and throughout the ceremony he played soft music on his crank organ. After the party, I posed for said guy in a plane, in front of a plane, shaking hands with Winslow, and all that hero stuff. It may appear in the *Pathétic Weekly* in a few weeks. (Note: *Pathé Newsreel.*)"

The next few days the weather continued to be unfavorable, with low clouds and rain for the most part. A few patrols were flown, Toul-Pont-à-Mousson-St. Mihiel, with no results other than on the 25th Lt. Rickenbacker fired a few shots at a single-seater which he observed carried "a black and white (center black) cocard, tail of orange color." On the 26th, Lt. Gude answered an alert and later landed at St. Vincent reporting heavy anti-aircraft fire. The action heated up on April 29 when in the afternoon about 6:10 p.m. Captain Hall and Lt. Rickenbacker attacked an Albatros single-seater at 2000 meters between Baussant and Montsec. Hall and Rickenbacker fired 200 rounds and the enemy machine dove, with both men following, continuing to fire. During the dive, a cloud of smoke poured from the enemy machine and continued until they lost sight of him at 700 meters near Les Hatten Chatel. They requested confirmation and on April 30 the Regimental Intelligence Office of 102 U. S. Infantry reported:

> "Two of our planes appeared over Beaumont at about 6:00 P.M. and circled above the German lines in the vicinity of St. Baussant. A few moments later a third plane appeared on the scene. All planes were at a fairly high altitude. The two American planes separated, one going toward the W. (west), the other maintaining his position. Machine gun fire was then exchanged between the German and American plane. Our plane seemed to climb above his adversary and started to dive using his M. G. (machine gun), whereupon the German turned and dove for the earth followed by our aviator. The German landed so far behind the lines that it was impossible to see just where, as he was lost in haze that was quite heavy at that time. The movement that drove the German to the ground was nicely executed, our aviator leading him on and at the same time climbing above and turning suddenly and diving toward him.
>
> Signed, A. Fredrick Oberlin, 1st Lt. U. S. Infantry."

Rickenbacker, in his book *Fighting the Flying Circus*, describes this, his first victory, while in the company of Capt. Hall:

> "I quickly decided what tactics I would pursue. While Hall went in for his attack I would maintain my altitude and work towards a position on the other side of the Pfalz, hoping to cut off his retreat. No sooner had I changed my line of flight than the German pilot saw me clear of my sun cover. Hall was already halfway to him when the Hun nosed up and climbed furiously for a higher level. I let him pass me and found myself on the other side just as Hall began firing. I doubt whether the Boche had seen Jimmy's Nieuport at all.
>
> Surprised by discovering Hall just ahead of him, the Pfalz abandoned all ideas of an attack and instead banked around to the right and started for home – just as I had expected him to do. In a trice I was on his tail. Down, down we sped with throttles both full open. Hall was coming on somewhere to my rear. The Boche had no heart for evolutions or maneuvers. I was gaining upon him every instant and had my sights trained dead upon his cockpit before I fired my first shot.
>
> At 150 yards I pressed my triggers. The tracer bullets cut a streak of living fire into the rear of the Pfalz tail. Raising the nose of my airplane slightly the fiery streak lifted itself like the stream of water pouring from a garden hose. Gradually it settled into the pilots' seat. The swerving of the Pfalz course indicated that its rudder no longer was controlled by a directing foot. At two thousand feet

above the enemy's line, I pulled up my headlong dive and watched the enemy machine continuing on its course. Carving slightly to the left, the Pfalz circled a little to the south and the next minute crashed onto the ground just at the edge of the woods a mile inside their own lines. I had brought down my first enemy airplane and had not been subjected to a single shot!"

In his *Reconnaissance Report*, he was a bit more brief:

"Capt. Hall and Lt. Rickenbacker attacked Albatros monoplace at about 610 P.M. between Baussant and Montsec. Capt. Hall fired, and also Lt. Rickenbacker – 200 rounds. Enemy machine dove, Capt. Hall and Lt. Rickenbacker followed him, firing all the time. Cloud of smoke emerged from enemy machine and continued to pour out all the way down. Lost sight of enemy at 700 meters near Vigneulles and Les Hatten Chatel, still going down. Redressed at 700 meters. Confirmation requested."

In Hall's report which he signed "chief of patrol", he states that he fired 350 rounds and Rickenbacker 200. The "Albatros", as reported, was indeed a Pfalz and thus began the long string of victories to follow. German records seen to date show no losses on April 29 or 30 on the American front, but the daily report of Gruppe Gorz states that at 1920 hours (German time) a Pfalz of Jasta 64 was attacked by two single-seaters which damaged the Pfalz. Due to motor damage the plane descended near Essey flying at a low altitude, finally landing between Xammes and Dampvitoux. This had to be the same plane.

Doug Campbell's letter of April 28 recounts some of the frustration in the enemy's lack of activity and the poorness of the weather.

"Air Service, A.E.F.
April 28, 1918

I have had two fights this week, but both were unsuccessful. The first one I should have had; he threw out a black smoke bomb and I stopped shooting because I thought he was on fire – a foolish thing to do. Then he got away from me. The second I chased about 5 km. inside his own lines, but couldn't overtake. The next day I saw another one over the lines and went after him, but turned around when I discovered myself 4 km. behind the lines at an altitude of only 1000 meters with a strong wind behind my back – nearly out of gliding distance. To me the risk of the motor stopping seems worse than that of getting shot.

The weather has been pretty wretched lately; haven't had a perfectly clear day yet. I hope we shall get one soon because the Hun birds will surely come out then. Yesterday afternoon I flew along well inside their lines at 3500 meters for half an hour, hoping some of them would come after me, but they wouldn't come out. You notice I have much more confidence in my eyes than I did ten days ago, though there is still lots of room for improvement. Twice already I have been sent out as leader of a patrol of three.

The other day, when it was raining, a few of us went out to visit some of the artillery batteries near the lines. The day before, they had been catching hell, and it had rained during the night and all day, so we got a good idea of the discomforts of their life. But Gosh! But the pilots have it soft! Our work is all sport."

In summation, the month of April was a time of extremely poor weather which hampered aerial activity on both sides of the lines, only punctuated by Campbell's and Winslow's two victories of April 14, plus Hall's and Rickenbacker's shared victory of April 29, with several additional minor clashes thrown in. Probably this was a better way for an untested squadron to start new operations than meeting immediate heavy action by well-seasoned enemy combat veterans.

---

[1] As contained in the Gorrell Report. National Archives Record Group 120, A.E.F. (World War I) 1917-1923: *History of the U. S. Army Air Service 1917-1919* (Gorrell Reports), Series E. Volume 12, *History of the 94th Aero Squadron*.

[2] While serving with the Lafayette Escadrille.

A view of Gengoult Airdrome with Mont St. Michel in the background. April 1918.

Captain Dave Peterson, another combat experienced pilot who also flew with the Lafayette Escadrille gaining three victories before transferring to the Air Service and the 94th. *U. S. National Archives, RG III, SC 13412.*

Major John Huffer, 1st C. O. of the 94th with a freshly delivered Nieuport 28 which still bears the French markings. April 18, 1918. Note he wears the ribbons and decorations from his French service and on his collar the crossed flags of the Signal Corps of which the Air Service was a part. *U. S. National Archives, RG III, SC 11304.*

Major Raoul Lufbery, ex-Lafayette Escadrille, one of the experienced leaders of the untrained flyers of the 94th. He stands before a new Nieuport 28 at the Gengoult Airdrome, Toul, France, April 18, 1918. *U. S. National Archives, RG III, SC 11306.*

Nieuports on parade. Fresh from the factory, six Type 28s are lined up with a seventh in the background. The nearest ship N 6185 was later Squadron number 10, flown by Gude and the plane in which Lt. Kurtz was killed when it accidentally caught fire in the air. Next to 6185 is 6180, later Squadron number 18, and flown by Green, Sherry, Prinz, and Jeffers. The serial numbers on the other planes cannot be discerned. *Reed Chambers album, U. S. Air Force Museum.*

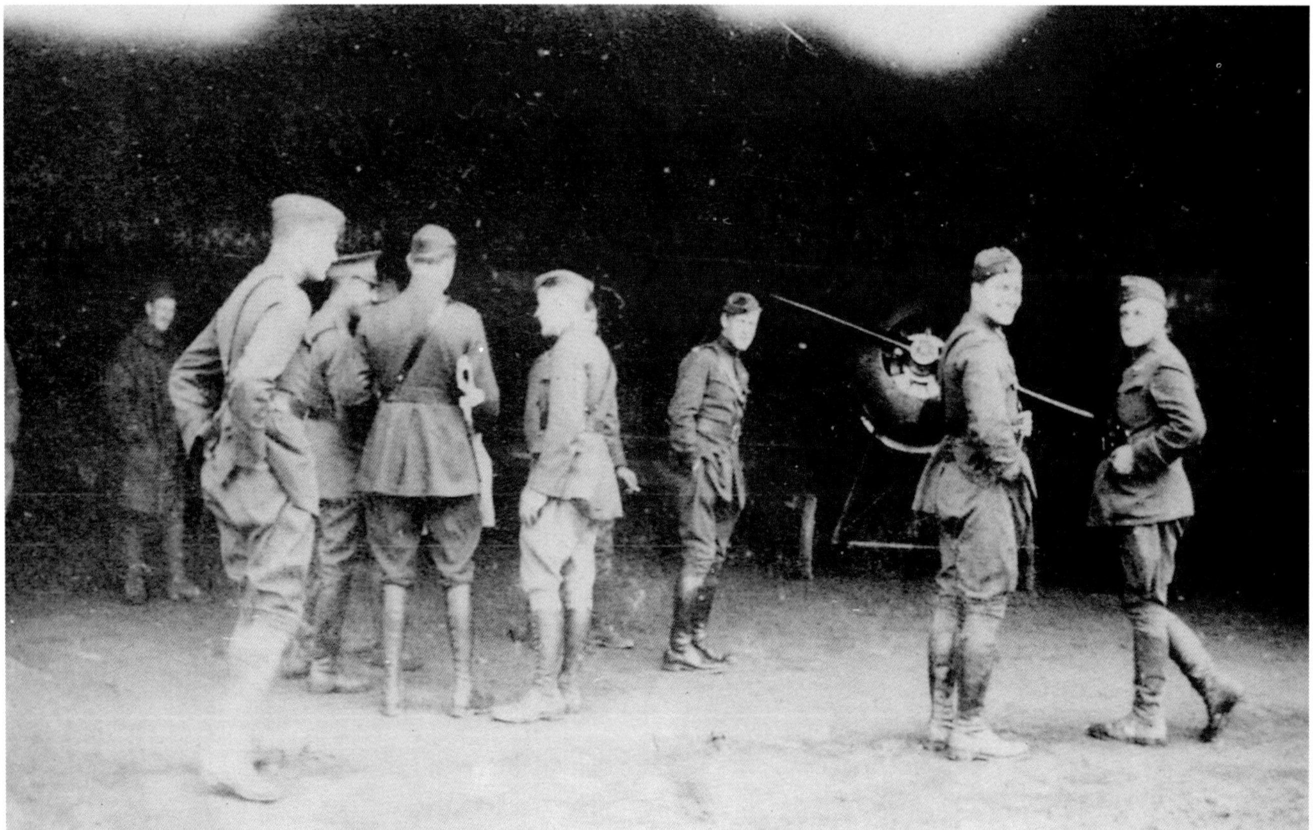

Alan Winslow, Art Cunningham, Eddie Rickenbacker, Reed Chambers, J. Gude, Doug Campbell and Ken Marr outside one of the hangars at Gengoult. April 1918. *Doug Campbell album.*

One of the new Nieuports with a single gun. Eddie Rickenbacker in the campaign hat and J. Gude wearing his French brevet wings seem to be pleased about something. Gengoult, April 1918.

"Madame" Sherry, Doug Campbell, Eddie Green, and Eddie Rickenbacker in flying gear at Gengoult Airdrome.

Eddie Rickenbacker and Eddie Green are making use of the 94th's Harley Davidson. Gengoult. April 1918. *Doug Campbell album.*

Left: Doug Campbell in flying togs seems to be relaxed before a patrol. The squadron Harley sports considerable French mud on its undersides. *Doug Campbell album.*

The 94th and the 95th gather at Gengoult. Ted Curtis, 95th, unknown, John Jeffers, George Zacharias, all 94th; Ned Buford 95th, Doug Campbell, Walt Smythe, 94th, Bill Casgrain, Russ Hall, Waldo Heinrichs, and Stuart McKeown from the 95th. April 1918.

"Madame" Sherry, Doug Campbell, Eddie Green, and Eddie Rickenbacker horsing around with the squadron Harley Davidson with side car. Gengoult. April 1918. *Doug Campbell album.*

Major Lufbery seated in his quarters showing things were Spartan even for a Major. This photo was probably taken at Villeneuve-les-Vertus before moving to Gengoult. The typewriter is an interesting part of the décor.

Major Lufbery's Nieuport 28 in French markings before any squadron insignia had been applied. This was N 6193 and later marked Squadron number 2.

J. Gude, Eddie Rickenbacker, Alan Winslow, and Raoul Lufbery. Gengoult, 1918. Note that Rickenbacker is wearing an open collar-style tunic which was much more comfortable when one was constantly turning his head while in the air. Lufbery wears a soft shirt with the collar turned over his tunic for the same reason.

94th mechanics take a break from oil and grease to cook up some chestnuts (?). Note the liberated monocle worn by the second man from the right.

Captain Jim Hall, adventurer, author, and ex-Lafayette Escadrille, poses by his Nieuport 28, number 6153, Squadron number 17. *Joe Dawson album.*

Standing, Major Davenport Johnson, 95th C. O., non-flying; Eddie Rickenbacker, Jim Meissner. Seated, Chester Snow, Alden Sherry, Reed Chambers, Doug Campbell, unknown, John Jeffers, and Bill Loomis. June 1918.

Captain Ken Marr, ex-Lafayette Escadrille. Marr later succeeded Major Huffer as C. O. of the 94th.

Jim Hall and number 17 prepare for a take-off at Gengoult. Note the permanent barracks in the background. April 1918.

Eddie Rickenbacker and J. Gude share a laugh by a single gun mounted Type 28 which had not yet received its squadron markings. April 1918.

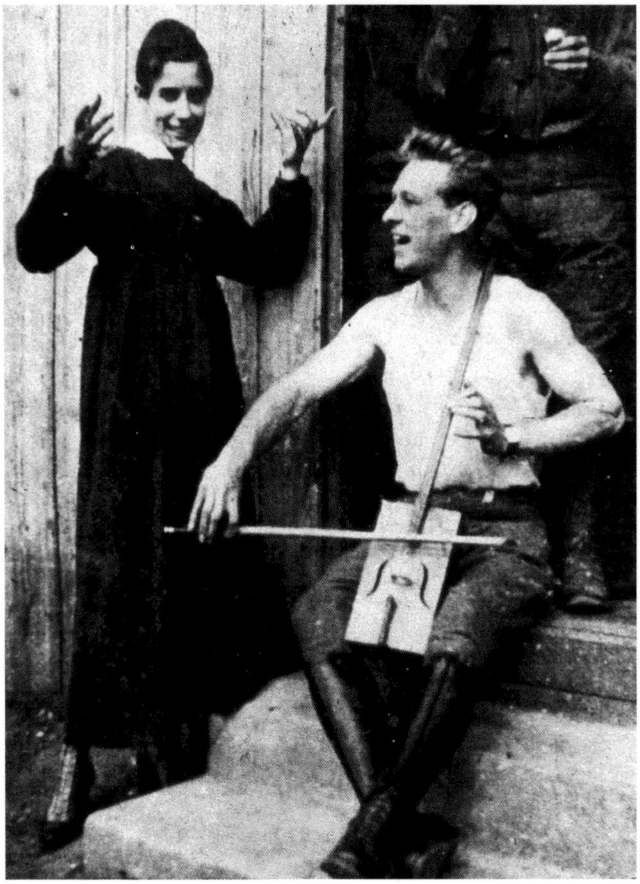

J. Gude, who if not heroic, was at least musical. Seen here entertaining one of the local talent with his homemade viola. An enlisted man stands in the doorway. *Via Alan Toelle.*

Major Raoul Lufbery stands beside one of the new N 28s bearing one gun and French markings. April 1918. *U. S. National Archives, RG III, SC 13359.*

Upsets in Type 28s were not unusual. Here we see Joe Eastman's number 6151 Squadron 14 on her back with Mont St. Michel in the background. *U. S. National Archives, RG III, SC 11314.*

Willing heads get number 14 back on her feet to be flown another day. Gengoult Airdrome, Toul, France, April 18, 1918. *U. S. National Archives, RG III, SC 11315.*

Nieuport 6195, Squadron number 8 was rolled over on April 20, 1918 by Jimmy Meissner. The landing gear appears to have suffered the greatest damage. *Reed Chambers album.*

Poor Joe Eastman seemed to have bad luck with some of his landings as evidenced by the condition of N 6149, Squadron number 21. The plane had originally been assigned to 1st Lt. Charlie Woolley of the 95th, then surrendered to the 94th when the Kicking Mules were sent off to gunnery school at Cazeaux.

Major Raoul Lufbery at Gengoult. April 1918.

Pals pose at Toul. Thorne Taylor, Bill Loomis, Jim Meissner, Eddie Rickenbacker, and Walt Smythe.

The same gang basically, but they exchanged Reed Chambers for Rickenbacker. Who among these original six members owned the camera?

Lufbery's Number 2 having her guns sighted. Gengoult Airdrome, Toul, France. April 1918.

Right: It took more than pilots to make a squadron run smoothly as can be attested by Lt. Charles A. Rankin, the 94th Engineering Officer who was sorely tried by keeping the 28s in the air.

94th Nieuports line up. The plane facing the camera carries a white cowling as was the habit of A Flight. Rickenbacker's number 12, N 6159, is next followed by Huffer's number 1, N 6169, and the last two cannot be identified. Toul, France. April 1918.

Walt Smythe readies for a flight, supported by Sgt. Jackson and the others of his ground crew. Smythe's Nieuport has a white cowl, marked with Squadron number 4, N 6230. Alden Sherry later flew this plane.

Both Ken Marr and Alan Winslow flew Squadron number 6. Records show there were two aircraft numbered "6", N 6172 which Marr wrecked when he collided with Taylor at Gengoult and N 6189. As no rudder markings can be seen, the actual plane cannot be identified.

The mechanical wizards, M. Sgt. Bertrandais, Chief of the Field, in the cockpit, and 1st Lt. Charles H. Rankin, Engineering Officer. Toul, France. April 1918.

Two more of the unsung enlisted heroes of the Engineering Section, both of whom are unidentified. Note the "94" in brass numbers on the left hand man's overseas cap.

Nieuport 28 number 6189 bearing the squadron white "6" is warming up at Gengoult. Two marking items of interest are the lack of the "Hat in the Ring" insignia and the spirals painted on the wheel covers.

Bill Loomis flew N 6181 Squadron dark-painted 15 which also bore painted rings on the cowling. The ship is being worked on by Loomis' mechanics. *Bill Loomis album.*

The same aircraft as in the previous photo having some serious tune-up work done on the engine. Gengoult Airdrome. April 1918. *Bill Loomis album.*

A 94th Nieuport line-up at Gengoult Airdrome, April 1918. Cunningham and Eastman flew number 14, Davis and Lufbery flew number 16 in which Lufbery lost his life on May 19. The Nieuport manufacturer's number of this plane was 6178. *Lt. Sumner Sewall album.*

Flying this airplane, N 6164, Doug Campbell scored one of the first official victories of the Squadron over a Pfalz DIIIa of Jasta 65 above Gengoult Airdrome, April 14, 1918. *U. S. National Archives, RG III, SC 19500.*

A Pfalz DIIIa in the later style German national markings, not over-painted Maltese crosses. This was the type of airplane shot down by Campbell for his first victory.

The smoldering remains of Campbell's Pfalz, with souvenir hunters hard at work. April 14, 1918.

Another view of the wreckage of Campbell's first victory. April 14, 1918.

A third view of the Pfalz with Campbell's picture superimposed on the left. These photos must have been made up for distribution as a souvenir of the event.

A view of another Pfalz with over-painted Maltese crosses on a ship built in 1917, Werks #8143.

Doug Campbell poses holding one of the Pfalz's Maxim machine guns and a belt of its ammunition. The gun was badly bent from the crash and the fabric ammo belt and its drum are in Campbell's right hand.

Campbell's Pfalz on display at the Toul city square, April 15, 1918. Not much to identify the Pfalz except the engine, a few spars, and the landing gear. *Lt. Sumner Sewall album.*

A slightly different view of the Pfalz remains and the nose of Winslow's Albatros D Va.

Campbell and Alan Winslow hold up an insignia cut from the upper wing of Winslow's Albatros. *Bill Loomis album.*

Winslow's Albatros right after the downing. As the German landed in close proximity to the American field, it didn't take long for the crowd to gather.

Winslow poses with his victim where it fell. April 14, 1918.

An Albatros DVa on a German field.

Another view of an Albatros D Va in its natural state on a German airfield somewhere in France.

This page and opposite: Eight photographs showing Winslow and his Albatros moving from the crash site to the Airdrome and finally to the Toul city square. The townspeople had never seen a German aircraft on the ground in such a complete state of being and it drew large crowds for several days.

Winslow, Campbell, and Major Huffer taken near the permanent buildings at Gengoult Airdrome not long after the two victories were scored. Note that Major Huffer wears spurs. April 14, 1918.

J. Gude is ready to take off in N 6154 Squadron 7. Gengoult Airdrome, late April 1918. *Lt. Joe Dawson album.*

Thorne Taylor poses in N 6148 Squadron 13. This Nieuport came from the 95th and when Taylor went to Spads, it was turned over to the 147th. The Greek letters of Taylor's fraternity, Delta Tau Delta, are below the cockpit.

Below: A nice view of Albatros fighters lined up at a German airfield. The earlier Maltese crosses were still in use and the German style aviation tent hangars can be seen on the left. *U. S. National Archives, 165 CN 4719.*

Reed Chambers in his Type 28N 6179 Squadron 11. This was the only Nieuport Chambers flew from March until the Spads arrived in July.

Thorne Taylor and John Wentworth relax before an alert at Gengoult Airdrome. Taylor's #13 is in the background. Late April 1918. *U. S. Air Force Museum.*

Major Raoul Lufbery stands by Rickenbacker's N 6159. Note the emblem by the cockpit. *Joe Dawson album.*

Captain Jim Hall with a French Spad in the background. April 1918.

Reed Chambers and Raoul Lufbery. Gengoult Airdrome, April 1918. *Bill Loomis album.*

Right: Reed Chambers. Gengoult Airdrome. April 1918. *Reed Chambers album.*

Commandant de la Forst decorates Campbell and Winslow with the Croix-de-Guerre at Gengoult Airdrome, April 18, 1918. L/R unknown French officer, Major Huffer, Lufbery, Campbell, Commandant de la Forst, Green, Winslow, Loomis, Chambers, unknown. *U. S. National Archives, RG III, SC 11316.*

Campbell and Winslow wearing their new medals. April 18, 1918. *U. S. National Archives, RG III, SC 11312.*

Major Huffer, F. P. Adams, an editor of the *Stars and Stripes*, and Major Lufbery attending the award ceremony for Campbell and Winslow. April 18, 1918. *U. S. National Archives, RG III, SC 11313.*

This page and opposite: Publicity photos of Campbell and Winslow before the medal ceremony. *U. S. National Archives, RG III, SC 11308, 11309, 11310, 11311.*

An Albatros D-type in Australian hands. Similar to Winslow's victim.

Alan Winslow, April 18, 1918.

Doug Campbell. April 18. 1918.

3

May - First Victories and Losses

May was to be an active month for the 94th which had both its triumphs as well as its share of tragedies. On May 1 the morning dawned with fog and rain, but by the afternoon it improved and three alerts were called that resulted in no action. Major Lufbery, who had responded to the third alert, developed engine trouble which caused him to prematurely land his Nieuport, turning over while he was performing a dead stick landing. Fortunately, the plucky Major walked away unhurt.

Rickenbacker had accompanied Lufbery on this 5 p.m. alert over Montsec, then on to Pont-à-Mousson and had observed that Lufbery's sudden dive which he thought to be an attack. Following him down, Rickenbacker observed Lufbery's propellor was not turning and discovered that he was looking for a suitable place to set down. A few kilometers south of Pont-à-Mousson a smooth field which turned out to be flat, was found, but unfortunately, it was very muddy. One slightly bent Nieuport was brought by road back to Squadron Repair and was to fly again.

The following day, May 2, the weather was officially reported as "Fairly good all day", which enabled the 94th to mount eight separate patrols. On the 11:23 patrol to protect a French photographic mission, Lts. Davis and Meissner encountered an enemy aircraft over Foret de la Rappe. Meissner's combat report only told part of the story: "Max. Altitude 5000 meters; Mission Protection Patrol; Narrative: Combat with monoplace Albatros at 4800 meters over Foret de la Rappe – Albatros shot down in flames at 12.03. I had to land at la Ferne de Nanceville because of wings damaged in the combat."

Meissner had experienced the first example of the structural problem which was inherent in the Nieuport 28, the collapse of the leading edge of the upper wing which led to the stripping of the upper fabric. This problem was caused by overstressing the aircraft in a full power dive, usually in the heat of combat. Meissner recounts the action in an unpublished account:

> "The (enemy) was going into a spiral when two tracer bullets went straight into its fuselage right back of the motor. Flames burst out from the cockpit instantly for I'd struck his tank, but to be sure the pilot was not alive and suffering, I kept up shooting. Diving with full motor in the excitement of the moment, I got so close that a lurch of the blazing enemy made me plunge almost vertically to avoid a crash. The strain was too great; with a crack, my top wing seemed to break loose and whip back overhead at the instant I shot under the Boche, so near I thought we had met. I wondered how soon the bottom wing would fold up and leave me in a wingless fuselage, pointed at Earth 15,000 feet below; what beastly luck to die just as my first victory had been won.
>
> But suddenly, I realized the top wing wasn't all gone, and the bottom wing hadn't folded up yet, the plane was still diving with motor cut off, still answering to the controls as I gently rocked the stick and pushed on the rudder. Surprised at still being alive, I looked up to see what really had happened to the top wing. All the entering edge, back to the main spar, had torn off, taking the linen completely off the upper surface from wing tip to wing tip so that only about two thirds of the covering on the lower surface was held against the ribs by wind pressure alone."

Meissner was flying Nieuport 28 6144 which had originally been assigned to Lt. Bill Casgrain of the 95th, who had been forced to give the plane up when he and the others of the

95th were sent back to Cazeaux Gunnery School. Number 6144 was returned to and repaired at Gengoult Aerodrome, then flown by Meissner until the Nieuports were replaced by Spad XIIIs. Under similar circumstances, and in the same plane, he was to lose the leading edge and the upper fabric again on May 30.

The *Compte-Rendu*, May 9, 1918, of the 8th French Army confirmed "Albatros-Monoplace-Down in Flames 12h 03 4800 mts. Foret de la Rappe."

The German two-seaters were having a difficult time due to the lack of fighter protection, being constantly attacked or driven back. A two-seater of FA (A) 298b on a photographic mission was driven back before it even reached the lines by four single-seaters. An hour later two additional two-seaters attempted to complete the photographic mission. They were attacked by two Nieuports and one of the two-seaters, a Hannover CL with the crew of Ltn. Hemmerle and Ltn. Neff, was brought down in flames over Foret de Vencheres. A report filed by Flakgruko 31 stated that one of the attacking Nieuports was damaged and presumably crashed or had to make an emergency landing. A section of fabric bearing an American cocard was found near the remains of the Hannover. As shown in Meissner's report, this is correct and how it actually happened, except that the downed plane was a Hannover CL, not an Albatros as Meissner reported and the French confirmed.

Earlier, at 11:00 a.m., 2nd Lt. Alan Winslow encountered an enemy biplace over Bois de Mort Mare, an action he described in his combat report. "Altitude, 4000 meters; Hour of leaving, 10:26; Hour of arrival, 11:22. Mission, Alert over Rambucourt; Route Camp – Rambucourt – Essey – Pont-à-Mousson. Encountered enemy biplace at 11:00 A.M. over Bois de Mort Mare. Chased enemy plane down below 1000 meters and into Germany about 6 kilometers past Essey. I fired about 100 shots at enemy from long range. Bullets entered German plane, but enemy kept on its course. No shots fired at me."

The weather held on May 3 and at 9:25 a patrol comprised of Captain Peterson, Lts. Campbell, Davis, Loomis, and Chapman engaged the enemy on three occasions. Dave Peterson who was Chief of Patrol, filed the following report of the action:

> "Time out 9.25, Time in 11.20; Max Altitude 4000, Mission Patrol; 10.00 A.E.G. biplace region Ancerville at 3000 meters, we chased it home. We could not get close enough to attack. Plane signaled by Archies. 10.25 4 Monoplace Albatros, region Harbouey, 3500 meters. We attacked driving them down to 1500 meters. 10.40 4 Monoplace, 1 biplace region Aurepierre at 3500 meters. We attacked, one of our planes hard pressed by enemy biplace on his tail, I disengaged him, saw enemy leave and Nieuport redress, then Nieuport dove vertically and burst into flames at 2000 meters. Fight continued at 10.45 with another Nieuport of our patrol. I attacked enemy monoplace from close range. He dove vertically then burst into flames and hit the ground near d'Amenencourt."

This was confirmed by *Compte-Rendu* of the French 8th Army, May 9, 1918.

The burning Nieuport was that of 2nd Lt. Charles W. Chapman, Jr., of Waterloo, Iowa. Chapman had enlisted in and was trained by French Aviation from June 1917 to February 1918, being commissioned 2nd Lt. U.S.A.S. February 21, 1918. He was assigned to the 94th on March 3, being part of Peterson's third flight which included Campbell, Loomis, Cunningham, Davis, and Eastman. On the day of his death Chapman was flying Nieuport 6138 with the Squadron number *0* which had originally been assigned to Lt. Harold Buckley of the 95th.

Later in the day, Captain Hall, Lts. Rickenbacker and Campbell, were on high patrol from 18h 39 to 19h 54 with Hall reporting:

> "Between Vigny and Soin (north of Nomeny) met one Albatros monoplace going towards Metz at 5000 meters. Time 19.30. Attacked from a distance. Capt. Hall's gun jammed after 20 rounds; enemy continued flight. Patrol too far in enemy territory to pursue. No other enemy planes sighted. Lt. Campbell fired about 20 rounds. Lt. Rickenbacker left patrol at Nancy."

Over the next three days, the weather began to deteriorate again, with one alert and one patrol flown on May 4 and no activity on May 5 and May 6. Skies were overcast on May 7, but conditions were good enough for the performance of a patrol of five Nieuports, as well as an early alert being called which stated that there were four enemy aircraft over Pont-à-Mousson. This alert was signalled at 7h 27 and was responded to by Lts. Rickenbacker and Green, led by Captain Hall. There are three recorded reports of this alert, two by Lt. Green and one by Lt. Rickenbacker, which are as follow:

> "Date May 7, 1918; Time out 7h 27; Time in 8h 16; Mission, Alert; 4 Boche over Pont-à-Mousson. Capt Hall, Lt. Rickenbacker and Green. Lt. Rickenbacker led to three enemy planes. I followed and attacked with Capt. Hall. One Boche went down in a vrille. Another monoplace attacked me from the rear. I turned and fired and he went down in a steep nose dive. I followed for a distance. One

Boche attacked a Nieuport below me and it went down in a vrille, apparently leveling out later. I joined the other Nieuport (Lt. Rickenbacker) and came home. M. E. Green, 1st Lt. ASSC. USR."

Green's second report read:

"Hdqrs. 94th Aero Squadron, S.C.

May 7, 1918.

Answering an alert, Lieutenant Rickenbacker and myself, led by Captain Hall, started north to the lines. On arriving east of Pont-à-Mousson, we turned west following the lines nearly to Fliery and on the German side at about 3500 meters. Lieut. Rickenbacker suddenly turned back and Captain Hall, with myself, followed. Lieut. Rickenbacker attacked first just northeast of Pont-à-Mousson and about four kilometers in the German lines, going down steeply on three German planes. Captain Hall and myself followed almost together. I dove twice, firing on a German plane, when I pulled up to arm my machine gun, which failed to work, during the second dive. I was just ready to go down again on the planes, when a fourth German monoplace attacked me from the rear. I maneuvered quickly and getting behind him fired several rounds. He went down in an almost perpendicular nose dive. I followed for a distance, firing, but could not dive steeply enough. At this time I saw a Nieuport plane five hundred meters or more below (myself being at about 1500) dive on a German plane, which was doing a tail spin. The German plane suddenly straightened out and came up and around in what appeared to be a sharp virage on the tail of the Nieuport. The Nieuport went into a vrille and leveled out very near the ground, disappearing over a forest. Another plane appeared and I went to meet it, proving to be Lieut. Rickenbacker.

Being at a low altitude and some distance over the lines, we started toward the lines, climbing, after waiting a moment for Captain Hall to appear, and not seeing him, we came to our post.

M. Edwin Green,
1st Lieut. ASSC. USR."

Rickenbacker's account of the engagement was:

"Hdqrs. 94th Aero Squadron, S.C.
May 7, 1918

Captain Hall received an alert about 7:30 A.M. of four enemy planes coming south, Pont-à-Mousson. Captain Hall, Lieutenant Green and myself left immediately, flying Northeast, Pont-à-Mousson, arriving over Pont-à-Mousson shortly before 8 o'clock at about 3500 meters altitude, but could not see anything of enemy planes. We then returned patrol east of Pont-à-Mousson for a short distance. Turning around, we again flew over Pont-à-Mousson at the same altitude, when I noticed one enemy biplace ahead of us just over the lines and about 1000 meters below. However, their anti-aircraft gave him signal of our approach, and he immediately dove into Germany. About the same time I noticed three enemy planes flying in formation approximately five or six kilometers in Germany and 1500 meters below us. I attracted Captain Hall's attention and reversed directions, upon which we peaked towards the Boche. I, of course, was ahead of him at the time, owing to my position.

I decided to attack one monoplace and was peaking close to him when another appeared from the rear. I left the first one, started climbing, and again peaked on another, firing approximately 50 or 75 rounds at him. The last seen, he was still peaking into Germany. While in a village, I noticed a Nieuport going down in a vrille. Of course, at the time I was unaware who it was. I then saw one of the patrol headed back towards our lines and immediately started climbing in the direction, as the enemy had been so scattered it was useless to continue the fight. Upon arriving at the field, I found that Captain Hall was missing.

(Sgd) E. V. Rickenbacker,
1st Lieut. ASSC., USR."

What in actuality occurred was the second failure of the leading edge of the Nieuport upper wing. Captain Hall entered the fray with Green and Rickenbacker and was diving after a Pfalz DIII of Jasta 64 when the wing edge collapsed, crippling his Nieuport. This was immediately seen by Leutnant Friedrich Hengst of Jasta 64 who attempted to force Hall to an even lower altitude. While this was occurring Hall's plane was hit in the engine by an anti-aircraft shell which luckily for Hall did not explode, but it killed the engine forcing him to land behind enemy lines. Captain Hall was injured, but not seriously, and became a guest of the Kaiser for the duration.

An interesting side to the story is that even though fire from M. Flak 54 finally brought the aircraft down, Ltn. Hengst was awarded the first victory for Jasta 64 as it was he who brought Hall down to the range of the Flak battery. This was his second victory, the first while flying as an enlisted pilot with Schusta 3, a two-seater outfit, which was over a FE 2b of 23 Sqdn. on March 11, 1917.

Doug Campbell in a letter home dated July 12, 1918 related the events of the previous week:

"Air Service, A.E.F.
France, May 12, 1918

For the last week this place has been pretty dead – raining all the time, no flying. About 10 days ago five of us got into a royal scrap with 5 Boche planes, and Capt. Peterson sent one of the Huns hurtling down thru space, but Chapman got himself into a corner and was brought down in flames. Just a week ago Capt. Hall got into a fight and was seen spinning down. But Ed Green saw him straighten out further down, and we are pretty sure that his motor got put out of business by a bullet, and that he spun down so as not to get shot, for he was out of gliding distance of the lines. Let's hope so, anyway, until we get definite news. (Note: Actually, a dud A. A. shell hit Hall's motor and stuck there, making his plane so out of balance that he spiraled into the ground and broke a few bones; he was a prisoner until after the Armistice.)

Hall's *High Adventure* is coming out in book form this spring, I think. If he is all right and lives thru the treatment he gets (his wounds of last June didn't leave him in too good shape), we will see "some" book after the war.

Wad is back from the front, and was supposed to come over from G— today, but it is after supper and he hasn't showed up. Eleventh hour interruption, I suppose."

Rickenbacker states in *Fighting the Flying Circus* that Lufbery within minutes of learning Hall was missing went on a solo flight into Germany and in a fight with "three fighting machines" he shot one down and the others retreated further into Germany. He also states that this was confirmed by an advanced post who witnessed the combat. There is no record of Lufbery's flight in the *Report of Operations*, nor was there any confirmation of this victory forwarded to the Squadron.

A patrol the same day of Captain Peterson, Lts. Campbell, Davis, Cunningham and Loomis headed out for Pont-à-Mousson where they intercepted three enemy Albatros in the area of Villers. There were no results of this encounter which Lt. A. L. Cunningham briefly described in his reconnaissance report:

"Left the field and was the high man on the patrol. When in the region of Villers met three Albatros. I attacked one of them, fired about 30 shots, and was attacked by two others above me; a jam in my machine gun caused me to maneuver around the other two and leave. My machine was shot in six places." Lt. Arthur A. Cunningham was listed on November 11, 1918 as "Pilot-Present. Interpreter and Historian."

He had two combats, and after the end of May did not participate in active combat flying.

On May 8, Rickenbacker was made Flight Commander filling the void left by Captain Hall. The weather that day turned to rain and overcast curtailing flight operations until the afternoon of May 11 when fair skies allowed him and Lt. Chambers to answer an alert over Thiaucourt. In that area they encountered three enemy aircraft which were put to flight. Rickenbacker's combat report stated: "Mission alert, saw three Boche planes. Had slight combat. No results. Vicinity of Flirey." Also on May 11, two new pilots, 1st Lts. Willard D. Hill and Walter W. Smythe, joined the Squadron and were immediately integrated into aerial patrols.

The next day all operations were suspended due to low overcast, but May 13 brought a clear morning with a few low clouds mid-day and a fine clear afternoon. Five patrols, St. Mihiel to Pont-à-Mousson were flown, as well as one reconnaissance and one alert which all produced "No results" in the "Operations Report", although the new man, Lt. Walt Smythe had a forced landing returning from the 19h 00 patrol. Rain and low overcast again on May 14, but the 15th was fair in the morning with alerts coming into the Squadron as early as 6h 03 and continuing until 18h 08 in the evening. The first active alert which departed at 9h 43 for the vicinity of Dieulouard consisted of Captain Marr and Lts. Winslow, Meissner, Hill, Wentworth, and Taylor.

Captain Marr, the only pilot who filed a report of the action, was a model of brevity in his combat report: "May 15, 1918. Altitude, 2000 meters. Hour of leaving, 9.46; Hour arrived, 10.15. Route, Villirs-sous-Puny, in Germany. 1 Biplace enemy plane attacked, 20 rounds fired. Went down in a vrille. Confirmation Requested. (Sgd). Kenneth Marr, Capt. A.S. USR."

The next alert at 10h 14 was to intercept an enemy plane flying towards the south near the Foret de l'Eveque. Lt. Rickenbacker led Lts. Green, Gude, Chambers, and Smythe, with the only report being filed by Chambers. "Combat Report of Lt. Chambers – Date May 15, 1918; Altitude (not entered); Hour of leaving, 10.33; Hour of Arrival, 11.37; Names of Pilots, Lt. Chambers; Route, St. Mihiel to Pont-à-Mousson. One German observation balloon north of Flirey 11.20 A.M. Fired 40 rounds of ammunition, large black cloud of smoke was seen after attack and no balloon when smoke cleared. Germans are evidently firing a lot of heavy shells. CONFIRMATION REQUESTED. (Sgd.) Reed Chambers, 1st Lt. ASSRC."

Less than two hours later, Lts. Meissner and Taylor departing at 12h 00 were on a patrol from Chateau Salins to Seicheprey when they encountered four enemy aircraft. Lt. Meissner filed the following combat report:

> "Coming west from Xammes at 13h 05 four Germans were seen about 200 meters below our altitude of 4500 meters. They started to circle. I dove on one, despite a jammed gun, in hopes Lt. Taylor would dive on another and break up the circle. My enemy dove straight down, and seeing two other enemy planes climbing, I did not follow. Lt. Taylor dove on the fourth firing, but his enemy also dove steeply and Lt. Taylor pulled up turning to find a biplace and headed south. As two enemy planes were now above us and climbing, we both returned to our own lines and were not followed."

The circle the wagons technique used by the Germans seemed to have been an effective defense turned into an offense in this situation.

Shortly before Meissner and Taylor's patrol, Captain Peterson was flying alone between Thiaucourt and Rembercourt when he ran into some decidedly heavy action which was described in his combat report:

> "At 11h 50 saw 2 Boche planes, region Thiaucourt at about 4000 meters. Staid (stayed?) above in the sun and waited for them. At 12.05 they turned towards our lines in single file, altitude 5200 meters. I swung in behind and attacked rear one from above, firing 50 shots. He dove almost vertical for 500 meters then burst into flames. In the meantime the other had attacked me from in front. I turned and attacked him from above. He threw out a cloud of smoke, then attempted a sharp bank and turn, when about a quarter thru, he slipped, the wings folded up, one of them becoming detached, and dropped. Could not see them hit on account of clouds and fog. 75 shots. CONFIRMATIONS REQUESTED."

These two victories were confirmed by the *Compte-Rendu* of the 8th French Army, May 27, 1918. These and his victory of May 3 were all scored while Captain Peterson was flying Nieuport 6158. This Nieuport had been a 95th Aero plane originally assigned to Lt. Waldo Heinrichs and was later flown by Lt. Joe Eastman and finally, for 20 days, by Lt. Doug Campbell until he was wounded in June.

Nine of the 94th's first eighteen victories were scored by Peterson and Campbell flying this old war-horse number 6158, which was quite a tribute to the Type 28, often criticized for its weaknesses.

The aerial activity of May 15 was supplemented by festivities on the ground in the form of a parade of French and American troops and decoration ceremonies by General Gerard of the 8th French Army. The award was the French Croix-de-Guerre with palm, and was to be presented to Captain Peterson, Lt. Rickenbacker, Lt. Meissner, Captain Hall in abstentia, and Lt. Chapman, posthumously. Prior to the ceremony, there was a great deal of kidding among the pilots and the recipients as to the French custom of kissing the cheeks of the hero after the presentation. General Gerard made the awards, and much to the relief of the gallant three in attendance, no kissing took place. The medals were given to Hall, Rickenbacker, Peterson, and Meissner for their victories and to 2nd Lt. Chapman for his valor shown on the day he was killed in action.

The good weather held and the alerts came in quantity. On May16 there were twenty-two, of which fourteen were actually responded to by aircraft.

In the afternoon, Lt. Jimmy Meissner was sent out on a mission called in his reconnaissance report an "Attack on Drifting Balloon" at an altitude of 4500 meters. The action he described follows: "Drifting balloon at 3500 meters, carried by south wind into German lines. Followed it some distance, lost it so attacked another balloon southwest of Mars la Tour at 6 P.M. Observer seen to jump in parachute while balloon was drawn down. 100 rounds fired at about 500 meters range, attacked by Albatros, and being at 1200 meters, returned to French lines."

The first balloon which was adrift belonged to Bz. 214[1] and its tether cable had been shot through by artillery fire and the second, which was brought to safety by its ground crew, belonged to Bz. 47.

As the war progressed, the 30-caliber Vickers machine gun was modified by Colt's Firearms Company of Hartford, Connecticut to fire an 11 mm bullet designed specifically for anti-balloon attacks. When these new guns reached the front, success in balloon kills rose dramatically and certain pilots like Frank Luke of the 27th and Lansing Holden of the 95th became proficient and expert in their use.

At 14:45, Lt. Doug Campbell departed on a patrol to Thiaucourt and ran into three German observation two-seaters, and filed the following combat report: "1 combat with 2 enemy biplace at 3.35 P.M. and 1 combat with 1 biplace about 4.00 o'clock, west of Thiaucourt. No apparent results on account of clouds, altitude 4500 meters." The day ended with a late protection patrol of 2 planes departing at 19h 35 and returning at 20h 20.

Alerts continued hot and heavy on May 17 with the first at 4h 42 and the last at 18h 35. At 4h 35, Lts. Eddie Rickenbacker and Reed Chambers set off on an early patrol from St. Mihiel to Pont-à-Mousson. Rickenbacker stated in his book that this patrol was to test out a plan to get a high altitude position over the German lines, reaching this position without alerting the German anti-aircraft or "Archie" batteries of their presence, and then as the Germans departed their field, dive down out of the sun for the kill. At 6h 24 when practically out of fuel, dauntless Eddie spotted three Albatros in the vicinity of Richecourt and began his attack. In his words he describes the engagement:

> "When the leader made the first swerve aside, I was less than two hundred yards from the rear Albatros. I was descending at a furious pace, regardless of anything but my target ahead. Fully two hundred miles an hour, my Nieuport was flying. Without checking her speed, I kept her nose pointing at the tail of the rear Albatros, which was now darting steeply downward to escape me. As the distance closed to fifty yards, I saw my tracer bullets piercing the back of the pilots seat. I had been firing for perhaps ten seconds from first to last. The scared Boche had made the mistake of trying to out dive me instead of outmaneuvering me. He paid for his blunder with his life."

He went on to say:

> "I believe I should (would?) have followed my first target all the way to the ground regardless of the consequences, so desperately had I determined to get him. So I perhaps prolonged my terrific speed a trifle too long. As the enemy airplane fell off and began to flutter, I pulled my stick back close to my lap and began a sharp climb. A frightening crash that sounded like the crack of doom told me that the sudden strain had collapsed my right wing. The entire spread of canvas over the top wing was torn off by the wind and disappeared behind me. Deprived of any supporting surface on this framework, the Nieuport turned over on her right side. The tail was forced up despite all my efforts with joystick and rudder."

Rickenbacker spun down over 10,000 feet by his estimation, at which time he put on full power which brought the Nieuport out of its spin and allowed him to reach the field at Toul. This became the third occurrence of the upper wing problem and the pilots of both the 94th and the 95th began to seriously consider the frailty of the Nieuport 28 under a full power dive. There were more of these incidents to come.

Rickenbacker's combat report of this event was short and to the point:

> "Time out 4h 35;Time in 6h 41; Mission Patrol; Had combat with three Albatros in vicinity of Richecourt at 6h 24; 1 Albatros was last seen descending in a vrille, the other two going into Germany. 1 plane evidently landed just behind German lines, badly damaged. Confirmation asked."

The confirmation was positively made May 27, 1918 in the *Compte-Rendu* of the 8th French Army.

Rickenbacker was flying Major Huffer's Nieuport White #1, serial number 6169 at the time of this engagement, records showing the wing was repaired that day and the aircraft was immediately back in service on May 18.

Later in the morning, Doug Campbell responded to a 9:00 alert and at 9:40 a.m. noted two Albatros biplace east of Thiaucourt at 3500 meters which he did not attack; at 9:45 he saw one plane over Frouard at about 4500 meters which he did not attack and five minutes later he engaged one of two Albatros biplace east of Thiaucourt at 3500 meters without results.

May 18 was very clear and the first patrol departed at 6:25 a.m. for St. Mihiel to Pont-à-Mousson at 3500 meters. There were six in the group: Major Huffer, Captain Marr, Lts. Hill, Meissner, Taylor, and Wentworth. Thorne Taylor spotted two enemy two-seaters at a higher altitude of 5500 meters. He rose to meet them and afterwards filed his combat report:

> "Combat at 7h 45 with one (1) German Rumpler and one (1) Albatros Biplace. Fired about 200 rounds. Albatros last seen descending in a vrille, over BUXERULIES, apparently no damage to the Rumpler, which I followed to THIAUCOURT. This enemy plane obtained higher altitude than I could get to. (one confirmation requested)."

This short narrative tells us two things about combat in May. One, the less experienced pilots expended large amounts of ammunition when compared to the old pros who would fire 50 to 75 rounds to the 200-300 of the novices. Secondly, the

Rumpler of all the two-seaters could easily attain an altitude to which our pursuit planes simply could not reach.

Later in the morning Major Lufbery, as was his style, went on a solo reconnaissance flight to Pont-à-Mousson and return which was to last but 51 minutes. During this flight he encountered some opposition about which he reported in his usual terse manner: "Time out 8h 11; Time in 9h 02; Max Alt 3500; Mission Reconnaissance Flight; Narrative, Major Lufbery met 6 German planes in the region of Norroy. He attacked, fired a few shots, his gun jammed and he had to return. Major Lufbery, USSC.US." Note he states "fired a few shots, his gun jammed;" "gun" singular, so on May 18 it would appear the 94th were still flying with a single gun. Photos of Lufbery standing by his "White 2" Nieuport 6193 bear out this unbelievable deficiency. It was not until almost the end of the 94th's stay at Toul in June that this was corrected.

At 8h 40 Doug Campbell mounted a voluntary patrol from the line St. Mihiel to southeast of Verdun. He was more successful than Taylor and Lufbery as his combat report reflects:

> "Time out 8h 40; Time in 10h 30; Max Altitude 5200; Mission Voluntary Patrol, 1 biplace 5200, 9h 20 about 10 klms. Southeast of Verdun. Attacked and saw bullets strike wing and fuselage. Enemy spiraled and piqued steeply into Germany. Followed to 2500 meters then turned back because of French anti-aircraft shells bursting at high altitude in the direction of Douaumont. CONFIRMATION ASKED. (Sgd) Douglas Campbell, 1st Lt. ASSRC."

Campbell's reaction to the French anti-aircraft fire without doubt was a prudent one as it was a warning and indicated the Germans were coming his way with an altitude advantage.

Campbell's confirmation was received the next day. "Lt. Campbell – enemy biplace – 9h 30 – 3200 mts. – Region Benzee –5-18-18. Confirmed by:Compte-Rendu of the 8th French Army of May 19th, 1918. Paragraph (3)." This was Campbell's second victory and number ten for the 94th.

This same day 1st Lt. Paul B. Kurtz joined the squadron, a temporary assignment for him to gain some combat experience before he was to be assigned as a permanent gunnery instructor. He had gone through his basic flight training with Rickenbacker, then sent to England for special aerial gunnery training and now was attending a "finishing school" with the 94th. Accompanying Kurtz was Lt. William G. Morrison who had the same temporary assignment.

May 19 was a day in which the squadron was dealt a savage blow. The first entry in the daily *Report of Operations* stated that "Weather very clear in the morning; clear in the afternoon until 16h 30 then showers and cloudy." Early patrols began with the first at 5h 10 until 6h 57 with Major Huffer leading Lts. Rickenbacker and Chambers. At 7h 30, Major Lufbery and Lt. Gude flew a patrol in a line from St. Mihiel to Pont-à-Mousson at the rather high altitude of 5400 meters, returning with nothing to report at 8h 41. Gude had made a test flight earlier at 5h 44 to 5h 54. Lts. Rickenbacker and Smythe answered an alert at 8h 36 to intercept an enemy plane over Commercy at 5000 meters, an alert which resulted in a combat with an Albatros at 9h 12 and a return to the field at 9h 42.

The *Report of Operations* stated that another alert was called at 8h 55 which was nineteen minutes after the one answered by Rickenbacker and Smythe. The "Report" says that the alert was answered by Lt. Gude, Major Huffer, and Major Lufbery. Lt. Gude filed a combat report as follows: "Date – May 19, 1918. Altitude 1500 meters. Squadron No. 94, Hour of Leaving, 8.35; Hour of Arrival 9.18; Names of Pilots, Lt. Gude. Mission – Alert – Toul . Combat with one Boche – 350 to 400 rounds – at 9h 00 to 9h 10. Attacked six times. Saw him go into a vrille near river southeast of Camp, near Foret de Haye. Conf'm Asked. (Sgd) O. J. Gude, 1st Lt. ASSRC."

Gude returned to the field at 9h 18 which was eight minutes after he expended his ammunition. Rickenbacker, who was in the air at the time, quotes in his book Major Huffer's account of events of that morning: "It was about ten o'clock when the anti-aircraft guns on top of Saint-Mihiel began belching white puffs of smoke overhead at a very high altitude. The alert came to us immediately that a German photography machine was coming our way and was at that moment almost directly over our field." This account starts to wander from the *Report of Operations* and Gude's combat report. The time quoted was 8h 55 and the altitude of the intruder was 1500 meters, not *about ten o'clock* and not *a very high altitude*. He goes on to say, "Lieutenant Gude was the only pilot on the field ready for flight. He was sent up alone to attack the intruder, an incident which brought regrettable results."

"It was Gude's first actual combat. His encounter with the enemy was seen by all the spectators who gathered about our hangers." Strange the *Report of Operations* names Huffer as one of three who answered the alert, but Rickenbackers's account says Gude was the only pilot ready. Huffer's Nieuport 6169, white number 1, was in service on May 19, even though Rickenbacker had collapsed the wing on May 17. It had been flown by Huffer for 60 minutes and by Colonel Mitchell for 48 minutes on May 19, and the early 5 A.M. patrol flown by Huffer himself on the fateful day would indicate his machine was in operation.

Rickenbacker's book continues:

"Gude began firing at an extreme range and continued firing until his ammunition was exhausted, without inflicting any appreciable damage upon the two-seater Albatros. As he came flying home, the Archie batteries in the neighborhood again took up the battle and poured up a violent barrage, which encompassed this lone enemy on every side. But to no purpose. The Albatros continued its retreat, climbing slightly and setting a course in the direction of Nancy."

Whether this is Huffer's account, or Rickenbacker's, the story continues:

"In the meantime, Major Lufbery, who had been watching the whole show from his barracks, jumped on a motorcycle that was standing in the road and rushed to the hangers. His own plane (Nieuport #6193 marked with the Squadron number white two) was out of commission. Another Nieuport was standing on the field, apparently ready for use. (Nieuport 6178 Squadron number white 16). It belonged to Lieutenant Davis. The mechanics admitted everything was ready and without another word, Lufbery jumped into the machine and immediately took off. With far greater speed than his heavier antagonist, Major Lufbery climbed in pursuit. In approximately five minutes after leaving the ground, he reached two thousand feet and had arrived within range of the Albatros six miles away. The first attack was witnessed by all our watchers.

Luf fired several short bursts as he dived in to the attack. Then he swerved away and appeared to busy himself with his gun, which evidently had jammed. Another circle over their heads and he had cleared the jam. Again he rushed the enemy from their rear, when suddenly old Luf's machine was seen to burst into flames. He passed the Albatros and proceeded for three or four seconds on a straight course. Then to the horrified watchers below, there appeared the figure of their hero in a headlong leap from the cockpit of the burning aircraft."

Major Lufbery's body landed in the garden behind a woman's home in the village of Maron.

There has always been a controversy as to whether Lufbery jumped or fell from his burning Nieuport. This will never be positively answered. When he hurriedly took off in Davis' machine, had he time to fasten his seatbelt? These early belts came over the shoulders with two straps and across the lap with two, all fastening into a central catch which could be a handful to assemble while taxiing or flying an airplane. It was later discovered that Davis flew with an extra pillow, which was actually a kneeling cushion from a church, on the seat. Royal Frey, one of the early directors of the Air Force Museum at Dayton, Ohio, was shown while on a visit to the area, the cushion which purportedly fell with Lufbery's body from the burning Nieuport. Could this extra seat height have had any effect which could have caused Lufbery to fall rather than jump from his plane? It is also reported that a finger had been shot off one hand and this wound could have made him lose control, abetting a fall. We will never know the answer for sure.

The two-seater, which was a Rumpler not an Albatros, avoided the heavy anti-aircraft fire only to be set upon by a flight from the French Escadrille Spa 68. The Rumpler was on a photo mission for *Reihenbildtrupp des A.O.K.C.* and was crewed by Ltn. Scheibe and Gefreiter Kirschbaum. During the attack by the French, Ltn. Scheibe who was manning the guns in the rear seat, fired at an approaching Spad and killed its pilot, Adjutant Baudry, with a single bullet through his heart. The Germans were then attacked by Sergent Dupre who was able to pour a stream of fire into them, at which time the plucky Germans, now out of ammunition, gave up and landed behind the French lines near the town of Flainval.

A single Rumpler on a photo mission, in spite of its own destruction, created, through Lufbery's death, a grave loss for the American cause, as well as the Baudry loss for the French and Spa 68.

Another alert was sounded at 10h 24 and was answered by Lts. Campbell, Loomis, Cunningham, and Eastman. Doug Campbell's combat report follows:

"Date, May 19, 1918. Altitude, 4500 meters. Sqdn No. 94. Hour of Leaving, 10h 24. Hour of Arrival, 11h 45. Names of Pilots, Lt. Campbell. Mission, – Alert. 4 planes at Pont-à-Mousson. Route, Pont-à-Mousson – St. Mihiel – Flirey. Sighted biplace at 4500 meters, 11h 35, four or five klms last of Flirey in our lines. Attacked. After two minute fight his right wings collapsed. CONFIRMATION ASKED. (Sgd.) Douglas Campbell, 1st Lt. ASSRC."

This victory was confirmed in the *Compte-Rendu* of the 8th French Army of the same day. The fight took place over Beaumont at 4800 meters when Campbell must have completely surprised Ltns. Bayer and Kämmerer of Flieger-Abteilung (A) 298b, as they found no time to defend themselves. Campbell's first bullets apparently hit the bracing wires of the right wing which broke off the aircraft, then fell straight down to crash near Flirey. This was the third crew loss of F.A. (A) 398b during May, which began to dramatically lower their morale and effectiveness.

Doug Campbell in his letter dated May 20, 1918, tells of this, his third victory, of which he shared the results with his visiting brother Wad who was serving with the U. S. Engineers:

"Alert House, Hat in the Ring Squadron
(don't use in address)
Air Service, A.E.F.
May 20, 1918.

Business is picking up. Wad came up here from G— day before yesterday in the evening and stayed over until yesterday after supper. He is looking awfully well. Just to show my brother what I could do, I went out yesterday morning and got me another Boche. We met over the lines north of here and had a nice fight. I soon succeeded in getting on his tail and started pumping him full of lead. It was an L.V.G. biplace, so of course the observer started shooting back at me; but I think I killed him soon, for he stopped shooting before I got very close to him. I kept on shooting, and was about 15 meters from him when his right wing crumpled up, and he fell from 4500 meters, hitting about a mile inside our lines. I tried to follow him down and watch him hit, but he went thru a cloud, and was going so much faster than I was that he had hit before I got thru the cloud. Realizing that it was up to me to strike for home and country, I struck for home at once, and announced my exploit by shouting my head off as I glided into the home field. The fall of the Boche had already been reported over the phone, but nobody knew who had got him until they heard me land.

Wad, Thorne Taylor, Rick, Major Huffer and I immediately got into a touring car and rode out to the front to look him over. His map showed that he was trying to photograph a certain battery, and I assisted him considerably, for the plane hit 50 meters from said battery and spread over a piece of ground 10 meters square. The pilot and observer were officers wearing the Iron Cross, and both were decorated with bullet holes in the head. I picked up a lot of souvenirs; the camera and plates were smashed, but a beautiful 4-inch Zeiss lens was uninjured, and will probably be used by the observation squadron of which Ken Culbert is a member.

The plane hit in a French sector, and an enthusiastic old Commandant must need to have the hero and his brother and friends dine with him. An excellent dinner in a little arbor in a wood 1 mile from the trenches, and trust the French to bring out a bottle of excellent Moet et Chandon to celebrate the occasion! The Commandant and I exchanged about 20 compliments during our stay at his post.

One never has good luck all the time. Major Lufbery tackled a biplace yesterday morning and was brought down in flames. I wouldn't believe it for a long time; he is always so sure of himself and goes at it so scientifically. To those who knew him well (I used to play bridge with him quite often in the evenings), he was a real man and a lovable character. There was nothing he liked better than to help us green pilots just as much as possible. It is hard to lose him.

Major Huffer got a French pilot to take Wad up for a little hop in a biplace machine, and I guess he enjoyed it a good deal.

I had 4 combats with biplaces on Thursday, Friday, and Saturday. The one on Saturday I am sure I hit, but didn't think I brought it down, and had to beat it because I was alone and some Huns were coming. It seems, however, that a machine came down at that place and time so it is possible that I will be credited with it, making 3 altogether. Not bad for a greenhorn, but I'm not swell-headed – yet."

The following day the 94th shared ten alerts with the 95th, none of which produced any type of success. On May 21, action picked up with a number of two, three, and four plane patrols, as well as single voluntary patrols flown, resulting in the following combat reports. Meissner, on a voluntary patrol at 8h 15, reported:

"Saw enemy plane (biplace) at 5000 meters over Gironville, flying north; attacked but machine gun jammed; fixed jam and attacked again northeast of St. Mihiel, firing twenty-five (25) rounds without result, when gun jammed again; combat took place at 9h 30. Enemy plane returned behind German lines."

Thorne Taylor on the 8h 44 alert filed two combat reports: "Saw 2 enemy biplace planes at 4800 meters over Gironville, flying north; attacked but without apparent result, firing about 75 rounds, following this plane inside our lines to Flirey, gaining altitude; No further combat." In his second report he wrote "Saw 1 enemy plane (Rumpler) at Flirey, flying southeast at approximately 6000 meters. Obtained position underneath this plane but could climb no higher than 5650 meters; followed over this field, when I descended, the enemy plane continuing its flight toward Nancy."

Lt. Willard Hill was a model of brevity. "Combat with 1 Boche biplace at 5500 meters, east of Flirey, without apparent results."

Alan Winslow, one of the two heroes of April 14, had been promoted to 1st Lieutenant and filed this report: "Saw biplace Boche attacked by another Nieuport at 11:00 above Hattonville. Boche went into a vrille; Nieuport left. I followed Boche down to 1500 meters. Boche then straightened out and I followed him to Gorze, firing 100 rounds, with no apparent results. My engine went wrong and stopped at 1000 meters directly above trenches; made a forced landing near Andilly."

This motor problem experienced by Winslow could well have been an example of the other frailty of the Nieuport 28. This problem was found in the earlier 28s, being the incorrect manner the gas line was attached from the fuel tank to the 150 hp Gnôme Monosoupape (single valve) Type 9-N motor. There originally was no flexible coupling in the line causing a tendency for it to crack due to the vibrations of the rotating engine. This vibration problem was exacerbated by the method used to control power which was not accomplished by a throttle, but by a switch firing one, three, five, seven, or all nine cylinders, as well as a button on the control stick which could kill all nine cylinders at once. Improper use caused misfires, which in turn caused vibration cracking the sensitive annealing of the copper tubing. This failure could result in unpleasant fires, as well as total loss of fuel and power.

May 22 was another black day for the 94th, when the temporarily attached Lt. Paul Kurtz plunged to his death at the end of a voluntary patrol with Lts. Rickenbacker and Chambers. At 8h 26 they met over the field to patrol the line St. Mihiel to Pont-à-Mousson. Lt. Kurtz was told not to attack unless the patrol had superior numbers. Rickenbacker's combat report states:

> "Saw three Monoplace Albatros 4500 meters over St. Mihiel at 9h 12 approximately. Attacked and followed them into Germany about six kilometers, separating one from the group which I again attacked and which fell. Shot about 100 rounds. Enemy plane last seen diving steeply north of Flirey. CONFIRMATION REQUESTED."

Rickenbacker's book says that after this fight he headed back to the Allied lines and was pursued by two "Germans" who turned out to be Chambers and Kurtz. While circling the field Kurtz suddenly went into a vertical dive and crashed to the ground. He stated it was later learned that Kurtz had confided to Lt. Morrison that he was prone to fainting spells after exposure to high altitudes and that was what must have happened just as he was about to land safely after his first patrol.

At the time Kurtz was flying Nieuport 6185, Squadron number 10, which was 1st Flight's spare aircraft and the same one which had been flown by Gude the day that Lufbery was killed. Rickenbacker's account of this event was in error and as recorded in the Squadron Flight Log and in Joe Eastman's diary, the plane actually caught fire which perhaps was caused by the rupture of the fuel line, a weakness of the 28s as was previously stated.

Rickenbacker's requested confirmation was made by the *Compte-Rendu* of the 8th French Army, May 22, 1918, paragraph (7). Strangely enough, no losses of any type were reported by the Germans for the day.

On another patrol, Lts. Green, Smythe, and Morrison, Kurtz's fellow gunnery instructor, ran into some German fighters on the St. Mihiel to Pont-à-Mousson route and Walt Smythe filed the following report:

> "Saw a plane dive over Pont-à-Mousson, at approximately 3000 meters altitude. Saw three other planes going towards Germany. Followed them from a height of 4200 meters and caught up to them when about five kilometers in Germany. They turned east and I came back. Do not know what make of plane I saw falling at about 10.05 A.M."

May 23 through May 26 were basically quiet days in the air. There was a fierce fight on May 23 between an L.V.G. of Flieger-Abteilung 46b and three pilots of the 95th which ended with Ltns. Will and Meisgang being badly wounded and the L.V.G. making an emergency landing at Vigneulles. Starting in the afternoon of May 24, the weather turned to haze, clouds, and rain, and did not clear for reasonably good flying weather until May 27. Smythe made a forced landing at Villers-en-Naye on the 23rd during an afternoon alert with Lts. Chambers and Morrison. Doug Campbell flew one voluntary patrol over St. Mihiel on May 24, Davis and Loomis answered an alert on May 25, Lts. Campbell, Loomis, Eastman, Davis, and Cunningham patrolled to Pont-à-Mousson on May 26, with nothing to report on any of these days.

The May 27 *Report of Operations* showed how good weather can notch up aerial activity in a big way. The summary listed five patrols, two protection patrols, two voluntary patrols, one trial flight, twenty-seven sorties, and four combats. The first patrol out was at 9h 04 of three planes at 5500 to St. Mihiel. The three pilots were Meissner, Hill, who was flying Nieuport 6142, Squadron number 23, and Taylor. Hill reported: "Route, Flirey – St. Mihiel. At 9h 40 I attacked a two-seater enemy plane, firing 30 shots. The same Boche was attacked at the same time by a Nieuport. Four scouts (Albatros) were close by and above. No result. Region of Essey.

About 10h 00 saw one two-seater protected by four Albatros, region Monsec, Haudicourt. One Nieuport attacked the formation. After, I attacked the two-seater, firing about 50 cartridges. Gun jammed and was re-arming gun when wounded by a ball in the left leg. Landed near Rambucourt and turned over." All indications point to the wounding being caused by Ltn. Otto Fritzner of Jasta 65. Meissner, on the same patrol, reported: "At 9h 55 attacked one monoplace north of Essey, at 2000 meters. Fired about 30 rounds, when enemy spiraled down. Confirmation asked. At about 10h 00 to 10h 10, engaged 4 enemy planes, firing several times without apparent results. East of Essey, at about 2000 meters."

At 9h 32, while the first patrol was still in the air, a voluntary patrol of Doug Campbell and John Wentworth took off to fly the route Pont-à-Mousson, Montsec and return. Campbell describes his fight with the German fighters:

> "At 10h 00 to 10h 06, altitude 3000-2500 in the region of Montsec, saw three enemy monoplaces. One went into a vrille and I shot at it about thirty rounds. Then I pulled out and chased two others. One did a renversement before I fired. I fired about 50 rounds into the other, I followed him into a dive, then I pulled out of the fight and when I looked around again a machine was falling in two or three pieces. A few moments later I attacked a biplace without results (apparently). He piqued steeply and disappeared into his own lines. CONFIRMATION REQUESTED."

Two confirmations were received by the squadron for an action which took place about 10h 00 on May 27. The first was from a French anti-aircraft artillery battery:

> "63rd Regt. of Artillery, Serifixed Post No. 136. Sous-Lieutenant Gassend commanding the A.S.A. post 136 certifies that he saw on May 27, 1918 at 9h 58 a combat between an airplane Type Nieuport and an Albatros to the north, northwest of the post at an altitude of about 2500 meters. It happened as a result of this combat that the enemy plane after being attacked twice, dove and descended in a vrille to about 1000 meters, then tried to straighten out but, apparently out of control, he continued his fall to about 500 meters. From then on it was impossible to see the result of the fall of the enemy plane as it was hidden by the camouflage branches of post 136. May 27, 1918. Signed and Sealed Sous-Lt. Gassend, Commanding. Translated 5/27/18 by Phillip J. Roosevelt, Capt. ASSC."

The second was from the *Compte-Rendu* 8th French Army, June 9th, 1918, paragraph Rectificates, "Enemy monoplace, 10h 00, 3000 mts. Montsec, 6-27-18." This was Campbell's fourth victory and the thirteenth for the 94th.

For the German side of the story, three references describe the action from their perspective. Four two-seaters of Flieger-Abteilung 46b departed their field between 1010 and 1025 with the mission to photograph the region of St. Mihiel, Apremont and Bauçonville. The first plane out was flown by Unteroffizier Eichner with Oberleutnant Stolze as the observer and during the course of their successfully accomplished mission, encountered no enemy action. The second plane, flown by Vizefeldwebel Simmerl, Ltn. Hoess observer, fought off an attack by a Nieuport in the vicinity of Apremont, while the third flown by Sgt. Mohr, Ltn. Brückner observer, was also attacked by a Nieuport over Loupmont that turned away after firing only a few rounds. The fourth plane with the crew of Ltns. Ortegel and Behringer on their return from the mission was involved in a brief fight over Heudicourt which bore no results for either side. When the four crews had returned, they reported to their intelligence, among other things, they had observed several air battles between German and enemy single-seaters near Xivray and witnessed two falling machines. Observer Oberleutnant Stoltze who was in the first machine out reported that one machine dove vertically and the second fell and crashed after what was thought to be a collision.

In that fight over Xivray, there were five Albatros of Jasta 65 and five Nieuports of the 94th Aero Squadron and three of the 95th. Further German reports for that morning describe heavy fighting with French Spads, one of which was shot down by Ltn. Fitzner near Apremont. The German report gives the time as 1100, but it must be remembered that German time was one hour ahead of Allied time. Within minutes, Offizier Stellvertrater Tiedje attacked another Spad which was in a fierce combat with his squadron-mate Ltn. Fritzsche. Firing at a close range he brought him down. Out of control, the French Spad rammed Fritzsche's Albatros which immediately broke up and crashed between La Perche and Montsec. Imagine the feeling of poor Tiedje knowing, because of his victory, his comrade was dead in the wreckage of the two planes. It is a difficult task to sort out what precisely did happen during that melee and who did what to whom, but without question, Campbell's confirmed victory had to be the unfortunate Fritzsche as he was the only German single-seater loss of the day. Interestingly, in Campbell's combat report he mentions: "When I looked around again a machine was falling in two or three pieces." Could he in the heat of combat have made a mistake and actually seen two aircraft falling rather than one?

Activities of May 27 ended with a German two-seater loss. While on its second mission of the day, L.V.G. C-V s/n 1752/18 with the crew of Ltns. Behringer and Ortegel, fell in flames to the guns of four Nieuports from the 95th which were flown by Lts. Ned Buford, Ted Curtis, George Fisher, and Alex McLanahan.

On May 28 the 94th and 95th, in cooperation, answered eleven alerts from 6h 47 until 19h 06. Doug Campbell and Eddie Rickenbacker, flying Huffer's N6169, Squadron number 1, set off on a voluntary patrol at 8h 16 on a route that would take them to Bois-de-Rate and return flying between 2000 and 2500 meters. Campbell's report stated:

> "At 9h 31, at 2000 meters, region of Bois-de-Rate, met six enemy planes. Attacked Albatros biplace and fired about fifty rounds. He went into a vrille, but I could not watch him. Fight continued for ten minutes, but I had no further good opportunities to fire."

Rickenbacker filed a combat report in which he wrote:

> "First noticed six enemy planes coming south at 9h 25, two Albatros biplace and four monoplace Albatros. Attacked one biplace Albatros at 9h 31. After firing 75 rounds saw him go into vrille and watched him crash in Bois-de-Rate. At 9h 35 attacked another biplace in region of St. Baussant, altitude, 2500 meters. Fired about 100 rounds. Last saw him going into a vrille, but could not see him crash. Then returned to our lines account of no gasoline. CONFIRMATION REQUESTED."

Captain Eddie had more to say about this in *Fighting the Flying Circus* in which he stated the day was beautifully clear and that he and Campbell headed for Pont-à-Mousson and then flew back and forth between there and St. Mihiel. No mention of Bois-de-Rate, but after an hour he noticed the six planes mentioned in the combat reports coming from the German field at Mars la Tour. He signaled Campbell and began to climb to a higher altitude that was obtained some 2000 feet above the two Albatros two-seaters and four Pfalz fighters. The account verbatim goes on: "So I withdrew into the sun and waited until the whole formation had crossed the lines and were well on our side before turning for the attack. As soon as we began our dive, we were observed. The two Albatros immediately turned tail and started for the lines. The four fighting planes drew closer to their formation and also turned back, keeping themselves between us and the machines they were protecting. Although the long range was hopeless, Campbell and I fired occasional bursts as we continued after them, always preserving our advantage in altitude and never permitting them a shot at us. In this fashion we all crossed the lines again and soon we were above the city of Thiaucourt, Campbell and I still holding the upper level." There ensued a lot of jockeying back and forth, the Germans attempting to lure the Nieuports into an attack where they could spring a trap. One of the two-seaters became slightly separated from the rest, possibly a decoy, and the narrative continues. "Like a flash we turned our airplanes and side by side dived swiftly down on the lone Albatros with our throttles full open. The Pfalz machines instantly turned to the pursuit. But even as they did so, they must have realized the futility of the chase, for not only did we have a mile or more handicap, but we rapidly increased this distance between us. As we neared our target, we nursed our machines until our gun sights were directly upon the enemy Albatros. About one hundred shots each we fired before we eased off our machines and began to climb away to regain our altitude. Looking back, we saw we had done a complete job with our Albatros. It swooped one way and then the other and, finally falling into a last spin, we saw it crash at the edge of the town of Flirey, just inside Ratta Woods." This most likely was Bois-de-Rate; in any event, there were no losses reported by the Germans on May 28. Flieger-Abteilung 46b completed all their missions without interference, although Flieger-Abteilung (A) 298b were involved in several air combats which caused them to turn back in spite of the fighter protection they had been afforded.

This sounds very much like the Rickenbacker-Campbell attack which, contrary to German records showing no losses, ended with a confirmation for Rickenbacker given that day by the *Compte-Rendu* of the 8th French Army, May 28th, 1918, paragraph 6. "Albatros Biplace, 9h 31, 2000 mts. Bois-de-Rate. 5-28-18."

Late in the afternoon, Lts. Chambers, Green, and Smythe departed at 17h 32 on a patrol to St. Mihiel – Pont-à-Mousson and return. Reed Chambers' report filed this narrative upon his return at 19h 12 stated:

> "At first I saw archie shells toward Pont-à-Mousson. Climbed from 3500 meters to 4000 meters and saw four Boche coming from Pont-à-Mousson (from Germany). I maneuvered to get above them and fired about 75 rounds at the top man at quite a long range 150 to 200 meters. He immediately dove and went through the clouds. I pulled away and kept climbing, looked back and saw four more

> Boche behind these. The three Boche came near me, and one dove under me, the other two coming straight ahead. I fired about 350 shots in all at the top men, when my gun jammed so I could not re-arm. Combat at 7.00 PM, 1 kilometer inside German lines, north of Flirey. First enemy plane attacked dove toward German lines about halfway between Pont-à-Mousson and Flirey. Could not tell exact location, as was above clouds."

Chambers did not request a confirmation and as seen previously, the Germans had no losses for the day.

The weather remained flyable on May 29 allowing two protection patrols, one voluntary patrol and one scheduled morning patrol consisting of Lts. Campbell, Loomis, and Eastman. They departed at 7h 28 making three round trips over the St. Mihiel to Pont-à-Mousson sector at an altitude of 5300 meters. Doug Campbell's combat report read:

> "Over Beaumont, 3500 meters, 8.05 A.M. Two enemy monoplaces chasing British plane into our lines. Attacked one of the enemy, firing about 30 shots at close range. He piqued vertically and I saw him start to level out once, then go into another vertical dive. Did not watch him further, as I went to attack the other enemy. The latter dived down into his own lines before I got near him. Over Pont-à-Mousson, 8.58 enemy plane at very high altitude. Lost sight of him in the sun, then at 9.05 saw French Schrapnel breaking south of Commercy. Boche was no where to be seen when we arrived at the location of the puffs."

Campbell went to the defense of a British reconnaissance plane returning from Germany and as shown by this good result, two further patrols were sent up for the sole purpose of protection of the British two-seaters. At 9h 02 Rickenbacker and Chambers were sent to cover the return of a British mission which proved to be a worthwhile effort as over St. Marier Farm near Montsec, they fought off five enemy attackers. Chambers reported firing 150 to 200 rounds, both stating "with no apparent results." The British crew in all probability felt the results were most positive.

At the end of the day, Captain Ken Marr took Lt. George Zacharias, who had not yet been officially assigned to the squadron, on a voluntary introductory patrol near Flirey which lasted 50 minutes, producing nothing to report.

Several hard fought battles took place on May 30, the results of which are somewhat in question.

At 6h 50, a seven plane patrol led by Captain Marr, with Lts. Rickenbacker, Campbell, Meissner, Taylor, Wentworth, and Winslow following, departed for the vicinity of Thiaucourt. During this patrol there were numerous combats reported with conflicting times recorded as to when they actually took place. The daily *Report of Operations* puts the patrol out at 6h 50 with the return one hour thirty-eight minutes later at 8h 28. Jimmy Meissner's combat report may have suffered from the squadron clerk's poor typing, as it reads:

> "Hour of Leaving, 6.56. Hour of Arrival, 8.11. Mission, Patrol. Route, Vicinity of Thiaucourt. At 8h 40 saw five enemy machines over Jaulny. Fired on two machines no apparent results. As several were above me, I drew out to the ____(?)____. At 8h 55 saw the enemy again east of Thiaucourt and with three other Nieuports returned to the attack. Piqued on an enemy monoplace and at the same time he piqued on me and hit my upper wings, ripping off the top surface. Headed to our line and was pursued by enemy biplace. Lt. Rickenbacker saw the situation and attacked biplace, which returned to its field. Lt. Rickenbacker returned with me to camp."

There were two time errors in the report as the times of the enemy sighting and the combat were actually 7h 40 and 7h 55. The reported collision was in error as it was another case of the structural wing failure of the Nieuport 28. Meissner made it home the second time with a wing failure of the same aircraft 6144, Squadron number 8, which was given a third wing and continued in service with Meissner through at least June 11. Meissner was given a confirmed victory over an "enemy monoplace" by the *Compte-Rendu* of the 8th French Army, paragraph (8). The time of victory was given as 7h 55 at an altitude of 4500 meters and the location as east of Thiaucourt.

Rickenbacker, who was still flying Nieuport 6169, Squadron number 1, in his report stated:

> "Had one combat at 4000 meters over Jaulney (his spelling) about 7.38 A.M. Five German planes, two of which I thought were Albatroses Biplace and three Albatros monoplace. Fired about 100 rounds and a biplace fell into a vrille after a few moments of combat. Attacked another monoplace a few minutes later, who piqued back into Germany. I then left the fight as the enemy planes were too low and too far into (Germany) to continue. Returned our lines and noticed four more planes coming toward the lines. I returned to the attack and found several Nieuports engaged in same, having arrived shortly before I did. Noticed Lt. Meissner piquing on one Boche and another piqu-

ing on him, at whom, I fired about 50 rounds. During his maneuvers, he and Lt. Meissner collided, Lt. Meissner losing most of his upper wings. Started for our lines with a biplace taking advantage of his damaged condition. Piqued on biplace and fired about 50 rounds. He then left the combat, Lt. Meissner and I returning to the camp. This combat took place about 7.55 A.M. east of Thiaucourt. There were two Nieuports engaged in combat with the balance of the Germans when I left. CONFIRMATION REQUESTED."

Rickenbacker received his confirmation in the same *Compte-Rendu*, 8th French Army, same paragraph as Meissner's victory. "Albatros Biplace 7h 38, 4500 mts, Region Jaulny 5-30-18."

An interesting coincidence of a victory claim comes from the German side for the same day, same time. German records show that our friend Offizier Stellvertrater Tiedje of Jasta 65 who had been possibly responsible for the collision and loss of a squadron mate by the destruction of a French Spad on May 27, was credited with shooting down a Nieuport south of Thiaucourt at 0900 German time for his second victory. Was he claiming Meissner while Meissner was claiming him? No losses were reported by either side with the exception of Bill Casgrain of the 95th, another victim of the Nieuport wing failure who crash-landed behind enemy lines and was captured by troops of the 5. Landwehr Division.

Captain Marr and Lt. Winslow were also engaged in this fight, both claiming gun jams and no results.

A Pont-à-Mousson to St. Mihiel patrol that departed the field at 7h 15 consisted of Lts. Campbell, Eastman, Davis and Loomis. Halfway between those two points, near Flirey and Beaumont, Eastman and Campbell found two enemy biplaces. Campbell's combat report tells the story:

> "At 8h 05 to 8h 10, over Lironville, about 2500 meters, met two enemy Biplaces. They separated and I attacked one, Lt. Eastman, the other. My opponent, during the 5 minute fight, exhausted all his ammunition without effect, and I was thus able to approach near and shoot with effect. He dived vertically, striking the ground just off the Limey – Montauville road, about halfway between these two points. CONFIRMATION REQUESTED."

The plane which crashed in French territory near Lironville was easily confirmed and made 1st Lt. Douglas Campbell, at the time flying N6158, Squadron number 0, the first American trained "Ace." The two-seater had belonged to Flieger-Abteilung (A) 242 of the 19. Armee with a crew, Sgt. Richard Strunk, the pilot and Ltn. Erich Külz, both of whom were killed in the crash.

Lt. Joseph H. Eastman, a Californian, joined the 94th on the same day as Rickenbacker and Meissner, keeping a fairly lengthy diary, which today is in the holdings of the Hoover Institution of War, Revolution & Peace. Eastman, from what he wrote in his diary, was plagued with both ultra-conservative indecision, as well as what he considered temperamental airplanes, a combination which gave him a great deal of inward concern and frustration. The May 31 entry from his diary was:

> "May 31st. Very much war today. In conjunction with an American raid 3:00 A.M. – Doug (Campbell), Bill (Loomis) and I went out on a 7:15 A.M. patrol for the purpose of snaring boche that might be up surveying the aftermath. After about an hour of the patrol Doug wig-wagged and pointed at a heavy barrage of black shrapnel with a few whites. He chose one of the two gray spots below and I lost track of him for the rest of the shift. He was merely bringing down a boche bi-place which makes the sixth he has handled in that manner and therefore somewhat a commonplace affair for Doug. On the other hand I had the extremely important task of learning another lesson – a not altogether rare thing with me at that. Yet the tale is not without its merits. One machine separated and curved over our territory back into Germany – at an altitude about 300 meters less than mine. I piqued around and under his tail – merrily fidgeting with selector, gas throttle, and gun lever the while. My two mistakes were in piquing too <u>far</u> under and too far behind – to the end that by the time I had used up my surplus speed I was still at too great a distance to maneuver effectively. This was really poorer judgment than it was conservative. I say that as someday I may look back on this and think otherwise. What convinced me I was following no Britisher (several days before he had almost attacked one in error) – was a sideward twist on the part of the man above – revealing a flash of yellow fuselage and a hot crackling of smoke tracers descending from an individual operating from the back pew and snapping close to my two sides. His manner was anything but impersonal. For my part – and this has been on my mind ever since – I passed up the one instant of good target offered me. There <u>was</u> an instant when he exposed a three-quarter broadside that – speed diminished thru climbing as it was – I might have pulled up long enough for a burst or two. But as I say, that might have happened. As an actual fact, he ran square into the sun where I could see him

in a renversement starting to dive on me. Further than that I had nothing to do with combat. It was a bi-place, higher than I and piquing down on me, also it was my first combat – so I chose to have no more dealings with him and viraged homeward with a fair show of energy. We haven't met since, but I sincerely hope soon again to have the pleasure."

Eastman mentions that the observer of Campbell's victim stood with empty cartridge belts flapping, looking at Campbell one hand on the exhausted gun and the other on his hip, "waiting self-possessed."

Laurence La Tourette Driggs, a writer who helped Rickenbacker produce *Fighting the Flying Circus*, and who wrote the foreword, took lots of liberties about this particular fight. He stated Campbell was on a solo voluntary patrol, but also agrees with Eastman's story that the observer, after expending his ammunition, stood up in his cockpit, arms folded wearing a haughty expression, daring Campbell to shoot.

Driggs, who had also written other early popular accounts of aviation in the World War I, *Heroes of Aviation* and *Aces Among Aces,* was working on the manuscript of Rickenbacker's book under two disadvantages; the first that Rickenbacker in 1919 was on a long and arduous speaking tour covering the United States and was unavailable to amplify specific events that might be questioned and secondly, he was using as a primary source Rickenbacker's diary for the narrative. Squadron and other official records were not available to him, so it is indeed amazing how close many of the dates and details actually are in much of the book, and also given the fact that Captain Eddie was not in the least bit shy when it came to making a good story better.

[1] Bz. was the German abbreviation for a balloon company, in this case Balloon Abteilung 214.

A nose-on view of Jimmy Meissner's Nieuport 28 N 6144, May 1, 1918. This photo was taken while the plane was having its machine gun sighted. The single Vickers can be seen at one o'clock above the cowling.

May 2, while in a successful fight with an Albatros, Meissner experienced the collapse of the leading edge of his upper wing, a weakness which caused some serious losses to the 94th and 95th Aero Squadrons.

A close-up view of the damaged upper wing of Meissner's Nieuport.

Meissner's dark number 14 showing the removal of the destroyed upper wing. Number 14 was the number assigned to the plane when it was flown by Bill Casgrain of the 95th.

Another view of the lost wing and also showing the Victory Loan poster applied to the lower right wing.

Meissner looking a little glum after losing his wing on May 2, 1918.

Lt. Charles W. Chapman shown wearing his French uniform. Chapman who trained with the French, was commissioned 2nd Lieutenant in February 1918 and was killed in action near Autrepierre in a fight with four German single-seaters. He was flying N 6138 Squadron O when he was brought down by Ltn. Wenig of Jasta 80b. *U. S. National Archives R.G 18 P-1124.*

Captain James Norman Hall in flying togs, posing by a French Spad.

Below: Hall's Nieuport 6153 Squadron 17 while having its single Vickers sighted in. Gengoult pits. *Lt. Eddie Green album.*

In a hotly contested fight on May 7, Hall lost the leading edge of his right wing and then had his engine hit by a dud anti-aircraft round which forced him to land in German territory.

Another view of Hall's Nieuport being inspected by German intelligence officers.

Hall's broken leg and nose have been attended to and he is off to interrogation by the Germans, transported in style. Note the dachshund in the German officer's hands, who in the following attempted to console poor Hall.

Hall and canine friend wait for the next phase of his ordeal on May 7, 1918.

The 94th had several squadron mascots, one of which was "Joe the Fox".

Major Raoul Lufbery prior to May 18, 1918. The Nieuport cannot be identified.

Left: Purported to be one of the Nieuport factory representatives sent out to Gengoult on various troubleshooting missions. He stands by number 8 which was the number applied by Meissner after the wing loss incident.

Bill Loomis' mechanics and his N 6181 Squadron 15. Note his unique oblique stripe-style cowl markings. *Lt. Bill Loomis album.*

Oscar J. Gude and a local French friend, photo taken in the village of Toul.

Lt. LeRoy Prinz who served a month with the 94th before being assigned to the 27th Aero early in July.

Doug Campbell with N 6164 number 10. The cowling on this plane was painted with red and black triangles. The white number "10" and the black triangles were not on the plane when Campbell scored his first victory.

Ready for a patrol, Eddie Rickenbacker in flight gear stands by his N 6159 number 12. Behind him is Hall's N 6153 number 17 dating the picture prior to Hall's loss on May 7. *Lt. Joe Dawson album.*

Doug Campbell stands by Alan Winslow's Nieuport 6189 number 6 which Winslow named "Priscilla". Note the victory cross on the hatband of Uncle Sam's hat in the ring. *Winslow Collection, U. S. Army Military History Research Collection, Carlisle Barracks, PA.*

Above: Eddie Green and N 6180 number 18, Gengoult Airdrome. Green shared this aircraft with Sherry, Prinz, and Jeffers. *Lt. Eddie Green album.*

Opposite: Jimmy Meissner looking somewhat like a bridesmaid dressed for high altitude flying, stands by his N 6195 number 8. *Lt. Eddie Green album.*

Right: Thorne Taylor and Jimmy Meissner on the field at Gengoult Airdrome. May 1918.

Eddie Rickenbacker tips the hat of John Wentworth's N 6168 number 5 at Gengoult, May 1918.

Alan Winslow and N 6168 number 5 showing Wentworth's snake design to good advantage. *U. S. National Archives, RG 111, SC 11885.*

Major John Huffer, C.O. of the 94th. Gengoult Airdrome, May 1918. *U. S. National Archives, RG 111, SC 13414.*

A group of the 94th mechanics at Gengoult. The Nieuport appears to be Meissner's number 8. *U. S. National Archives, RG 111, SC 13358.*

Taken at the same time as the previous photo was this picture of the 94th officers. Kneeling L/R Campbell, Meissner, Green, unidentified, Gude, unidentified, unidentified. Standing non-flying, unidentified, Lufbery, non-flying, Huffer, Marr, unidentified, Rickenbacker, Chambers, Wentworth, Cook, Loomis, Winslow, Smythe. *U. S. National Archives, RG 111, SC 13357.*

Ken Marr at Gengoult. mid May 1918. *U. S. Signal Corps photo.*

Eddie Rickenbacker and his N 6159 number 12 at Gengoult, mid May 1918. *U. S. Signal Corps photo.*

Jimmy Meissner. Gengoult. May 1918.

Right: Alan Winslow is all smiles as he stands by Rickenbacker's number 12. Mid May 1918. *U. S. Signal Corps photo.*

Awards Day, May 13, 1918. The 94th officers line up on the left with French officers on the right. Among those in the front row are Rickenbacker (2nd), Meissner, Green, Loomis, Chambers, Sherry, unknown, and a ground officer on the end.

The 94th Nieuports line up for the May 13 ceremony. L/R Campbell's number 10, Smythe's number 4, Gude's number 7, Rickenbacker's number 12, and Green's number 18. Note Smythe's plane does not carry an upper wing number.

Another view of the same line-up which shows the American band in the background and Hill's N 6142 number 23 which carries an unusual camouflage pattern on the upper wing. Hill was wounded in action in this plane and, as a result, it was wrecked behind our lines.

Major Raoul Lufbery and his N 6193 number 2 at Gengoult shortly before his death. On June 2, 1918, Lt. Phillip Davis was killed in action flying this Nieuport.

On the morning of May 19, Major Lufbery was shot down and either fell or jumped from his burning Nieuport, landing on this fence in the yard of a woman's home in the village of Maron.

The remains of Nieuport 6178 number 16 which Lufbery was flying when he was shot down in flames.

Another view of N 6178 when the remains were brought back from Maron to Gengoult.

Flowers for the funeral services of Major Lufbery and Lt. Kurtz. Taken at Gengoult before the burial service.

Lufbery's coffin being carried to the gravesite.

On the day of Lufbery's death, Doug Campbell scored a victory over a two-seater LVG of FA 298b. The LVG fell in Allied lines and Campbell was able to view the wreck with his brother who was visiting him at the time of the downing.

Campbell amidst the wreckage of victory number 3. Ltn's. Bayer and Kämmerer were the unfortunate crew of the LVG. *Doug Campbell album.*

Right: Campbell and some French officers at the site of victory number 3. *Doug Campbell album.*

Rickenbacker sighting the Vickers gun on Huffer's N 6169 number 1 at Gengoult. Note the tri-colored cowling on this aircraft.

On May 17 Rickenbacker in a dive collapsed the leading edge of the upper wing of N 6169. He scored a victory in this fight, but came home on a wing and a prayer. Rickenbacker in flying clothes can be seen on the left. Gengoult.

The gallant Eddie looks a little shaken after losing his wing while diving Huffer's number 1.

Not to be outdone by Rickenbacker's wing failure of May 17, Meissner does it again on May 30, flying N 6144 number 8, the same plane in which he caused a wing failure on May 2. This, too, was the upper left wing shown in this *Signal Corps* photo. *U. S. National Archives, RG 111, SC 15160.*

Rickenbacker and the collapsed upper left wing looking a little happier than he did in the preceding picture. Interestingly the aircraft N 6169 was back in service the following day.

Another *Signal Corps* photo of Meissner's May 30 wing failure. *U. S. National Archives, RG 111.*

Jimmy Meissner and his often rebuilt N 6195 with its new number 8 at Gengoult, late May, 1918.

Opposite: Doug Campbell with John Wentworth's number 5 in the background. *U. S. National Archives, RG 111, SC 11888.*

Left: Rickenbacker ends the month pleased with the action of the previous 31 days, but still awaits that second Vickers machine gun for his plane.

4

June - The Squadron Matures

The first day of June began for the 94th with a voluntary patrol flown by Meissner and Wentworth who departed at 7h 23 for St. Mihiel to Pont-à-Mousson and were later joined by Winslow who left at 7h 50, returning at 8h 30, ahead of the others by 20 minutes. All had nothing to report.

At about the same time, a scheduled patrol was mounted by Rickenbacker flying 6169 with the Squadron number 1, Chambers in 6179, number 11, Green in 6180, number 18, and Smythe in 6230, number 4. The route of this patrol was St. Mihiel to Verdun and return at 4500 to 5000 meters. East of St. Mihiel at 8h 22, Eddie Green flying at 3500 meters encountered an enemy aircraft. He fired 50 rounds at him with no results; ten minutes later over St. Mihiel at 4500 meters, he fired another 50 rounds at an enemy before his guns jammed, also attaining no results. Over Flirey he spotted five more enemy planes which turned and returned to Germany. Reed Chambers at 8h 03 flying at 5200 meters had a scrape with an enemy biplace, firing 150 rounds during which he had to contend with five or six gun jams. The enemy dove to 3000 meters returning to the German lines. At 9h 30 north of St. Mihiel, Chambers fired 100 shots at another enemy plane with his guns again jamming several times due to bad ammunition.

Eddie Rickenbacker at 8h 22 ran into the same Rumpler that Green had met east of St. Mihiel and fought with him for eight minutes during which time he also experienced four gun jams that he, too, attributed to bad ammunition.

From the experience of this one patrol it would seem that there was a serious problem with the quality of ammunition supplied to the 94th and in use at this time. Rickenbacker briefly mentions this same action in his book, but makes no reference to the ammunition problem.

A mission to protect a Salmson on a photo reconnaissance near Thiaucourt was flown by Lts. Davis, Cunningham, Loomis, and Eastman who encountered no enemy activity; later, another scheduled patrol was flown by Meissner, Wentworth, Zacharias and Winslow at the 2000 meter level up to St. Mihiel with no reportable results. The squadron received four new Nieuports from Colombey-les-Belle: Numbers 6349, 6260, 6275, and 6297. These planes were ferried in on a six-minute flight by Captain Marr and Lts. Campbell, Taylor and Winslow.

Eastman in his diary comments on the protection patrol:

> "Bill (Loomis), Cunny (Cunningham) and I protected a Samson (Salmson) for photography some seven or eight kilometers over the lines. In a way he needed it – the protection – as six of the 95th planes tried to embarrass us from the rear. Then someone made a false move that set all nine of us to swooping at one another like a swarm of flies. We must have thought there was a joker (German) in our party as we spent fifteen minutes in the silly game of "cherchez le boche"! I inadvertently, like others present, lost track of which was the Samson, and the next thing was a grand diversion of five of the pack dropping down on two unoffending "A.R.s." On top of which, friend Bill and I eventually collected and set after another fictitious boche and dove at him to discover him to be a Spad! It's high time this foolishness stopped; and now that there are two more green squadrons, "The Canadian Circus" (he was referring to the 27th and 147th Aero Squadrons who had received some of their training in Canada) are on our field; a fellow's no longer safe flying over the lines. But they are full of promises to carry out their patrols regularly fifteen miles or so in Germany – and as I know the temper of these motors, they won't remain with us long."

An early alert began the activities of June 2 with Campbell, Davis, Cunningham and Eastman responding at 6h 44, flying to Lironville and achieving no results while spending an hour in the air. Meissner and Taylor flew a voluntary patrol from St. Mihiel to Bey at 5000 meters, while Reed Chambers voluntarily flew up to the lines, all of which ended with no results.

In the afternoon at 14h 43, Doug Campbell led a flight consisting of P. W. Davis, flying Lufbery's N. 6193, Squadron number 2, Loomis, Eastman, and Cunningham on a protection patrol over Thiaucourt. At about 15h 10 the patrol ran into six Pfalz of Jagdstaffel 64 in the region of Buxières-Maizerais and a furious fight ensued. In this fight Lt. Davis, in his second trip over the lines, was shot down by Leutnant Friedrich Hengst, the same man who was credited with bringing down Jim Hall in the collapsed wing and anti-aircraft dud affair of May 7. Davis' Nieuport burst into flames and crashed in the area of Bruley-Wold, north of Montsec, and his body was recovered by the Germans from the wreckage. How strange that Lufbery was shot down in flames flying 6178, Squadron number 16, which was assigned to Davis, and Davis was brought down in flames in Lufbery's 6193, number 2!

Lt. Eastman, upon returning from this action, filed the first of his few known combat reports:

"COMBAT REPORT of Lt. Eastman
Date – June 2, 1918, Altitude, 5000 meters
Hour of Departure 14.45; Hour of Arrival, 15.36
Name of Pilot, Lt. Eastman
Mission, Protection Patrol – Route, Thiaucourt

At 15h 12, 1500 meters, had combat with Pfalz biplace (the Pfalz was a single-seater), firing 20 rounds. Enemy plane went down in a side slip from which he never redressed, as far as I could see. I followed him down to 800 meters, but had to withdraw owing to gun jamb and enemy anti-aircraft activity. Enemy down Northwest of Maizerais. CON'F REQUESTED. (Sgd) J. H. Eastman, 1st Lt. ASSRC."

Writing of this episode in his diary, Eastman gives further details:

"We were all taking an afternoon nap in our room – Cunny, Davis and I – when Doug called us out to meet the British over the lines – eleven of them with a promise of any number of Huns tagging after them. My mechanics weren't there, so for some reason everything sounded wrong after leaving the ground. I imagined a knock, a trace of smoke in the nacelle and a few others – so left the three others to return to the field. Over camp I decided I was apprehensive without reason – and again turning soon joined the others. Five minutes later Doug balanced his wings, and all four of us dove. I was three quarters of the way down when I discovered our objective. There were six enemy planes at about 2500 metres, and in another instant I was close to one shooting away with my gun. It jammed and I viraged away quickly fixing it. In the virage I could see what a mad melee we had dropped into. Our planes, boche planes swooping and firing, smoke ribbons of tracers up, down, at you and away from you far and near. I had always known that the first big fight I ever got into would be my last, and there was a biplace quite a way to the right peppering me from his side, and here another swinging around on my tail. Another thing I had always known was that in a real fracas I'd be helpless because of my poor execution of acrobatics. This man on my tail was at the point of straightening his turn to fire when without figuring how to do it or where it led I did a renversement that brought me out on a slow dive directly head-on line of flight with the enemy. He was a trifle lower and diving beneath me. He gave me a vivid impression of red. Red on his tail and red upholstering in the seat, and then he passed directly thru my line of fire under me. I swung on down after him to get a short burst and another jam – his plane limply falling in a long wing-slip. At the moment he appeared to be about to crash – still wing-slipping at about fifty meters altitude – a brilliant explosion somewhere to my starboard brought me to my own predicament. My altimeter read 800 metres, and as I gave it full motor I looked around to see not a plane of all the combat in sight but a terrifyingly growing barrage of "archies" in all directions. If I wasn't frightened during the combat, certainly I was in jack-rabbiting at 800 metres over those guns that had me at less than their minimum range!"

In his diary, Eastman makes no comment regarding his confirmation request, but certainly gives us insight into his lack of confidence as a pilot and the inner struggles he constantly faced with his concerns about the dependability of his plane and the awful fear of anti-aircraft or "Archie" fire. One would wonder if it was his conscience which spoke to him causing him to return to the patrol rather than the smoothing out of his engine?

Further combat reports on this fight were written by Cunningham and Campbell.

2nd Lt. Arthur S. Cunningham from Medford, Massachusetts, was a member of Campbell's 3rd Flight, a plucky pilot, but plagued by poor eyesight, often flying wearing eyeglasses which without doubt cut down his effectiveness as a combat pilot. This was later corrected by making him full time Operations Officer and later Squadron historian:

"COMBAT REPORT OF Lt. Cunningham
June 2, 1918. Altitude, 300 meters.
Hour of Leaving. 14h 41; Hour of Arrival, 16h 06.
Protection Patrol, Route, Thiaucourt.

At 15h 12, had a combat with one Pfalz monoplace, firing about 50 rounds. Enemy plane went down in a nosedive and while still following my gun jammed, when I pulled up. Repaired jam in gun and attacked second time from underneath, firing about 30 rounds when my gun jammed again. I turned away my engine missing, and pulled myself into a vrille, falling 400 meters. Repaired second jam and while repairing, was attacked by an enemy plane, who put several bullets in my plane before I was able to attain his level, when my gun jammed again. Left the fight and was rejoining Davis when he burst into flames just behind his seat. He fell in a vrille, watched him until he seemed to pull out of the vrille and began side-slipping down to the ground. Meanwhile the flames had subsided. Watched Lt. Davis until he landed. His upper wings were intact, but after landing the plane started burning again. Two combats. (Sgd) A. S. Cunningham, 2nd Lt. ASUSR."

Doug Campbell's combat report ends the story of this unfortunate fight:

"COMBAT REPORT OF Lt. Campbell-
June 2, 1918. Altitude, 3000 meters – Squadron, 94th
Hour of Leaving, 14h 43; Hour of Arrival, 16h 05
Mission, Protection Patrol. Route, Thiaucourt.

At 15h 10 attacked six monoplace in region of Maizerais, at 3000 meters. Approached one to within 50 meters before shooting, when I fired about 20 rounds. Saw bullets strike fuselage, but was unable to observe results. The melee continued about five minutes, but had no further opportunities for effective fire. About one or two minutes after the fight, just as we were reforming, Lt. Davis' plane burst into flames from the side gasoline tank. He went into a vrille but seemed to regain control of the machine and for some moments the fire was not visable. Later it broke out afresh but I cannot really say whether he lost control of the machine before landing. His plane was seen burning on the ground just across the lines from Richecourt. (Sgd) Douglas Campbell, 1st Lt. USUSR."

Campbell provides a summary of events of the previous two weeks in his letter home written on June 2:

"Air Service, A.E.F.
France, June 2, 1918.

Gosh! I haven't written you for almost 2 weeks! I've been too busy making the world safe for Democrats. (Note: A gag current among servicemen at the time, parodying President Woodrow Wilson's solemn pronouncement about "making the world safe for democracy.")

The first week of the two was pretty dud, for though the weather was fine the Boche stayed in his nest. But the last week has been a corker! On Monday, May 27, John Wentworth and I went on a voluntary patrol, leaving the ground just after breakfast. As we usually do when the sun is on our side of the lines, we climbed to a fairly high altitude rather far inside our lines, twisting, turning, and alternately raising and lowering the nose of the plane so as to see better. Flying like a ship in a heavy sea, and always going up, up.

Ah! White (French) bursts of anti-aircraft shells over the lines in the middle of our sector! We made a bee line for the place, making a couple of turns now and then to make sure that there were no Boche planes at higher altitude than the bursts. And now, getting close to our objective, we rivet attention on that part of the sky. There is a little yellow-jacket, with black wings and orange body, circling about among the shrapnel bursts. That's an Albatros, and there's another, and a third, and two further down – five in all.

The nearest one of the top three is the best target, for he is separated from the rest, and possibly he doesn't see me. Down goes my nose for a dive, with the motor singing with increased speed and the wires whistling. I'm 300 meters from him now, and he doesn't – yes, he does see me, and puts himself into a spin before I shoot. Now I'm in a vertical dive over him, and put a few shots in his direction although it's not much of a chance to hit, but don't follow him too far, old boy, because those other two are just waiting for that. I pull out of the dive, and my speed carries me up the two or three hundred meters that I lost; there are the other two of the upper three, just turning to run into Germany. I'm pretty close now, and the rear one turns over on his back in a pretty renversement and dives. I guess I'm supposed to follow him, so the other one can turn and dive on me, but I'll just keep chasing the one that's left, and see what happens; John is right back there, and will take care of the first one if he tries to come up at me. Getting within 50 meters, I lean on the trigger and see tracers hitting the Boche machine. He turns and dives at the same time, and I try to keep the tracers hitting him, but I have to break all the principles of aerial flight to do it. Now he's spinning, and I don't know where the other Boche are, nor where John is, but those other two Allied planes that I saw just before the fight must be here by this time, so I'll climb up and out of the melee to get a comprehensive view of it. The comprehensive view shows 4 Boches whipping their Mercedes motors so they will carry them home a little faster, and 3 Americans running after them hell-bent for election. The fifth Boche seems to be – for the love of Mike what's that down there?

It looks like a piece of Boche wing fluttering down, and there's another piece, and way down there the body with a couple of stumps of wing on it, giving the pilot the fastest and shortest and most unfortunate ride he ever had, though probably he has been shot and doesn't know it. That last one I shot at must have been rendered unconscious and have gone into a spin with full motor, which could easily overstrain the wings. The Boches are too low and too far back now, and the Americans have turned back, so I pick up John and we go home.

Tuesday morning Rick and I found 6 enemy planes and attacked them. Four of them ran away, and we fired at one of the others simultaneously, making him spin down and crash into a wood on the German side of the trenches. The other one tried to play decoy for the 4, who were waiting behind their lines, but we didn't bite.

Wednesday morning I had the pleasure of saving an English plane and the lives of pilot and gunner. A group of English bombers had gone far into Germany before daylight, and one of them got separated from the bunch on the way home. I was patrolling the lines at 8 a.m., and saw a plane coming out of Germany (everything beyond the lines is called "Germany" by us) with two Boches on his tail. He was in a bad way, and I dived on the enemy just in time, for the pilot was already wounded. The Huns ran away. That afternoon I received a very nice message of thanks from the British squadron.

Thursday morning about four of us had a wonderful mix-up with 5 Huns, but without results. Friday, I found 2 biplace observation planes this side of our lines and had slick fight with one of them. We manoevered all over each other for about 5 minutes, and the gunner shot away all his ammunition without hitting me. Then I brought him down inside our third line trenches. The gunner was a true sport. He tore up his map and stood up to take his medicine.

Yesterday I didn't fly.

The infantry observer who reported the fall of the plane Rick and I got together, balled up his report, so we may not get credit for it, but he's a dead gone Hun anyway, and besides I have 5 official victories to my credit without it.

One of our boys was pretty badly wounded on Monday. (Note: Willard D. "Jud" Hill). A bullet of the armor-piercing type split up on the seat of his plane and tore a big hole in the flesh of the thigh. He landed all right just this side of the trenches and was taken right to a hospital. He's getting on, but will be laid up for some time. He was lucky, though; there were about 25 bullet holes in his machine. We figured that one of them missed his cheek by 2 inches.

Since I last wrote, Ken Culbert has been killed in an accident."

June 3 was a day in which the squadron mounted three voluntary patrols, answered five alerts while flying twenty sorties with no results. The action returned on June 4, starting with a voluntary patrol leaving the field at 4h 45, flown by Lts. Rickenbacker and Smythe who headed for Pont-à-Mousson which was Rickenbacker's favorite early morning hunting ground. Rickenbacker found Smythe to be a valuable companion in the air due to his "reliability and good judgement," pairing up with him on many occasions. This first patrol was to prove fruitless and they returned an hour later, refueled, and at 7h 48 took to the air again heading for Dieulouard at 5000 feet. This time they spotted two Albatros biplace coming from Pont-à-Mousson, which they soon engaged:

"COMBAT REPORT – Lt. Smythe
June 4, 1918. Altitude, 5000 meters. Squadron, 94
Hour of Leaving, 7h 57; Hour of Arrival, 8h 53.
Mission, alert. Route, Dieulouard

I saw two enemy planes coming from Pont-à-Mousson towards Flirey at an altitude of 5000 meters. I was at 4500 meters. I turned towards sun and climbed, then gave chase. They separated and I followed the one nearest me. He headed into Germany and I could not catch up. Fired several bursts without result. Time about 8h 30. (Sgd) W. W. Smythe, 1st Lt. ASUSR."

"COMBAT REPORT OF Lt. Rickenbacker
June 4, 1918. Altitude, 5000 meters. Squadron, 94th
Hour of Leaving, 7h 48; Hour of Arrival 9h 07.
Mission, Alert. Route, Dieulouard

Met two Albatros bi-place at 8h 35, but as they had altitude on me headed towards France, when I noticed a plane over Toul at 5000 meters, being shelled by anti-aircraft. I started for him over Menil-la-Tour, got on his tail and fired four shots, when gun jammed. After fixing gun, I attacked again but could not get within range again. Followed to about four kilometers in Germany, when I was piqued on by two Albatros biplace. I then left for home. (Sgd) E. V. Rickenbacker. 1st Lt. ASUSR."

In *Fighting the Flying Circus*, Eddie tells a different and more embellished tale. He describes the plane he attacked as a Rumpler with the number "16" in big black letters and an orange rising sun just ahead on the fuselage and speaks of the gun jam, but reports the two attacking Germans as single-seaters who put a few bullet holes in his wings. The following day, June 5, he states he went on a solo patrol in Smythe's plane, ran into "16" again coming from Metz with two single-seat escorts, who turned and flew into Germany. He attacked, the two-seater went up and over him and began firing a machine gun mounted to shoot through the floor.[1] Rick's gun jammed again, but he cleared the jam and kept attacking from above. He states he chased the German well back into their lines and while firing a farewell shot, his guns jam again, the pilot waves, the gunner fires "a last cheery burst from his 'tournelle' guns" ending the festivities, almost. He states that he had been in the air for two hours and thirty-five minutes with an oil supply of two hours fifteen minutes. Therefore, the engine froze from lack of lubrication, and he then glided back over the lines and safely landed near Menil-la-Tour.

The 94th Alert Log for June 5 shows that Rickenbacker, flying N. 6283 Squadron number 16, Smythe, flying N. 6230 Squadron number 4, and Winslow flying N. 6189 Squadron number 6 departed on a voluntary patrol St. Mihiel-Bey at 7h 48, Smythe and Winslow returning 8h 50 and 8h 58, respectively. Rickenbacker's return was noted in the Log at 10h 15, indicating a forced landing at Menil-la-Tour. Interestingly, Rick had made a 21-minute test flight in N. 6283 the morning of June 4 and Smythe made a 10-minute test flight in the same plane on June 8, although Smythe's assigned plane was N. 6230 Squadron number 4.

The June 5 *Report of Operations* confirms the Alert Log showing a voluntary patrol flown by the three aforementioned pilots and combat reports were filed:

"COMBAT REPORT of Lt. Smythe
June 5, 1918. Altitude, 5200 meters. Squadron, 94th
Hour of Leaving, 7h 50; Hour of Arrival 10h 15
Mission, Voluntary Patrol; Route, Bey to St. Mihiel.

I was at Flirey going East at 5000 meters, when I saw barrage near St. Mihiel. Turned, but enemy plane was too far in Germany to follow, time 8h 10. Later saw several planes north of Thiaucourt; followed them going east. They led us into Germany. I turned back and saw two planes low down 800 meters. Piqued and shot several bursts then came back as several planes approached. No results. (Sgd) W. W. Smythe, 1st Lt. USUSR." In this report, Smythe's arrival time is shown as 10h 15, not 8h 50 as shown in the Alert Log.

"COMBAT REPORT of Lt. Rickenbacker
June 5, 1918. Altitude 5000 meters. Squadron, 94th
Hour of Leaving, 7h 50; Hour of Arrival, 10h 15
Mission, Voluntary Patrol. Route, Bey-St. Mihiel

Met a biplace Rumpler over Void, flying at 6000 meters. Attacked him over Vaucouleurs, after gaining equal altitude, but was unable to do anything but harass him owing to lack of being able to maneuver with him. The fight continued until over Commercy, when both my guns had jams which I was unable to fix in the air. However, I continued to maneuver as though attacking him, until about six miles north of St. Mihiel, in Germany when my motor stopped owing to defective bearings. Started gliding for home and landed at Menil-la-Tour at 10h 15. Combat started at 9h 20. No apparent results. (Sgd) E. V. Rickenbacker."

While all this was occurring, Doug Campbell departed at 9h 12 for a voluntary patrol to Pont-à-Mousson flying at 5000 meters. Ten minutes later Jimmy Meissner also departed on a voluntary patrol, joined by Thorne Taylor and George Zacharias, which was to take them to the area of Lironville. Campbell had two fights with two-seaters, the first with no results, while the second was to have some rather profound results. The second engagement was of some duration and during the fight Meissner saw Campbell on the attack and joined in. His combat report tells more of the story:

"COMBAT REPORT of Lt. Meissner
Date - June 5, 1918. Altitude, 5300 meters. Squadron, 94th
Hour of Leaving, 9h 22; Hour of Arrival, 10h 40

Name of Pilots, Lt. Meissner
Mission, Alert. Route, Ourches

Barrage thrown up over Nancy shortly before 10.00 AM. At 3000 meters found Lt. Campbell chasing a Rumpler which was about 3700 meters. Stayed beneath Rumpler until it started to descend, about 10h 20. It spiraled and glided down, Lt. Campbell and I following and shooting repeatedly, until within 1000 meters of ground, at 10h 25. The Rumpler appeared to land between Eply and Mailly. CONF' REQUESTED. (Sgd) J. A. Meissner, 1st Lt. ASSRC."

Both Campbell and Meissner were credited with the Rumpler victory, Campbell's confirmation finally being made by American Military Authorities on September 27, 1918.

In this action, Campbell was wounded by an explosive bullet that hit the bottom of his seat and struck a wire, exploding the round inches from his back. Part of the bullet traveled up along his spinal column and stopped in the lower shoulder muscles. He was able to bring his plane safely back to the field at Toul and was able to climb from the cockpit without assistance. His letter of the following day describes the events rather tersely.

"Air Service, A.E.F.
France, June 6th

Yesterday was not my lucky day. At 9 a.m. I took to the air, and had been up only 10 minutes when I saw a Boche far in our territory at a great altitude. It took about 15 or 20 minutes to climb up to him and then we had a fight. He was a biplace, but did some fine manoeuvring; and I did some rotten shooting, so between the two he got away. Then almost immediately I saw another machine of the same type at a high altitude, and went after him. Again it was a case of good manoeuvring on his part and poor shooting on mine, and we fought from 5200 meters all the way down to 500. He had a jam, apparently, about halfway thru the fight, so just at the end I approached him from a dangerous angle. He had fixed the jam, however, and shot at me as I turned away, putting about 8 bullets in my machine. I heard a loud crashing sound and felt myself hit in the back; it appears that a bullet struck a wire just behind me, and one of the fragments lodged in the flesh of my lumbar regions.

Fortunately, it didn't disable me for flying, and I made a beeline for home, landing safely. Inside of half an hour the bullet had been located by X-ray. I kicked against taking ether, so they used cocaine for local anaesthesia, and I never felt a thing. The wound is perfectly clean, and they sewed it up tight.

Day before yesterday I had supper with Major Joe Flint, whose hospital is located 10 miles from our field. The hospital where I am is the best of the American Surgical Hospitals, and is a mile from our field. (Note: Evacuation Hospital No. 1, near village of Sebastopol, near Menil-la-Tour.) I am sleeping and eating well, and am as comfortable as could be expected with a hole in my back.

It is reported that the Boche who got me is down, but whether he fell or landed in uncertain. (Note: Landed, apparently with motor not functioning, in No Man's Land, and the artillery demolished the plane.)"

Rickenbacker flying Huffer's N. 6169, Squadron number "1", departed at 7h 40 on a solo voluntary patrol at an altitude of 6000 meters up to Pont-à-Mousson, returning at 9h 59. The "Alert Log" gives his altitude at 6000 meters, while the *Report of Operations* shows the altitude of 5000. If Rick was out to get the German morning photographic plane, his lusted after "16" with the orange sunrise insignia, he may have given the 6000 figure as his desired height. He claims in his book that he could get no higher than 19,000 feet (6000 meters). In any event, Rickenbacker returned at 9h 30, empty-handed once more.

He was feeling feverish at this time and after one patrol the next day, he took some well-deserved R & R in Paris, returning to the air on June 12. The balance of the day there were three alerts and an afternoon voluntary patrol flown by Loomis, Cunningham and Eastman up to Flirey with no results obtained.

During the time of June 3 through June 9, there were nine additional pilots assigned to the squadron which had lost seven pilots through enemy action or disciplinary grounding and transfer. The new faces included Alden B. "Madame" Sherry, George W. Zacharias, Robert Z. Cates, William W. Chalmers, Edwin R. Clark, Harold R. Tittmann, Chester Snow, plus Leroy J. Prinz and Fred I. Ordway who were transferred from the 27th Aero Squadron which had more pilots than airplanes. They were quickly absorbed into the squadron and began making patrols at once without a great deal of orientation or familiarization of the front.

On June 7, while on his third patrol, "Madame" Sherry had a forced landing in N. 6154 number 7, the plane previously assigned to the grounded and transferred Oscar Gude. This landing ended this aircraft's useful life, and ineffective career. While on the same patrol, which included Chambers, Green and Smythe, a combat occurred. Chambers' combat report stated "Had a combat east of St. Mihiel with two enemy planes – biplace. Fired about 50 rounds. Attacked them twice with no apparent results at an altitude of 5500 meters, as they flew back into Germany."

Joe Eastman, who had been on a late morning protection patrol, filed the following combat report. "At about 12h 05, while on protection patrol in region of Thiaucourt, sighted two Boche. Attacked one at long range and followed him down to 2000 meters without any apparent results." The day ended with a total of four patrols, one alert, two combats and eighteen sorties.

Jimmy Meissner had an encounter with a biplace on the morning of June 8, which occurred north of Regniéville, with no apparent effect. The next day in the company of Wentworth, Winslow and Taylor, he tried again. "Attacked Hannover biplace at 8h 15 to 8h 25 over Lironville fighting him beyond Thiaucourt. Altitude, 4000 to 2000 meters. Lt. Winslow fired 200 rounds and had two jams, Lt. Wentworth, 50 rounds, Lt. Taylor, 100 rounds, two jams, Lt. Meissner, 140 rounds, two jams. Enemy pilot and observer very skillful. No apparent results." From this report it would be safe to assume that the bad ammunition problem was still plaguing the squadron and Meissner may have felt that one way to bring it to the attention of the upper level chain of command was to state it thusly in his combat report. A combat report might get wider distribution than verbal grousing.

June 10 and 11 were quiet with only one alert; June 12 was a day of target practice, trial flights and two alerts, with no results. There were four reported combats on June 13 and the last confirmed victory for the 94th in the month of June. The day began with a voluntary patrol led by Meissner, followed by Winslow and Taylor departing 7h 15 for St. Mihiel to Pont-à-Mousson. No combat reports can be found which pertain to this patrol, but the *Compte-Rendu* of the 8th French Army of June 13, 1918, Paragraph (8), credits the three pilots with a Hannover biplace down in flames near Thiaucourt at 8h 15. This confirmation made Meissner's fourth, Winslow's second, and Taylor's first victories official. Ten minutes after the voluntary patrol departed, a scheduled patrol consisting of Green, Chambers, Rickenbacker, returned from Paris, and Smythe headed for Bey-Pont-à-Mousson-Flirey; flying for two hours and 12 minutes, they had no results.

Bill Loomis filed a combat report when he returned from a patrol from the St. Mihiel-Pont-à-Mousson-Bey triangle. He had combat with two "Boche" in the vicinity of Thiaucourt, and drove them down to 2000 meters when they left for their lines with no apparent damage being done.

At this time the Germans were flying in larger and larger formations, making life more difficult for the three and four man patrols of the 94th. Someone of authority felt that the squadron should copy the German approach, so on June 15 the *Operations Report* indicates a "Trial Flight, Squadron Formation 15 planes" was flown. One can't imagine what a circus that must have created, as it was attempted again with sixteen planes on June 19 and on June 25 a patrol of twelve planes was mounted and a mission was flown.

On June 17 the squadron was joined by Hamilton Coolidge of Boston, Groton, and Harvard, a close friend of Quentin Roosevelt and Doug Campbell, and a pupil, like Campbell, of a unique flight training program at Issoudun. The reader may recall that Campbell and Coolidge had been given heavy responsibilities in the creation of the U. S. Training Center at Issoudun. Most of the men who had come over with them from the ground schools in the States were in the basic flying school at Tours, learning on Caudron G IIIs, with French instructors, graduating with a pilot's brevet, then moving to the advanced schools now ready at Issoudun. The training that Coolidge and Campbell received put them right into two-seat Nieuports which more closely approximated the machines they were to later fly in combat. Both men were outstanding to begin with, but if one traces their flying careers at the front, one has to wonder if their training was more suitable than the old prescribed method. More of Ham Coolidge to come, but his introduction to the front is described in his letter of June 19 to his mother:

"Toul, June 19, 1918

Beloved Mother,

Here I am at last after all these months of impatient waiting, and indications point to a busy time. We are very comfortably installed here and the spirit and atmosphere are inspiring to say the least. A pilot at the front is no longer treated as a schoolboy. In my own case I have little to complain of in this respect, but I had it much better than did the students at the 3rd A.I.C.

The day after arriving our captain sent me up for a trial flight and to get used to the new machine a little. That evening – it was last evening, come to think of it – I went out over the lines with three of the older pilots. It was most bewildering, because there was so hopelessly much to think about. The "Archies" or anti-air craft guns kept a steady fire at us, but meantime it was necessary to regard the instruments on your machine, to keep in touch with your comrades, and continually to watch for the Boches.

We sighted a Boche patrol way below us, but they turned back when they saw us. We were only over the lines a few minutes and saw very little in the evening haze.

The real fun started at 3 o'clock, this morning, when a tremendous bombardment started up. It waked me up at once. Shortly afterwards our flight leader tapped on my door and said, "I guess we had better get up, it looks as if the Huns were starting something." When we came over the lines, we could see hundreds of brilliant little flashes twinkling out of the twilight here and there. Our job was to remain an hour and a half over a certain place, and jump on any Hun planes who might come out to regulate the fire of their artillery. Well, Mammy, there was a layer of clouds that just suited the Boche anti-air craft gunners. For an hour and a half we circled round over the place amid an incessant storm of shrapnel burst. Sometimes, they came so close that I could feel my whole plane give a great bounce from the concussion, tho' no fragments actually hit me. We circled, twisted, squirmed and dived and always the black bursts appeared at the spot where we had been only a fraction of a second before. It was absolutely thrilling. As the sun rose we could see more and more of the trenches, and bursts of smoke from exploding shells. The joke is that the Boche started using gas shells exclusively. Then the wind shifted completely around and blew his gas right back on him. There was no infantry action for some reason, merely a violent bombardment, and never a single Boche plane appeared. It was a surprisingly sudden baptism for me, but the sooner one gets used to the Archies and to being continually alert, the better it is, and I was mightly glad they were willing to send me out so soon (some of the pilots ahead of me have been waiting around for days).

Q. is in the same group and on the same field, but in a different squadron, darn it all! We are trying to work out some way of having him transferred to this squadron, because both of us know more of the boys in it than in the others.

My official address is – 94th Aero Squadron, 1st Pursuit Group, Z. of A., American E. F.

Your
Ham."

A patrol was sent out at 4h 03 on the 19th destined to fly to Beaumont, Flirey and Seicheprey, at an altitude of 2500 meters. Seven pilots took part in this mission: Lts. Rickenbacker, Green, Taylor, Coolidge, Loomis, Meissner and Winslow. Rickenbacker's combat report tells much of the story:

"Mission, Patrol. Route, Beaumont, Seicheprey and Woods S.E. of Seicheprey.

Enemy artillery fire concentrated on Beaumont, Seicheprey and territory up towards Flirey, thus making a sort of triangle. I harassed the enemy from about 500 meters for approximately half an hour, firing 500 rounds of ammunition. Strafed enemy's trenches, from Flirey to Beaumont, with 500 rounds of ammunition. Emptied guns on them. 500 meters altitude at about 5.00 o'clock. Saw clouds of gas as far as five kilometers in Germany. The gas from shells being thrown by the enemy was being blown back over their territory. (Sgd) E. V. Rickenbacker, 1st Lt. USUSR."

Rickenbacker who was flying N. 6383 number 16 and had expended all his ammunition, returned to the field at 5h 02, quickly warmed up N. 6179 number 11 and returned to the fray at 5h 24.

This is a good example of Rick's aggressive nature and his eagerness to get to the enemy. He went back and strafed the trenches from 300 meters expending another 300 rounds of ammunition. Thorne Taylor filed an almost identical combat report to Rick's, although he only used 350 rounds firing at an enemy artillery emplacement rather than strafing the trenches, returning at 5h 20.

Special Orders No. 221, June 7, 1918, assigned 1st Lieuts. W. W. Chalmers, R. Z. Cates, and H. H. Tittmann to the 94th Aero Squadron.

Harold H. Tittmann, Jr. attended Yale University, received and passed his Reserve Military Aviator training at Rantoul, Texas, finished his flight training at the 3rd Aviation Instruction Centre, Issoudun, and his gunnery training at Cazeaux. He was assigned to the 1st Flight which was led at that time by Reed Chambers. The first two letters written home told of Tittmann's first few experiences in front line flying and his letter of June 19 mentions the first of the trench strafing missions:

"94th Aero Squadron
A.P.O. 709
Zone of Advance
June 10, 1918
Dearest Mother,

I am very proud to state that I have been permanently attached to the 94th Aero Squadron, address as per above. It was just luck. There was an opening and I was next in line. Lufberry was at the head of this squadron at the time of his death; Douglas Campbell, the only American trained "ace;" Kenneth Marr, an "ace," who is now C.O.; and several other celebraties. Furthermore it is the oldest squadron (American on the Front). Therefore I believe I am in luck. Dod's Squadron, the 147th, is filled up, so I can't get in there, but they are on the same field. So we see quite a bit of one another.

As I have just arrived, I have no machine as yet, but I'm promised one tomorrow. Maury Hill's squadron is only a couple of miles from here. He is driving a bi-place observation and photographic plane. Three of them took their first trip over the lines yesterday, protected by four monoplace "chasse" machines from our squadron. The German "Archies" were very active and gave them several scares. It was their own fault as they were flying too low – only 3000 meters. I much prefer to drive a monoplace "chasse" machine, as they are the fastest thing on the Front up to 5000 meters, German machines not excepted. There are several Yale men in the Squadron, one being Alan Winslow – very nice.

The Americans seem to be really in it now around Château-Thierry. It may be interesting to know that I was on the last train that went through Château-Thierry from Nancy to Paris. I was 9 hours late and I never saw so many troops and supplies in my life. Very interesting. Even ferrying machines out to the eastern part of the lines involves some risk, as you have no communication and the "boches" are fairly near.

The work on this field consists of patrols and "alertes." Some machines stay on the ground to answer "alertes," that is, when a "boche" plane crosses the lines in our sector, it is alerted to this field by our listening posts, the height and place of crossing being given. The only trouble with that is, by the time you get cranked up and over where "bosches" are supposed to be, the latter are usually headed well into Germany.

Patrols are more interesting. They are at different altitudes up to 5000 meters. The "bosche" photographic planes go that high usually.

Our quarters are very comfortable and we have every convenience – plenty of orderlies. Our insignia on our planes…is supposed to be "Uncle Sam's Hat is in the Ring." The 94th Squadron was the first, you will remember.

Much love
Harold"

"19 June
Dearest Mother:

This morning we were awakened at three-thirty by most intense artillery fire at the Front – it shook our barracks. Eight went out and took the air, as we did not know whether the Germans were on us or not. But it proved to be the first American gas attack with American gas. They say it was a remarkable sight as the heavy artillery chimed in with the gas guns. It was just a "strafe," as the infantry did not go over. We have no official report as yet, but we believe the "strafe" was highly successful. Two days ago the "boches" tried a raid, 800 coming over. But they walked right into our machine gun cross-fire and were pretty hard hit. We are not taking many prisoners any more, owing to the tactics of the enemy. They would come up to a machine gun emplacement with their hands up yelling, "Kamerad." On the back of their hands they had hand grenades strapped. When they got near enough they would throw the grenades, kill our soldiers, and take the gun position. So now they do not pay much attention to this "Kamerad" idea.

One of our men, Lt. Rickenbacker, went low over the trenches. It was the first time that we have done any trench "strafing." The boys up above him were under very hot fire at 2000 meters and came down with much shrapnel in their machines. In Maury Hill's squadron, a piece of shrapnel hit the entering edge of the top wing and bounced back into the observer's cockpit. He now has it as a souvenir.

Several days ago three paper balloons were seen coming over the field – like these 4th of July balloons. One landed on the field and proved to be a "boche" propaganda balloon. To it were attached newspapers and cartoons disparaging England. Probably to try to cause dissention between the two armies. I doubt very much their effectiveness.

I forgot to tell you that Jimmy Meissner when he was over the barrage this morning saw a big shell at the peak of its trajectory – just at an almost dead center. Rather interesting to see a shell in flight, don't you think so?

My bus is laid up today with three broken pistons in the motor. There has been quite a bit of sabotage connected with the aeroplanes for our Army (French makes of course) but I don't believe mine is a case of this, however.

I am feeling fine and am very much interested in all that is going on. I haven't had any mail for a week because my address has been changed so often.

Very much love,
Harold"

Activity over the next four days was at a minimum with only two patrols flown, plus a series of test flights and gunnery target practices. On June 24 Rickenbacker led a patrol consisting of Chambers and Tittmann departing at 7h 19 and returning, in part, two hours later. Rickenbacker and Chambers filed the following combat report:

"COMBAT REPORT of Lt. Rickenbacker and Lt. Chambers.
Date June 24, 1918. Altitude, 5000 meters; Squadron 94th.
Hour of Leaving, 7.19. Hour of Arrival, 9.18
Names of Pilots, - Lts. Rickenbacker, Chambers, and Tittmann
Mission, Voluntary Patrol; Route, Merville and Lucey.

Lt. Rickenbacker and Lt. Chambers had combat at about 8.55 with an enemy plane near Merville. Lt. Rickenbacker fired about 20 rounds of ammunition and both guns jammed with broken bullets. Apparently no results. Lt. Chambers fired about the same amount of ammunition at the same Boche, when both guns jammed also. No apparent results. Returned to field. Gave instructions to Lt. Tittmann to stay over lines and above in case of fight, which he did? During both combats (he) was last seen above patrol about 9.00 A.M. probably 5000 meters high over the lines. (Sgd) Lt. Rickenbacker and Lt. Chambers."

The fledgling Tittmann became lost and had almost landed in Switzerland. There were reports of a plane seen going down in flames which led some to think he had been shot down. He, in fact, headed incorrectly east, exhausted his fuel, and finally landed safely. Rickenbacker was not pleased with this turn of events and mentions so in his book. Two days after the event Tittmann and Nieuport were returned to the Gengoult airdrome.

A large patrol of twelve planes departed Gengoult on the morning of June 25, the first plane off at 4h 06 heading for the region of Pont-à-Mousson. The *Operations Report* states there were three combats, but the only combat report found was that of Lts. Loomis, Wentworth, and Eastman which stated:

"Lt. Loomis and Lt. Wentworth saw two balloons at East of Pont-à-Mousson about 4.45 and fired 200 rounds of ammunition with no apparent results. Lt. Eastman reports to have seen balloons in flame on Lt. Loomis' territory. (Sgd) Lt. Loomis, Lt. Wentworth, Lt. Eastman."

The whole affair of June 25, according to Rickenbacker, was designed to be a balloon busting party with pilots assigned to specifically known balloon sites. Various theories were expanded as to the reason for the total failure of the event, including jammed guns, morning dew dampening the balloon's skin, the quick passage of the bullet through the envelope which did not allow time for the ignition of the gas, and heavy ground fire which made the attack more than difficult. Ham Coolidge describes his part in the show:

"(Toul) June 25, 1918
Dearest Mother,

My head is heavy as I write these lines. We got up this morning again at 3:30 to stage a little "stunt." My rôle was to go out with our Capt. and patrol a certain length of the lines, drawing anti-craft fire and generally carrying on in such a way as to divert attention from certain of our comrades, who were the chief perpetrators of the stunt. I performed my duty exceptionally well, as I afterwards found out, though I must make the admission that it was entirely unknowingly that I did so. You see I never have been over that part of the lines before, so I did not realize when we reached them. Moreover I didn't see any of the black shrapnel puffs, that generally inform one that he is over hostile territory. A few "onion," or incendiary, rockets, and incendiary bullets came up, but still it did not dawn on me. The Capt. seemed to be acting queerly, too, and a few minutes later I lost sight of him. I circled around hoping he would pick me up again, and in the meantime I saw a distant plane that might have been anything. But no, it was one of five Boche machines that had their eye on us and were looking for a chance to bite if we crossed their lines. They must have known I was lost more or less because the Capt., who saw them all the time, said they all started to get together and come my way. About five minutes later the Capt. found me wandering around and he motioned "home." Back we came "tout de suite," and then he told me how they were aiming to trap us! It just shows how little the green fighter sees. Anyway I did distract the Boche's attention for a while!

I have another plane as my first one was wrecked a few days ago. The motor stopped suddenly when I was very low and over bad country. A good landing was impossible, and I was very lucky to get out of it with wrecking my machine, but not myself. You see these little buses are very small and fast, and dependent greatly upon the motor. Without it, the wings are so small that you have to descend rapidly and land very fast. Obviously, a smooth field is the only one adapted to that kind of work.

This is a great life, and much different from what I pictured life at the front to be. There is little noise, except for occasional artillery activity. We have wonderful quarters, and delicious food: also hot and cold shower baths. Of course, this is a quiet sector, so one must make allowances. Other places are not nearly so good.

I've got to go up on patrol now. A bunch of us will protect some observation planes.

Best love, dear Mammy,
Ham."

June concluded with the 1st Pursuit Group moving en masse to the old French field at Touquin which lay some twenty-five miles south of Château-Thierry. During the move entire flights of people were hopelessly lost, some had forced landings, motor troubles were constant, and things generally were in a state of utter confusion. To add to those miseries, many of the 94th pilots were suffering from bouts of the three-day flu which added to the lack of successful aerial activity of this final period of June and lowered morale considerably. One positive note on the move to Touquin was the billeting of the squadron in a château south of the field. The owners had closed it in 1914 when the German advance seemed unstoppable and when opened to make living quarters for the 94th it proved to be luxurious by any comparison. Furnished with 18th century furniture and surrounded by ponds, gardens and lovely scenery, the château seemed a long way from the horror of the trenches and war in the air.

Coolidge tells of his reaction to life at this new part of the front in two letters home, written at the end of the month:

"(Touquin) June 29
Dearest Mammy,

I find myself rather restricted in the news I should like to tell you, on account of the censorship regulations. Naturally one must be particularly careful about such things in the zone of advance.

We are now living in a most superb château! Never have I seen such splendid grounds and gardens, though of course they are not adequately cared for in these times of war. The gardens have beautiful roses, and many other kinds of flowers, but something which interests us even more is the abundant supply of fresh vegetables which they offer. On the grounds of the château is a small lake with loads of fish. There are stone steps leading down to the water's edge, and you almost expect to find a gondola waiting there. Really this place is the sort of thing you read about. It seems hardly real. It certainly is up to us to show some good results in our work to justify such luxurious living conditions.

In the line of our work, I have nothing new to tell you since that experience of which I have already written you. You remember, it was the time when I didn't see four Boches who "did" see us, and when our Capt. saved the situation for me. Two nights later we were raided in magnificent style, and had to take to our "abris," though most of the time we stood just outside watching the show. We could plainly hear two Boche planes overhead. Searchlights swayed to and fro over the sky in their efforts to find them, and the brilliant shrapnel bursts which dotted the sky were quickly followed by the boom, boom, and crash as they came more directly over us. Soon after this we drew into our "abri" and almost immediately afterwards four bombs fell about a quarter of a mile off in an open field. They made flashes which we could plainly see through the end of our tunnel-like "abri." The whole earth shook, and we could feel the concussion of air against our faces. Out we came again, but Mr. Boche returned once more. This time instead of dropping bombs he sailed over, fairly near a searchlight emplacement, and spat down a vindictive little stream of glowing incendiary bullets from his machine gun. Satisfied with this demonstration he sailed away to Hunland, soon followed by a companion, whose destructive efforts we had plainly seen at a neighboring town.

We have some active work ahead of us, and are keen as ever about it. It was published in the paper that Capt. James Norman Hall of this squadron was using a new type of Nieuport plane when he was captured. Did you see his good article in the June *Atlantic Monthly*? Do read it. It is so infinitely superior to these awful articles we find in the *Saturday Evening Post, Colliers*, etc., which make such painful misstatements and are so obviously written by a short-story writer and not an experienced pilot.

Your loving, Ham."

"(Touquin) June 30th, 1918
Dearest Lu,

I'll slip in a line to you before it's time to go out on our next patrol. It will take us some time to feel thoroughly at home in this sector, and I spend my spare time staring at my map. You know P.A. always used to make more or less fun of the fact that he was the only one of the family who ever took the slightest interest in maps. Well, I wish he could see his little son H. these days. My map is unquestionably the best friend I have. It really is impracticable to carry a map in your plane, because the minute you start to look at it some wily Boche is "on your tail" in an instant out of nowhere. Lu, it's painful how many things you have to watch simultaneously in this game. Let me just enumerate some of the more important things to do all at the same time – 1. Keep a continual watch out for Boches. 2. Continually watch your patrol leader. 3. Look at the ground to see where you are going and where you want to go. 4. Watch out for the steady fire of anti-aircraft shrapnel ("Archies"). 5. Watch your instruments which give you the dope on your motor, your altitude, etc. You can easily see how staggering all this is to the newcomer, and really I still place myself in that class. I have not as yet had any combats. I've had some interesting times over the lines looking for Huns, and dodging Archy, and have seen a few Boches on several occasions. No longer are there any of these trips alone over the lines. A lone man is practically certain to be nailed. On all our voluntary patrols we must go at least six strong in formation. As "chasse" or fighting planes our function is to patrol certain areas between certain times in search of Huns, and to offer protection to Allied reconnaisance, réglage, or photographic planes. We also do "alert" duty, during which time we sit around waiting a telephone call reporting boche planes over such and such a place, at a certain altitude and going in a certain direction. Then we hustle on up to meet them.

We are living in a château with wonderful lawns, gardens, pine groves, and a small lake full of fish! Did you ever hear of such luxury? Will write when something exciting has happened. Haven't heard from you for "ages."

Yours, Ham."

[1] Later in the war Junkers developed an armored plane with guns that fired through the floor.

Eddie Rickenbacker, Doug Campbell, and Ken Marr stand by one of the white cowling N 28s of A Flight. Note the white painted propellor hub, plus the pair of Vickers guns. This would date the photo late June 1918.

Jimmy Meissner, his mechanics, and N 6144 number 8. Gengoult.

LeRoy J. Prinz was a dancing instructor before his time with the Air Service. He served about a month (June) before transferring to the 27th Aero Squadron.

Eddie Green, Alden "Madame" Sherry, John Huffer, Jimmy Meissner, and Bill Loomis check out a French chateau on a sightseeing tour. June 1918.

Lt. Smith, Charles Alexander, and Edwin Clark at Saints. August 1918.

Front row: Ed Clark, Walt Smythe, Jimmy Meissner, John Jeffers. Standing: Joe Eastman, Bill Chalmers, Fred Ordway. Seated: Harold Tittmann. Photo taken between June 6 and June 20, 1918. *USAFM*.

One of the 94th's mobile machine shops. Its four operators pose between repairs. Note the rather primitive rope and chain arrangements for better traction with a shovel also available just in case. *Lt. Eddie Green album*.

Right: John Jeffers. Saints Airdrome. July 1918.

Rickenbacker astride Huffer's number 1 chats with Ken Marr before a patrol. From this picture one can get a sense of how small the Nieuport 28 actually was.

Rickenbacker with his Nieuport sporting two Vickers guns. *U. S. Signal Corps photo.*

Jimmy Meissner at the wheel and John Mitchell of the 95th as passenger in one of the 94th squadron's touring cars. Saints. July 1918.

Alden "Madame" Sherry and crew with his twin gun N 28.

Ken Marr and Dave Peterson before Peterson was assigned to the 95th Aero Squadron on May 16, 1918.

Weir Cook, unidentified, John Jeffers, unidentified, Willie Palmer, Willey Sparks, Art Cunningham, Eddie Green, and Thorne Taylor with the squadron canine mascot, "Spad". July 1918.

On occasion the 94th officers were brought up closer to the front for familiarization and some unofficial souvenir hunting. Here we see Reed Chambers, Eddie Rickenbacker, and Jimmy Meissner with three other officers on one of these trips.

Right: Fred Ordway during his brief stay with the 94th, June 6-24. Ordway went on to the 27th Aero.

Below: An excellent group photo of the 94th pilots late June – early July 1918. Front Row: LeRoy Prinz, Harold Tittmann, Fred Ordway, Walt Smythe. Second Row: Bill Loomis, Chester Snow, Eddie Green, Alan Winslow, Ken Marr, Eddie Rickenbacker, Jimmy Meissner, Thorne Taylor, George Zacharias. Top Row: Ham Coolidge, Art Cunningham, Bill Chalmers, Joe Eastman, Alden Sherry, John Wentworth, E. Z. Cates, Ed Clark, John Jeffers.

LeRoy Prinz sitting on Eddie Green's number 18 which they both flew for a short period.

Right: Private F. J. Passarelli, who Joe Dawson claimed to be "the world's greatest orderly". *Joe Dawson album.*

Below: On July 7, Bill Chalmers was shot down and captured while flying N 6181 number 15. Chalmers was able to land behind German lines and his plane was captured intact. This photo was taken when the plane was in German hands.

Another view of Chalmers' Nieuport undergoing testing in German hands. July 1918.

94th Aero Squadron enlisted men exploring the ruins of Château Thierry, France.

On June 7, 1918, "Madame" Sherry, while on his third flight with the 94th, had a forced landing in Allied lines causing the end of N 6154 number 7. He is seated on the right with a group of French and American soldiers who came to his assistance. *Joe Dawson album*.

Pat Maloney tries his hand with a Colt .45 caliber M1917 revolver. It is of interest to see the quantity of M1917 revolvers rather than M1911 .45 automatics that were issued to Air Service personnel.

Bill Loomis stands near what appears to be a squadron truck loading barrels of gasoline. June 1918.

Toul, June 1918. Front row: Reed Chambers, Jimmy Meissner, Ken Marr, Lt. Cooper (ground officer), Thorne Taylor. Rear: Joe Eastman, Doc Walters, Walt Smythe, Eddie Rickenbacker. *U. S. A. F. Museum photo.*

Lt. Donald Herring, ordnance officer, and Chester Snow, pilot, who joined the 94th June 9, 1918.

Left: Joe Wehner, five victory Ace of the 27th Aero, later killed in action, leans on the door of one of the 94th touring cars; Eddie Rickenbacker and LeRoy Prinz behind the car; Walt Smythe and an unidentified friend in the rear. Saints. July 1918.

J. Loy "Pat" Maloney joined the squadron in July and was still a member during the Occupation of Germany in 1919.

Ham Coolidge joined the 94th on June 17, gaining eight victories before he was killed in action October 27, 1918. *U. S. National Archives, RG 18 P-1463 A.S.*

Below: A rare view of Ham Coolidge in his Nieuport over Château Thierry taken by Alden Sherry. June 1918. *U.S.A.F. Museum photo.*

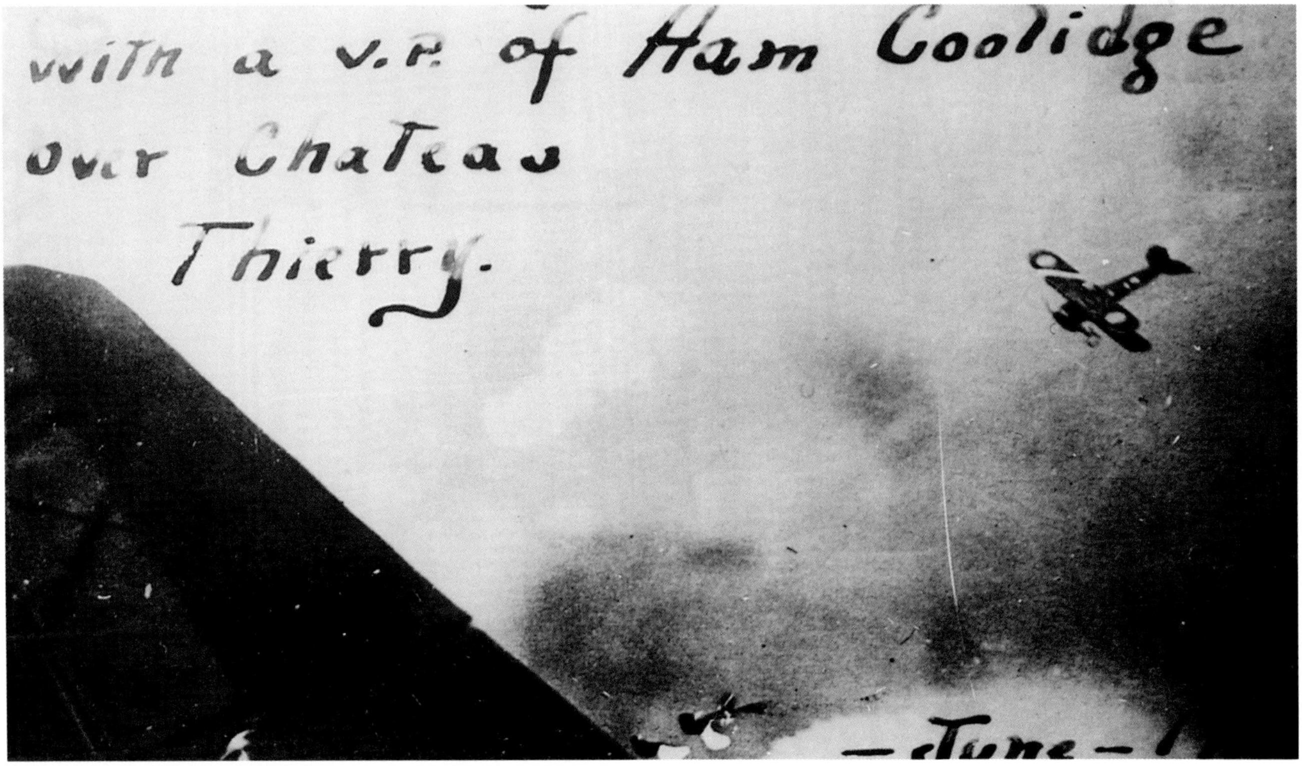

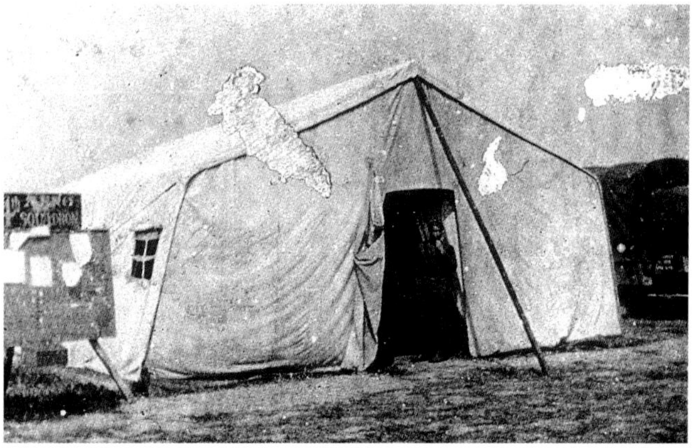

The 94th operations tent with the daily schedules on a bulletin board to the left.

The target butts at Gengoult Airdrome. *Lt. Eddie Green photo.*

94th pilots off duty. L/R Rickenbacker, unidentified, Maloney, Eastman in the doorway, Marr, Campbell, Taylor, unidentified.

George Zacharias joined the 94th June 5, 1918.

Reed Chambers catching up on the news in the alert tent. June 1918. *Reed Chambers album.*

Jimmy Meissner in a squadron staff car. Note the Air Service roundel on the door.

A view of another staff car which bears a small 94th insignia. It can be seen between "Jim" Beam, the armament officer and Lt. Smith, the Adjutant.

Reed Chambers and N 6179 number 11 in the early single gun days at Gengoult.

Above: A great group shot in front of Hangar 1, Gengoult Airdrome. L//R: Unidentified, Doc Walters, Eddie Rickenbacker, unidentified, unidentified, unidentified, Thorne Taylor, unidentified, Reed Chambers, Ken Marr, Bill Loomis, LeRoy Prinz, John Jeffers, Jimmy Meissner, Joe Eastman, Chester Snow, Alden Sherry, George Zacharias, Eddie Green. *U. S. Signal Corps photo.*

Right: Taken the same day and the same place, Jake, the 95th Aero mascot, goes through his paces for a mixed group of 1st Pursuit Group officers. *U. S. Signal Corps photo.*

Left: Eddie Green dressed up in his best uniform and swagger stick. June 1918. *Joe Dawson album*. Center: Wiley Sparks and Weir Cook. July 1918. Right: Alden "Madame" Sherry. Gengoult Airdrome. June 1918. Note the popular cane, the aviator style open collar tunic and the U.S.R. (United States Reserve) insignia.

July at Saints. The Spads began to arrive at the Squadron in early July. Sam Kaye at the controls of Spad 15130 number 16.

George Zacharias has solved the neck chafe problem of the high-collared tunic by wearing a soft shirt up and over the offending cause. July 1918.

Pat Maloney with his Spad named "Babe", Spad 15056 number 23. His flight crew share the picture. Saints. Mid to late July 1918.

Thorne Taylor and two of his crew stand in front of Spad 15021 number 13 which Taylor flew from July 14 – September 29, 1918.

Rickenbacker with cane stands by Spad 4523 number 1 which he flew from July 7, 1918 through 1919.

Above: Reed Chambers and crew with Spad 4526 number 11.

Above right: Reed Chambers atop his Spad 4526 number 11 at Saints. July 1918.

Right: Thorne Taylor and Spad 15021 number 13. Saints. August 1918.

Below: Spad 15003 number 15 was assigned to Charles Crocker and is surrounded by his crew, Bill Loomis, Wiley Sparks and an unidentified officer in the background. Number 15 lasted from July 14 to September 14 when it was wrecked at Hill 334, St. Mihiel.

Rickenbacker with "Spad" the squadron mascot.

Chester Snow tipping Uncle Sam's hat on the side of Spad 15225 number 6 which was flown by Chambers during the month of September.

The business end of a Spad XIII showing its twin-mounted Vickers.

From the cockpit looking over the windshield at the gun sight and the twin Vickers.

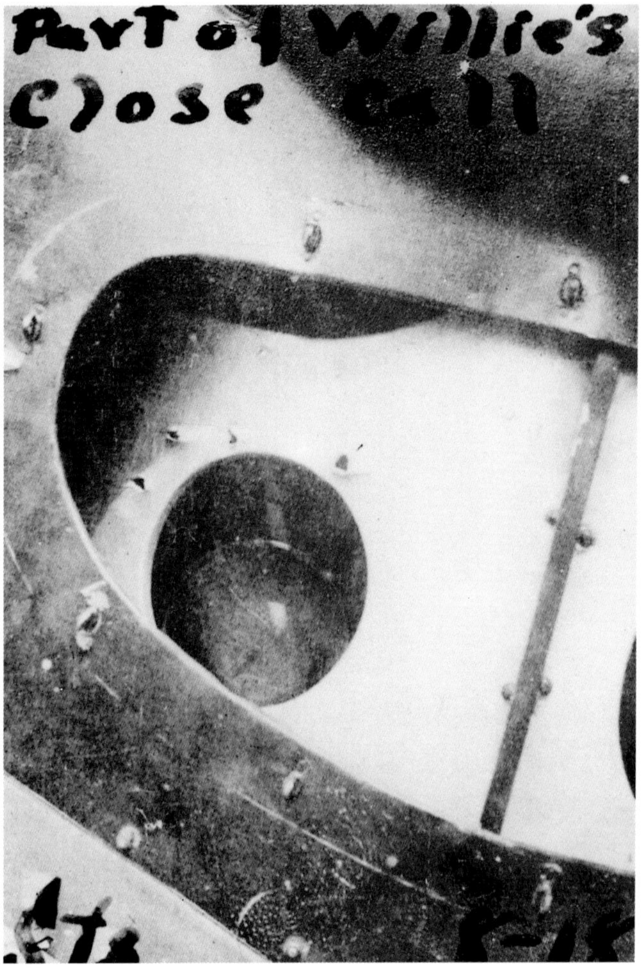

A photo showing battle damage to Willie Palmer's Spad when he was operating out of Saints. July and August 1918. Four bullet holes are seen on the top of the round opening, but the rugged Spad made it home.

Thorne Taylor in the cockpit of Spad 4589 number 3 which he flew from July 14 – September 15, 1918.

Campbell was ordered home, much to his disgust, to check out the fighter training in the United States. This photo, taken with an admiring crowd of 94th enlisted men, was just prior to his departure. *Doug Campbell album.*

Pat Maloney and a line-up of Spads. Saints. August 1918.

At the end of his recuperation from the back wound he received on June 6, 1918, Campbell went on leave to Biarritz where he was photographed in the center. His two companions are unidentified.

Right: Reed Chambers. Saints. July 1918. *Joe Dawson album.*

Alden Sherry and "Spad". Saints. August 1918. Joe Dawson's caption in his album was "Fat chance to teach that dog anything." Perhaps Spad was not too bright. *Joe Dawson album.*

Eddie Rickenbacker. Saints. August 1918.

Reed Chambers and one of his mechanics. Saints. August 1918. Note the red, white, and blue bands on the forward landing gear struts. These show up on Rickenbacker's plane, but may have been on others.

Sam Kaye and his mechanics pose by his Spad. From August 3 to September 26, Kaye regularly flew Spad 15130 number 16.

Reed Chambers and Spad 4526 number 11. Saints. August 1918.

Rickenbacker and number 1. Saints. August 1918.

5

July - Spads and their Shortcomings

The daily *Report of Operations* for July 1, 1918, states that one patrol was flown from Belleau to Château-Thierry at an altitude of 3500 meters. There were six planes piloted by Lts. Meissner, Wentworth, Zacharias, Cates, Tittmann and Green. The patrol departed Touquin at 14h 53 and at 15h 45 they were jumped by six enemy single-seaters. Jimmy Meissner's combat report gives his side of the story:

"COMBAT REPORT of – Lt. Meissner
Date – July 1, 1918; Altitude, 3500 meters; Squadron 94th
Hour of Leaving, 14.53; Hour of Arrival, 16.35
Names of Pilots, Lts. Meissner, Wentworth, Zacharias, Cates, Tittmann, and Green
Mission, Patrol/ Route, Belleau, Château Thierry

In vicinity of Boureaches, at 15h 45, 3500 meters, six enemy monoplace, believed to be Fokkers, piqued down from the sun at us. Two of them came within range and fired a few rounds, but turned away when shot at by other Nieuports. We turned west to climb and were not followed. Lt. Tittmann was missing, but no machines were seen to fall. Lt. Cates left the patrol at 16h 05, turning south from lines and is still missing. (16h 15). Lt. Meissner fired 25 rounds and Lt. Green 10 rounds. (Sgd) J. A. Meissner, 1st Lt. ASUSR."

Lt. Harold Tittmann from all reports was flying the upper left position of a vee formation which was being led by Meissner. When the enemy came out of the sun, he was the first in line to be attacked. Tittmann nearly collided with one of the attackers who had separated from his formation and then proceeded to try and get on the enemy's tail to attack.

The rest of Tittmann's fight was described by eyewitness, Captain H. H. Barnhart of the 109 Machine Gun Battalion, 28th Division:

"At 4:30 p.m., July 1st 1918, the attention of those on the ground who were operating in the vicinity of Château-Thierry (Charly, to be exact, which is southwest of Château-Thierry on the banks of the Marne) was drawn to the air by intense machine gun firing. One Allied single-seater pursuit plane was seen maneuvering among five German pursuit planes (Pfaltz-type) at a low altitude. Soon one German plane abandoned the fight and climbed toward its own lines apparently out of ammunition. After about three minutes more circling around, another German plane was seen to dive precipitately and disappear behind a hill. It was not on fire, as far as the onlookers could tell, but it did not rise again and all the officers present are certain that it crashed. It was out of control in descending. As there were no other Allied planes in sight, it is certain that the German was destroyed by this particular Allied plane.

After several minutes more fighting, the Allied plane, which was piloted by Lt. H. Tittmann, U.S. Air Service, was apparently seeking a landing field, as it persisted in flying around in a circle. It was thought that the pilot was going to land on a very good field on high ground, quite far back from the Marne on the South Bank. Both banks of the Marne looked like good landing ground from the air because wheat was growing there. Barbed wire entanglements, however, had been put up here several weeks before by some Italian Engineers. The wheat had grown up around the wire, hiding it from view from the air.

Whether Lt. Tittmann intended landing on the south bank or the north bank is not known. At any rate he failed to avail himself of the good high ground and, going at a speed of 90 mph, struck the barbed wire with the undercarriage. The plane turned over on its back. The shock caused the screws that held the seat to the fusilage to give way and Lt. Tittmann with seat still strapped to him was thrown 30 feet clear of the wreckage. This fact probably saved his life, because if the seat had not been torn loose, he would have been crushed beneath the whole plane. Captain Barnhard and Lt. Sleeth were the first to reach him and they administered first aid. The latter made tourniquets out of an Italian blouse that they cut up. His right arm and both legs were bleeding profusely. It was found that Lt. Tittmann was shot through the right lung, right arm, and right foot (probably from the same burst) and his left leg was broken by the fall."

In the seat were found nine bullet holes and approximately 200 were counted in the whole plane. This means that 100 bullets found their target. Captain Barnhart unloaded both machine guns and found twenty rounds left out of the original five hundred.

Barnhart continues:

"The Italians on the other side of the river began to swim across to the plane, but the German planes stayed around and machine-gunned everybody and everything in sight. So they thought better of it and took cover again. Lt. Tittmann remained conscious after the crash and gave his name and address. The only piece of clothing that was fit to salvage was the helmet, which Lt. Sleeth sent to his family through the YMCA. Lt. Tittmann was taken to a nearby power house by a French doctor and thence to a chateau where his wounds were dressed by Major Moore, M. C. Engineers (105). He was then sent back to La Ferté-sous-Jouarre in care of the 103 Field Hospital 26th Division."

Tittmann survived his terrible injuries and began a long journey through field hospitals, the 10,000 bed hospital at Bazoilles-sur-Meuse where, fortunately, he was assigned to the Johns Hopkins Unit, and finally to Walter Reed Hospital in Washington, D.C., from which he was finally discharged on 3 May 1920. Dr. Simon Flexner, Director of Laboratories of the Rockefeller Institute for Medical Research conferred on Tittmann, "the reputation of being the worst wounded-in-action American soldier to have survived, not only in World War I, but also in any other conflict in which the United States had been engaged."

The morning of July 2 a patrol consisting of Lts. Chambers, Wentworth, Green, Sherry, Chalmers, Smythe and Coolidge was sent out to fly at 5000 meters "over the lines." This may well have been another familiarization flight over their new territory. Six enemy planes were spotted by Eddie Green whose combat report stated, "Saw formation of six Boche at 10.15. They turned into Germany. I shot about 50 rounds at a very long range. Did not continue the attack as they were above us. Saw two other Boche formations way back behind the lines. Lt. Chambers left patrol about 9h 50 west of Château-Thierry. Anti-aircraft active, but very poor. We also saw several formations of French planes as well as several Nieuports."

The 147th Aero Squadron was very active July 2 and experienced a number of combats while flying basically in the same Château-Thierry area, which may explain Green's Nieuport sightings. The missing Cates returned to the squadron and was on patrol the afternoon of July 2, 1918.

There was little to no flying on July 3 and 4, but two protection patrols of eight planes each were flown on July 5. The first departed at the early hour of 4h 04, returning at 5h 19. Green's combat report stated: "Lt. Cates left the patrol with bad motor at 4h 20. Met five Boche over Verdilly while waiting for the Salmsons. I fired about 25 rounds at 4h 50. Formation again reassembled with four men following the Salmsons which appeared at 5h 00. Lt. Jeffers lost the patrol and came home. Lt. Winslow has not returned at six-fifteen. Lt. Gude has not returned at this time. Anti-aircraft very active. Visibility very bad. Salmsons apparently succeeded in taking their pictures. Last saw Lt. Gude and Lt. Winslow over Verdilly at 4h 50."

The second protection patrol of eight Nieuports, consisting of Lt. Green, Patrol Leader, Lts. Winslow, Gude, Coolidge, Jeffers, Chalmers, and Cates, was to protect three Salmsons photographing in the Verdilly area. In Green's second combat report of the day, he states that at 16h 50 before they met the Salmsons, they ran into five enemy planes at 4000 meters. Green fired 25 rounds without results. Four Nieuports protected two Salmsons with no mention of the other four Nieuports or the other Salmson. The photo mission was accomplished and Winslow went missing again.

A mysterious note to these two patrols is the re-appearance of Lt. Oscar J. Gude after being inactive since the Lufbery downing. The re-appearance was short as he was only heard of one more time as a member of the 94th.

One large patrol was flown on July 6 with Green again leading and reporting "Saw one white balloon southeast of

Château Thierry, probably a propaganda balloon. Saw one plane probably enemy east of Château Thierry at about 6500 meters. Saw three American reglage planes at 17h 00 north of Château Thierry. Anti-aircraft very active about Neuilly at front. Saw fires on ground northwest of Château Thierry near Etreville. Lt. Jeffers landed on field just the other side of Oneaux."

A protection patrol was ordered to cover the 1st Aero Squadron on the morning of July 7 in the region of Château Thierry. Lt. Jimmy Meissner led the patrol consisting of Loomis, Smythe, Green, Coolidge, Winslow, Cates, Chalmers, Sherry, Wentworth and Rickenbacker. The only pilots not on the patrol were Chambers, 1st Flight, Zacharias, 2nd Flight, and Eastman, 3rd Flight.

Two combat reports of the mission survive, the first by Lt. Cates and the second by Alden "Madame" Sherry:

"Date – July 7, 1918. Visibility near lines, Very Good.
Mission. Protection Patrol for the 1st Aero Sqdn. Photographic.
Route actually followed, Epaux, Bonnes, Priez, Griselles.
Names of Pilots, - Lts. Meissner, Loomis, Smythe, Green, Coolidge, Winslow, Cates, Chalmers, Sherry, Wentworth, Rickenbacker.
Hour of Departure, 8.25. Hour of Return, Panned.
Altitude, 5500 meters.
Enemy planes seen, 1 Biplace Rumpler, E. A. Encountered, 1 Biplace Rumpler.
Time 9.50. region, Bonnes. Altitude, 5000 to 900 meters.
Enemy planes seen, 1 Monoplace Fokker. E. A. Encountered, 1 Monoplace Fokker.
Time 10.00. Region, Griselles. Altitude 2500 to 800 meters.
Combats, 2. Number of Rounds fired, 300.
Plane struck by several enemy bullets.

Narrative: While protecting a Salmson from the 1st Aero Squadron, I encountered one enemy Biplace Rumpler at 5000 meters, following it to 900 meters and firing 300 rounds. Lt. Meissner and another Nieuport also firing. The tail of the enemy plane burst into flames about 3000 meters at 9h 55 over Griselles. At 10h 00 Fokker piqued on me from the side, forcing me down to 800 meters. CONFIRMATION REQUESTED. (Sgd) R. Z. Cates, 1st Lieut. USUSR."

The format of Cates' report is different from reports filed earlier by other pilots and it is not known if this was a new format introduced this day. From the report it would seem that the encounter with the Fokker may have had something to do with his reported "panned" end of the flight.

"Report of Lt. Sherry.
Date, July 7, 1918. Visibility near lines, Very Bad. Sqdn. 94th. Mission, Protection Patrol
Names of Pilots, Lts. Meissner, Loomis, Smythe, Green, Coolidge, Winslow, Cates, Chalmers, Sherry, Wentworth and Rickenbacker.
Time of Departure, 8.26. Hour of Return, 16.00. Altitude, 5200 meters.
Number of Planes seen, 2. E. A. Encountered, one biplace.
Time, 9h 50. Region, Recourt. Altitude, 3500 meters. Type, Rumpler.
Combats, 1. Number of Rounds fired, 60.

Narrative: While protecting Salmson from the 1st Aero Squadron I saw 2 biplace enemy machines and attacked one of them firing about 60 rounds, at the height of about 4000 meters. During that time three or four Nieuports were attacking the other machine. Apparently no results. The last time I remember of seeing Lt. Chalmers was last seen when we left the field. Forced to land at Griselles, gas pump broken, borrowed some gas and returned safely. (Sgd) A. B. Sherry, 1st Lt. ASUSR."

Lt. William W. Chalmers was shot down during this patrol, landed, and was taken prisoner by the Germans. His name appears in Sherry's report because of his missing status at the end of the day, some 7 1/2 hours after departure. The confirmations for victories attained this day, made by "American Military Authorities of July 20th, 1918," seem to be rather confusing. They were given to Coolidge for an "enemy plane (down in flames) 9h 50, 3000 mts. (near Griselles) 7-7-18;" to Lt. Cates same place, but at 9h 50, not 9h 35; to Lt. Cook who was not listed on the patrol, for an "Enemy Fokker" at 9h 35 at 3000 meters in the region of Verdilly-Besuit; to Bill Loomis for "Enemy down in a Vrille" same time, same place; and to Eddie Green with the same language as Loomis'. Cates, Loomis and Green all ended the war with one victory for which this confirmation may have given them credit. The Germans lost three two-seaters on July 7, one from FA 46b which had been in scrapes with the 94th before, when they were at Toul.

Ham Coolidge in his July 7 letter to his mother gives more details of the fight:

"(Touquin) July 7

Dear Mother,

I got a Boche today – or rather Jim Meissner and I got one together, but as we were too far inside their lines for our observation balloons to see it, we shall probably not receive official credit. Four of us attacked a single bi-place Rumpler and we all peppered away without result for several minutes. He was fighting for his life and gave us all a good fight! Suddenly it occurred to me that it would be much more to the point to get under his tail where I should be out of range from his rear gun and at the same time have a chance to soak some shots into him at close range. Just as I did so he started to dive, and at the same time Jim Meissner appeared; the other two of our gang had jammed guns and left the scrap. We both shot at the Boche and a second later great hot, red flames burst out from beneath his fuselage. I shall never forget the sensation of seeing a stream of flaming tracer bullets from my guns sink into its body and almost instantly flames bursting out as we dove at great speed through the air. At 2000 meters both my guns had jammed, so I left the battle pursued by a group of Fokker monoplane (monoplace) fighters who had come up in the meantime. Jim dove after the Boche a little further, gave him a final salvo of shots and followed me. He scared off a Boche whom he said was hot on my tail. I had lost Jim, my only thought was home for dear life before the mob nailed me. We out-distanced them and Jim pulled up beside me just as we crossed the lines. Golly, I was glad to see him as I didn't know what had become of him. We did not stay to see our victim crash, but from his predicament at 2000 meters from the earth we do not doubt that there are two less Germans in the Imperial Air Service tonight.

H."

To give the reader a clearer idea of how the Squadron operated, the following information is included. The Squadron was broken up into three flights, plus Captain Ken Marr and 1st Lt. Eddie Rickenbacker who were not assigned by flight. A breakdown of flights, pilots and aircraft gives one a clearer idea of how the 94th operated during the Nieuport era. Much of this information comes from a June Squadron Condition Report:

Pilot	**Plane No.**	**Sqdn. No.**	**Remarks**
Marr, Captain	6236	17	ex 95th Aero
Rickenbacker, Lt.	6283	16	
Rickenbacker, Lt.	6169	1	ex Huffer & 95th Aero
Rickenbacker, Lt.	6159	12	Flown by Zacharias
First Flight			
Chambers, Lt.	6179	11	
Green, Lt.	6297	3	Went to 147th Aero
Sherry, Lt.	6154	7	ex Gude
Smythe, Lt.	6230	4	Also flown by Sherry
Spare a/c	6180	18	Prinz and Jeffers
Second Flight			
Meissner, Lt.	6144	8	collapsed wing twice
Taylor, Lt.	6148	13	ex 95th Aero to 147th Aero
Wentworth, Lt.	6168	5	to Colombey-les-Belles
Winslow, Lt.	6189	6	also flown by Marr
Zacharias, Lt.	6159	12	ex Rickenbacker
Spare a/c	6340		
Third Flight			
Campbell, Lt.	6158	0	ex 95th Aero. Also Peterson
Loomis, Lt.	6275	2	to 27th Aero. Lt. Sands KIA
Eastman, Lt.	6151	14	Also flown by Cunningham
Cunningham, Lt.	6260	20	Also flown by Eastman
Jeffers, Lt.	6181	15	Shared w/ Loomis, Chalmers
Spare a/c	6163	9	Cunningham, Coolidge, Clark

At this time, the rumors were getting stronger that the 1st Pursuit Group was about to be equipped with Spad XIIIs which would end the use of the perceived to be undependable Nieuport 28s.

The weather conditions were poor on July 8, but in spite of that a patrol was flown from Favorelles to Château-Thierry departing at 8h 45 and which resulted in a scrap with a biplace and five Fokkers. Of these events, Meissner and Rickenbacker filed a joint Combat Report.

"COMBAT REPORT OF Lt. Rickenbacker and Lt. Meissner.
Date – July 8, 1918. Visibility near Lines, Poor. Squadron, 94th.
Mission, Patrol – Favorelles to Château-Thierry.
Names of Pilots, Lt. Meissner, Flight Commander, Lts. Sherry, Winslow, Coolidge, Green, Rickenbacker, Loomis,

Taylor. (Lts. Rickenbacker, Green and Loomis in patrol above other.)
Hour of Departure, 8.45. Hour of Return, 10.35. Altitude, 4500 meters.
Enemy planes seen and encountered, 1 biplace and 5 monoplace Fokkers.
Time, 9h 35; Region, Etrepilly, Verdilly, Bezuit.
Formation, 1 biplace and 5 monoplace Fokkers, in "V" formation with last man high and afterwards milling in a circle.
Combats, 2. Number of rounds fired, 260.

Narrative: Saw six planes diving on Lt. Meissner's patrol, 1 biplace and 5 monoplace Fokkers. Time 9h 35, 9h 40. Region, Etrepilly, Verdilly, Bezuit. We attacked the biplace. I fired 150 rounds, Lt. Green 50 rounds, and Lt. Loomis 50 rounds; Altitude, 4500 meters. The biplace was last seen in a vrille. Then a monoplace attacked me in the rear and was driven off by Lt. Green. The fight lasted about 5 minutes, then the enemy retired. We descended to 500 meters over Château Thierry. Fired about 150 rounds into the German trenches. Heavy enemy artillery noticed at Longpont and Coincy. CONFIRMATION REQUESTED. (Sgd) E. V. Rickenbacker, 1st Lt. ASUSR.

Narrative: Intense artillery activity between Longpont and Coincy between 10h 00 and 10h 30. Many enemy aircraft in the German lines. Lt. Winslow has not returned at 10h 50. Last seen going South, region southwest of Château Thierry ahead of patrol (Sgd) James A. Meissner, 1st Lieut. ASSUSR."

On July 9 the Squadron began its next move, this time from Touquin to the field at Saints. Lts. Sherry, Taylor, Rickenbacker, Coolidge, Smythe, Snow, Loomis, and for his final 94th flight, J. Gude, Wentworth, Green, Winslow, Cates and Prinz departed Touquin in the morning for this short flight. Of note were Lt. Prinz's crash at a French farm and Lt. Wentworth destroying his Nieuport at Saints. The field at that time was undergoing repairs which made it difficult to attempt many active flights. One eight-man patrol went out on July 10, but with no results, and nothing was flown on either July 11 or 12.

Ham Coolidge speaks of his close friend Quentin Roosevelt in a letter home of July 10:

"(Touquin) July 10
Dear Mammy,

Quentin and I were not assigned to the same squadron. We are in the same group, consequently operate from the same base and see each other frequently. Let me tell you of the splendid *coup de main* he sprang today: While on patrol with some eight or nine of his comrades over the lines, the formation became broken up in some quick manoeuvering. Q. suddenly found himself alone. After circling around a few minutes he saw three planes in formation not far away and hastened to rejoin them, falling into place behind them. It seemed a little queer that his leader should be going so far within the enemy lines, but he thought no more about it until the leader made a sudden turn exposing to full view upon his rudder – a large black cross! "Wrong again," said Q. to himself, but his brain kept right on working. Sneaking close up behind the rear man who either did not see him or supposed him to be one of his friends, Q. took careful aim and let him have a stream of bullets from his machine gun. The plane wavered a second, then toppled over and fell spinning in a spiral like a winged stone. Q. reversed and headed for home at full speed pursued by two bewildered Huns whom he gradually left further and further behind as his little Nieuport roared along. A quick backward glance revealed his victim still spinning after a fall of some nine or ten thousand feet; he then disappeared in a cloud bank.

Isn't that one of the most remarkable *true* tales you ever heard? It's doubtful if his Boche is confirmed – too far inside their lines. In my experience here I cannot recall a *single* instance when the Boche would come out and fight in our territory or even over the lines. Invariably we must go to them. They are always to be found, often in large numbers, but they seem to have the homing instinct to a high degree. If our Boche of the other day is confirmed, there are three of us who will receive official credit. In a mix-up like that it is often impossible to tell who delivered the telling shot, and often the men who did but little shooting were the biggest factors in the combat by forcing a situation or so distracting the enemy's attention that some one else had a chance to sneak in at close range and put in some telling shots. I know my bullets hit him and that he burst into flames as they entered his fuselage, but I haven't an idea that mine were the only ones that hit him, and I'm sure that another boy's shots fired after I was through (with both guns jammed) was what finished anything there may have been left to finish. It was really a very funny affair at first. Four of us were peppering away indiscriminately, ineffectively, while he banked his old ship up first on one side, then the other in order to give his observer a chance to shoot first at one of us, then at another. The end of the scrap would have been sad had we been fighting with human beings, but I frankly confess that a thrill of pleasure came over me as I saw the flames burst out.

The tactics of air fighting are fairly complicated and we frequently have to admire the old Boche for his keen knowledge of them. They say the Yanks are quick to learn, however. It really looks as if the Huns had to be very careful about losing men and planes. They do only what is absolutely necessary, crossing the lines only when a definite mission is to be performed. This policy would be good if they were very insistent that Allied planes should not cross their lines, but they seem somewhat indifferent about it.

Love,
Ham."

On July 12 Doug Campbell wrote his family from Biarritz:

"I don't remember when I last wrote, except that it was a long time ago. On the 19th of June I left Base Hospital 15 for 3 weeks' sick leave, and "sick leave" has certainly proved to be an excellent name for it.

I spent almost two weeks and many francs in Paris, where for 10 days I had a delightful time. Almost every morning I went to a place just outside the city where there are a lot of planes, and I flew quite a bit on Spads, which is the type of machine our Sqdn. will probably have when I get back. Then in the afternoon I would return to Paris and invariably meet old friends. Anybody who wants to see friends has only to sit in the "Crillon Bar" – really a sort of men's clubroom, delightfully furnished, in the Hotel Crillon on the Place de la Concorde – from 5:30 to 7:00 p.m., and he will meet most of the American officers in Paris, particularly Harvard men and pilots. It is really getting to be almost an institution; officers on leave in Paris drop in there every afternoon, not for the purpose of drinking, but to meet old acquaintances. I ran across Archie Roosevelt, two or three Harvard classmates, Ken Smith, some Harvard Second Football teammates, and oodles of pilots that I hadn't seen since January. Vive le Crillon!

I was in the pink of condition and thinking about going back to the Sqdn. when I collected the 3-day grippe which is going the rounds, and spent a couple of days in bed. Then I packed myself off to Biarritz, and no sooner arrived here than a couple of young ptomaines dived on me out of a hors d'oeuvre or something, and kept me in bed on a liquid diet for 4 days. I'm just getting up again. Now it will be 10 days before I'm fit to go back to the front, where one is comparatively safe. The Sqdn. has moved near where I was in March, and Ham Coolidge has at last got rid of his Issoudun testing job and joined us, so I am more anxious than ever to get back to work. I've been a liability for six weeks now, which is pretty rough on Uncle Sam's Liberty Funds, even if I have cost the Imperial German Government some $300,000. – (That's 10 pilots or observers at $25,000. – apiece, plus 6 machines)."

Campbell wrote in the 1960s:

"Note: A few days later, when en route to rejoin his Squadron, which was the 94th, in the 1st Pursuit Group, the writer was intercepted and given orders (to his infinite chagrin and disgust) to proceed to the United States to inspect the training of chasse (fighter) pilots there and make suggestions for improving it. Despite his efforts to shorten this mission, in which he soon found that he could accomplish little because the fault lay in the sluggish, underpowered aircraft then available for this training in the United States, red tape and Army bureaucracy kept him from returning to Europe until November, and he was crossing the Atlantic eastbound when the Armistice was signed.

So, although he did rejoin his beloved squadron for a few weeks in November/December, he did not succeed in again going WHERE THE ACTION IS."

July 13 must have seemed an unlucky and red letter day. The *Operations Report* was extremely brief, stating:

"1 Trial Flight. One plane from 12h 33 to 12h 59. Col. Mitchell" followed by "Spads available 1; Spads unavailable 13. 14 Total"

The day had come for the long awaited Spads to arrive and now with it came the frustrating time to get these fourteen machines airworthy and combat ready. The Engineering Officer's report of July 14, 1918 shows the same statistic as the day before, "Planes available 1, Planes Unavailable 13. 14 Total. Installing guns." It seems unusual that the guns were not supplied at the factory or even at the depot at Colombey-les-Belles. In any event, the planes had arrived and they were #4505, which was given Squadron number 4; 4523, which was Rickenbacker's number 1; 4526, Reed Chambers' number 11; 4589, Jeffers' number 3; 15003, Crocker's number 15; 15004, unassigned, but number 10; 15006, Eastman's number 19;

15011, Green's number 18; 15014, Marr's number 17; 15015, which was quickly wrecked; 15021, Taylor's number 13; 15022, Sparks' number 5; 15042, Zacharias' number 12; 15052, Sherry's number 8. The following day 4573, Palmer's number 20, was delivered, two more Spads on July 16, 15027, Clark's number 2 and 15056, number 23 which was wrecked. The last five came in on the 18th, 4538, Snow's number 7; 15026, which for some reason was soon condemned; 15031, Cates' number 9; 15034, Coolidge's number 22; and 15067, Winslow's number 6. Along with the new Spads came new pilots. On July 17, Samuel Kaye, Jr., Wiley S. Sparks, and William W. Palmer joined the ranks of the 94th.

Coolidge was ambivalent about the new Spads in two letters home:

"(Touquin) Sunday, July 14
Dear P. A.,

Today is the great French national holiday. We are making a brave show of all the French and American flags we can scrape up. It's the least we can do after the fine way they honored our Fourth of July. As it happens, too, our squadron is off duty, because our splendid new planes which arrived yesterday are being all fitted up with guns and equipment, so until they are ready we do nothing, having rid ourselves of our old planes yesterday. Our new ships are the famous Spads, single seater chasse planes of two hundred and thirty horsepower, and very well constructed. Our last planes were very fast and handy, but now that they are gone I will confess to you that they were *not* reliable planes. Every time we went far over the lines we had qualms because the motors frequently gave out and you never could tell when it might happen.

A few days ago occurred the most important event since our arrival on this sector. Some mail from home arrived!

In a little over a week now I shall be putting on my second service stripe – one year of foreign service. It's hard to realize that I've been away a whole year unless I judge the time by my longing to see my family. When will these vain fools come to their senses? Not till they've had some harder knocks than any they've yet received I'm thinking.

Love to all,
Ham."

"Dear Lu and Dickie,

This is the first chance I've had to write since your letter came about a week ago. I've been cheated out of a lot of action at a most interesting time, because when our brand-new planes arrived, mine turned out to be a lemon. After days of struggling with it I had to have a new one, which takes a few days to equip and get into shape. They are splendid machines – 230-h.p. Spads (monoplace) – and no experiment.

This is the queerest life you ever saw. One week we live in a château, the next we are billeted in dingy farmhouses. Sometimes we eat like kings; again we almost starve because of all being broke! You understand there's plenty of food to be had, but occasionally our pay gets waylaid and out of our last pay we may have bought uniforms, etc. Then we are all broke for a while until two months' revenue suddenly comes, when we are tremendously rich! In general, though, I manage to keep ahead of the game. This letter is hopeless; I can't seem to collect my thoughts, so will try again soon.

Affectionately,
Ham."

With the arrival of the new Spads, the headaches seemed to multiply to unimaginable proportions for the Engineering Department. Between July 18 and the end of the month, there were 124 problems concerning these brand new airplanes. Overheating, oil leads leaking, faulty oil pumps, faulty carburetors, faulty magnetos, broken gauges, faulty gas tanks, plus the replacement of entire engines. Several of the July delivered Spads became total wrecks due to crashes caused by this shoddy workmanship by the French.

Two patrols to Château-Thierry and return were possible on July 18, but produced no results. They were of 2 hour and 1 1/2 hour durations and the Engineering Department had to cope with nine different problems from these two patrols.

On July 19 ten out of twenty-three planes were available with which the 94th attempted three patrols. On the first patrol, Lt. Kaye developed problems severe enough to cause a forced landing; Lt. Sparks had a similar experience on the second; and Lt. Sherry had to return to Saints with motor trouble on the third. One might imagine that the morale at this point was more than a trifle low. Patrols were flown the following day with six or seven planes participating and emergency landings continuing, including one at the 1st Observation field which occurred during a test flight.

Lt. Meissner, while on an intermediate level patrol, reported: "Great cloud of gray smoke in region about five kilometers south of Soissons observed rising to a height of 1500 meters at 15h 45. It appeared to be an ammunition dump blown up. Many camions and dark masses, as though of troops, on the roads southwest of Soissons."

July 21 saw poor weather in the morning and fifteen out of twenty-six airplanes were found to be in commission. The weather cleared in the afternoon, allowing a seven-man group to fly an intermediate patrol in the evening from 19h 30 to 21h 05. Chambers led Meissner, Coolidge, Loomis, Sparks, Taylor, and Clark and as a result of the flight, a Reconnaissance Report was filed:

> "Narrative – During the whole patrol three fires were distinctly observed region of La Ferté-Tardenois. The town itself must have been burning and something on either side of it – Lt. Coolidge.
>
> A plane being chased was seen on fire in the region south of Brecy at about 20h 15, altitude 3500 meters. – Lt. Loomis
>
> Fère (Ferté) Tardenois on fire, Saponay and Villemoyenne also burning. Very large explosion occurred just over road southwest of La Charnel at 20h 30. – Lt. Taylor."

Before the evening patrol, Ham Coolidge penned this letter to his mother.

> "(Saints) Sunday, July 21
> Mother Dear,
>
> I was just sitting outside basking in the sun when three little girls came running by, playing tag. They were all dressed in their very best, and I, putting two and two together in my cleverest manner, decided, "Ah, this must be Sunday!" It's the only way of telling around here. This morning's patrol failed to materialize because of the bad weather, which, however, was not quite bad enough so that we could lie in bed and sleep. No, we had to get out to the field and wait in case it did clear up. We shall try again this evening.
>
> You never knew such an interesting sector with such interesting things to see and others to do. But I cannot give much in the way of detail. From the air it is often very difficult to distinguish where the lines are or tell just what is going on. What you do see are thousands of shellholes, the frequent flashing of guns, and a great quantity of smoke; sometimes large heavy columns of it, more often hundreds of little streaks of smoke.
>
> Last night, we flew at a very low altitude, quite peacefully for a while, until suddenly, woof! A fierce shock rocked my little ship, and in a few seconds there were many of those disturbing black puffs all around and among us. We all began to squirm and twist and that throws off their aim, but golly, how a close shot makes one jump when it arrives unexpectedly! A group of six Huns appeared, obviously trying to pick a scrap – because why? We were in their territory and half a gale of wind was endeavoring to push us further in. They knew that all they had to do was to keep us bothered for a short while after which our gasoline supply would be insufficient to carry us home against that heavy wind. Even if they did not shoot a single one of us down, we should be forced to land in their territory and become prisoners. But we saw the situation as clearly as did they (for a wonder) and refused to delay a single minute. You can see that it is important to grasp the situation quickly and *not* to fight when conditions are strong against you, even though there appears to be a tantalizing prey. I'm afraid that that is how poor Quentin was lost. You knew about his loss surely? I think he forgot about the strong wind against him when he saw the Boches. Undoubtedly he fought splendidly, but when it was over, he had drifted still further into Bocheland and had insufficient fuel to come out. Probably also they kept bothering him every foot of his way.
>
> Really it is almost laughable the way you move and countermove, retreat or advance, in preparing a big combat of "dog-fight." These do not often happen because circumstances usually make it foolhardy for one or the other patrol to fight. The ordinary case is where a whole patrol picks on a few planes over which it has an advantage of position etc. Then frequently another formation comes to the rescue and you have an unpremeditated "dog-fight."
>
> You know I often think of old Cousin Sam Langley, a man with the courage of his convictions all right. I've always admired him immensely. And now I'm happy because my fondest dreams have come true. War provides *such* a good justification for flying! Surely he too has "heard the heavens filled with shouting, and there rained a ghastly dew from the nations' airy navies grappling in the central blue."
>
> Your
> Ham."

The following day, on the morning of July 22, thirteen out of twenty-six Spads were available for flight and at 11h 00 to 12h 30, twelve of them patrolled the region of Bezu with no results. By 16h 30 in the afternoon, the Engineering staff had one more airworthy and a patrol of fourteen planes headed for St. Fère and Oulchy-la-Villc. The *Operations Report* for the day reports:

> "Five combats, see reports of Lts. Chambers, Taylor, Clark, Cates. One confirmation requested. Three planes struck by enemy bullets. Lt. Palmer landed damaged plane slightly wounded in the leg. Lt. Wentworth according to Lt. Meissner's report seen to be having motor trouble as he was sinking out of sight of the patrol before he reached the lines. Lts. Winslow and Wentworth panned at La Ferté."

This large fourteen plane patrol stirred up a hornet's next of activity which can be best described by the following two combat reports:

> "COMBAT REPORT OF Lieut. Taylor and Lt. Chambers. Date – July 22, 1918. Visibility near Lines – Good. Mission – Patrol.
> Region, Mont St. Fère – Oulchy-la-Ville.
> Names of Pilots. – Lts. Meissner, Loomis, Coolidge, Chambers, Smythe, Wentworth, Cates, Winslow, Palmer, Taylor, Clark, Sherry, Green, and Kaye.
> Hour of Departure, 16.50. Hour of Return, 18.00. Altitude 3000 –3500 meters.
> Enemy planes seen, 24 Enemy Planes Encountered, 24.
> Time 16h 55 to 17h 10. Region, Oulchy-la Château. Altitude 3000 – 3500 meters.
> Type of E.A. – Fokker monoplaces and biplaces.
> Combats, 5. Number of rounds fires, 500
>
> Narrative: Encountered 24 enemy Fokker monoplace in region of Bruyeres. They followed diving and firing over our lines. One put holes in my plane, turned and shot at Lt. Palmer on my left; I could see splinters fly back off his seat. I turned and shot but guns jammed. Lt. Palmer piqued and landed in France. Time of fight, 16h 55. (Sgd) T. C. Taylor, 1st Lt. ASUSR.
>
> Narrative: Saw white anti-aircraft upon arriving. Saw about twelve enemy planes below us and started to dive on them and I noticed about twelve more above us about four kilometers away, and pulled away. These twelve came down after us. A running fight followed in which one Boche went down. Region, Oulchy-la-Château, time 16h 57. Altitude, 3000 meters. CONFIRMATION REQUESTED. (Sgd) Reed Chambers, 1st Lt. ASUSR."
>
> Narrative: Lt. Cates saw one formation of seven enemy planes above patrol and the formation of five below. The lower formation attacked coming up from under us. Lt. Cates' guns jammed. No results. Lt. Palmer panned at May-en-Multien with a hole through his gas tank, his prop shot away, and with a slight wound in his leg. Lt. Clark went down with Lt. Chambers on a Boche but he went up again and the six Boche started to shoot up Lt. Palmer. Lt. Palmer's machine had seven holes in it, and his guns were jammed. (Sgd) Lts. Cates, Palmer, and Clark."

From reading this account, one would gather that the formation of twenty-four Germans broke into two groups of twelve, then one broke up further into seven staying up high and five below acting as bait and then attacking with the upper seven joining the fray. With thirty-eight planes circling, firing, diving, climbing and making all manner of maneuvers, this combat must have been something to behold. The eighteen pilots available for duty this day flew a total of two patrols, four trial flights, twenty-nine sorties and had five combats, most all of which occurred after noon.

From July 23 through July 28 only four patrols were flown with poor weather conditions being partially responsible. Lts. Alexander Bruce and J. Loy Maloney were assigned to the 94th Aero. On one of these four patrols, six pilots had to leave because of motor troubles. This patrol from which Joe Eastman had to depart caused him to write the following morose and negative entry in his diary:

> "July 24th – The run of luck that I have been experiencing as a pilot is soon due to alter for the better, or it will finish me in some manner – of which the mad-house looms up as an imminent possibility.
>
> My Spad after five changes of oil pumps was again given me to make a practice flight this morning in preparation for the squadron patrol at 15h this afternoon. I no more than cleared it off the field when something – a connecting rod – broke, smoke blew into the pit, the entire plane shook with vibration and I was hardly able to regain the field again without accident. This was my lot after nearly a week in fussing with the tub. – Rankin, (the Engineering officer) at luncheon told me to take Number 10 which he said was in good condition. Later I learned that it was the machine that Coolidge and Sherry had unsuc-

cessfully attempted to use. I went out to it, and found it still in the process of repair. I waited until time for the patrol, and learned in that time further of its disquieting departures from a machine in "good condition." The motor is of an unheard of make; the throttles are offset and require a new technique in manipulation; its gas thumb-lever needed a pair of pliers to move; and neither guns nor sight had ever been tested. Although my habitual appearance is one of cow-like docility and temperamental imperviousness – I left the ground in a state of mind that jumps out of its chair when a door is closed above a whisper. After two minutes in the air I began to gather the evidence of my switchboard. Both air and oil pressures were less than half the normal figure – and the important little temperature hand was doing a comedy skit in the region of 105° or 25° hotter than is conducive to peaceful flying. A few minutes spent hopefully in pursuit of the patrol failed to influence the gauges for the better. I piqued for the field and instead of the temperature cooling it continued to augment in its own cheery fashion. The motor stopped firing over Coulommiers; I juggled it to life, it coughed, missed, and revolved feebly by turns letting me down nearer and nearer to an unpromising landscape – which, by the true grace of God, I was enabled to clear. At the hangar I climbed out of the boiling creature of misfortune and was able only by a considerable effort to keep myself from braking down completely. It bothers me no little to find that my nervous force is bordering the point where it can't be held in leash by willpower. What the outcome of this is to be is more than can be foreseen, though I'm confident that with a spell of normal flying conditions I can regain my stride. The demoralizing feature of it is that everything I touch or fly seems to suffer as from a plague of ill-fortune with my contact. This makes without relief or interval – six flights that beginning with two smashes have all ended disastrously. Except for the 2nd smash I'm satisfied that in the same planes anyone else would have had the same fate."

Poor Eastman was not gaining any confidence, which he sorely needed, from the introduction of the new Spads. He states that others less timid than he would have experienced the same problems that he was having, but one would have to wonder as he also was continually having problems with his Nieuport. More of Eastman to follow.

Poor weather and poor Spads kept operations to a minimum over the period of July 23 to July 29. Four patrols were flown with as many as sixteen pilots departing on July 28, but there was little enemy activity. The Engineering people under Lt. Rankin were able on one day to have twenty-one out of twenty-six Spads available for flight. Problems continued with jammed gun feeds, broken pistons, dud carburetors and general unreliability of all sorts. Coolidge had a piston rod exit out through the crankcase, but he was able to land safely.

Action heated up again on July 29 when fourteen Spads went out on an afternoon Protection Patrol, departing at 17h 45 for the region of Oulchy-Fère-Verneuil. Nine combat reports were filed at the conclusion of this patrol:

"COMBAT REPORT OF Lt. Bruce.
Date, July 29, 1918. Visibility, Poor. Squadron, 94th.
Mission, Protection Patrol. Route, Oulchy-Fère-Verneuil.
Hour of Departure, 17.45. Hour of Return, 19.15. Altitude 3500 mts.
Enemy planes seen, 14 and others above. E.A. Encountered, 9.
Time, 16h 23. Region, Oulchy-la Château. Altitude, 3000 mts.
Type, Biplane Fokkers. Combats, 1. No. rounds fired, 20.

Narrative: I saw formation of machines above which I mistook for part of my own patrol until they had approached closely. I then piqued with full motor and was followed by two. One kept on my tail, firing, till we reached 500 meters. I turned once and fired about 20 rounds with one gun. Both jammed. Landed later at Montautin with motor trouble. (Sgd) Lt. Bruce"

COMBAT REPORT OF Lt. Wentworth.-
Narrative: Attacked Fokker biplane at 3500 meters, maneuvered several minutes, first firing about 45 shots at very close range. No apparent results. Motor stopped during the fight and I did a few turns to vrille. Leveled out at 1000 meters, where he stopped following then saw no planes fall. (Sgd) Lt. Wentworth"

COMBAT REPORT OF Lt. Jeffers.-
Narrative: I was in lower patrol, in formation of five. We were attacked by over 10 German planes. I emptied about 50 rounds of ammunition on German plane without results and pulled up to the right, and looped around. One Spad was going down in a spin with German planes hovering around. (Sgd) J. N. Jeffers, 1st Lt. ASUSR."

COMBAT REPORT OF Lt. Winslow.-
Narrative: My flight of four planes, Lt. Coolidge, Lt. Cates,

and Lt. Wentworth and myself were above the other flight; the lower flight engaged 10 Huns. I saw about six others above our flight. I signaled to my flight to stay together to protect lower patrol from upper Huns. Two of my flight dove and joined the fight. However, immediately, the upper Huns dove past mc, made a dive at the lower flight, I glided into Germany. I saw a Spad and a German go down in a spin. (Sgd) Alan F. Winslow, 1st Lt. ASUSR."

COMBAT REPORT OF Lt. Loomis.-
Narrative: We were attacked in the region of Oulchy-la-Château by two patrols of Fokkers. One at 4500 meters and the other at 5000 meters. Both patrols dove on our lower patrol and in the mix-up I saw one Boche fall in a Vrille. Time 18h 25. (Sgd) Lt. Loomis, USR."

COMBAT REPORT OF Lt. Chambers.-
Narrative: I was leading a patrol of nine planes at 3000 meters over Fère-en-Tardenois protecting a Salmson which was operating in that vicinity and I saw about thirty-five or forty planes over Oulchy-la-Château and both black and white Archies. I started towards them and saw another bunch of about seven planes above us and pulled away. Two of our planes however left the patrol and dove on the Boche below evidently not seeing the Boche above who in turn dove on the two Spads. One Spad sent a Boche down in a spin. I dove on a Boche that was chasing this Spad and fired about 20 shots. Both guns jammed. I didn't see either of the other two Spads which are missing. Lt. Bruce, Lt. Coolidge and Lt. Snow are missing. (Sgd) Reed Chambers, 1st Lt. ASUSR."

COMBAT REPORT OF Lt. Snow.-
Date, July 29, 1918. Visibility, Misty. Squadron, 94th.
Mission, Protection Patrol. Route, Oulchy, Fère, Verneuil.
Pilots on Patrol, Lts. Loomis, Cates, Snow, Coolidge, Winslow, Wentworth, Cook, Kaye, Green, Chambers, Bruce, Jeffers, Sherry and Clark.
Hour of Departure, 17.15. Hour of Return, 18.35. Altitude, 3800 mets.
Enemy Planes seen, 17. E.A. Encountered, 5. Time, 18.35.

Narrative: I left formation about 18h 30 because of motor trouble and started to glide S.W. Shortly after I saw a large formation about 1000 meters above and to my right with white shrapnel breaking in it. While watching these planes I was attacked from above and behind by 5 Fokker biplanes. One with red nose, apparently their leader, did all the shooting. The other four remained above. I dived steeply turning, but going S.W. They left at about 1000 meters and I then continued in a flat glide, landing and crashing near Marigny. (Sgd) Chester A. Snow, Jr., 1st Lt. USUSR."

COMBAT REPORT OF Lt. Cates.-
Narrative: I saw a large formation of machines off to one side of our formation and I was carefully watching these when we were attacked from above. Two machines were on my tail before I realized what was on. I fired with both guns, one jammed and I fired about 75 rounds at the other. Saw one Spad go down in a slow spin. Altitude, 3000 meters. CONFIRMATION REQUESTED.

COMBAT REPORT OF Lt. Coolidge.-
Narrative: Was flying close to Lt. Winslow in second formation over Oulchy-le-Château when several E.A. Fokkers dove on us from above. Swerving sharply around to avoid their dive I observed most of the others diving steeply. I climbed as hard as possible going towards the sun. Met three of our Spads but they did not climb as I continued upwards to get altitude on a formation of seven Boche hovering over the melee. I lost the others at this time and met a French Spad (XII). We continued upwards for a few moments when he dove away at 5000 meters. I was still slightly below Boche patrol. I remained as close to them as I dared for 20 minutes in case they dove or in case I should be able to out-climb them. Came home followed by them part of the way towards Château-Thierry. Landed at La Ferté Gaucher for gas. Lt. Coolidge."

Ham Coolidge penned the following letter to his mother before departing on the late afternoon patrol described in the previous combat reports.

"(Saints) July 29, 1918
Dearest Mother,

During the past week we did not "prove" much in the air – our squadron, I mean. Bad weather frequently robbed us of patrols, and when we did go out we seldom saw Boches. Once, however, we saw more than we cared about. Nine of us on patrol saw a formation of six Boches planes below and our leader signaled to attack. Just as we started down, however, *eighteen* more Boches appeared over the edge of the clouds. We saw at once that we were in a bad fix. We swung round as quickly as possible, but they were by this time close "on our tails" and the "tracers" began to fly past us. I don't mind saying I was thoroughly scared – twenty-four against nine is poor odds especially when one is over enemy territory. Looking back I could plainly distinguish every feature of the enemy planes nearest me. They were single seat Fokker biplanes. We became somewhat scattered in our hasty retreat, so I can speak only for myself. I kept my motor open wide and kicked my rudder to and fro which gave my machine a zig-zag motion and made it a difficult target. As luck would have it my plane didn't suffer any bullet holes. Fortunately our Spads are very fast: surely that was all that saved us.

Mammy, you have no idea how exciting the times are. Of course you know from the papers exactly what has been happening about this time, but I have had the good luck to go up to the front one rainy day last week and see some of the most interesting sights. I saw several of the steel boats in which the Boches crossed the Marne. Everywhere was debris and plunder of every kind. On the way home we passed an ambulance train and someone yelled "Hi, Ham Coolidge!" Looking back I recognized Phil Shepley in a black leather coat waving his arms. Our captain was in a hurry so we couldn't stop.

Yesterday the motor of my beloved Spad went to pieces, luckily over a French aerodrome near the lines. Meanwhile I use the plane of a comrade *en permission.*

A letter of greeting arrived from Uncle Arch. Would that I might have seen him. Mother, Doug Campbell is now on his way home. If he comes to Boston give him a *time*; he's one of the finest boys in the world, besides being a great friend of mine, and an "ace" with seven official Boches!

Your loving,
Ham.

P.S.
Many thanks for congratulatory cable!"

July 30 was a less active day with one patrol of eleven planes being flown in the morning with no reportable results, the day ending with nine out of twenty-six Spads in an unserviceable state.

The last day of the month an 8h 00 low patrol of thirteen planes was sent up to the region of Oulchy at 600 meters. Lt. Sherry had to return to the field with motor trouble, Lt. Green had a forced landing at La Ferté, and Lt. Palmer landed with motor trouble at Frenchville being out of oil. Nothing resulted from the patrol, although Lt. Chambers did report: "Saw archies about 3000 meters above and could see five enemy machines one larger than the rest. Flew very low to the ground, about 5 or 6 kilometers past our balloons, which were on the ground. At this distance saw no troops of any kind and was not shot at."

A high patrol of thirteen went out at 19h 00 heading for the region of Oulchy-la-Château at 4000 meters. Lts. Jeffers, Sherry, Maloney and Clark were all forced to return with motor troubles and our friend, Joe Eastman, managed to land near Vaux with an unreported problem. During the patrol there were three combats reported and Lt. Loomis in a Reconnaissance Report stated: "Lt. Loomis, leader of the upper patrol, saw formation of six Boche approach the lower patrol led by Lt. Winslow from the sun, but the Boche patrol probably catching sight of Lt. Loomis' patrol turned back into Germany."

Lt. Thorne Taylor's narrative continues the story:

"Lower patrol headed by Lt. Winslow composed of Lts. Cates, Taylor and Palmer piqued on the enemy for action. Lt. Palmer piqued on an E.A. and fired about 30 shots but was forced to pull away on account of motor trouble. He had to dive out of the fight in order to catch his motor. Apparently no results, Lt. Taylor."

COMBAT REPORT OF Lt. Cates.-
Date, July 31, 1918. Visibility near lines, Poor.
Names of Pilots – Lts. Green, Kaye, Clark, Coolidge, Jeffers, Sherry, Winslow, Cook, Cates, Loomis, Taylor, Maloney, Eastman and Palmer.
Hour of Departure, 19.00. Hour of Return, 20.15. Altitude, 4000 meters.
Enemy Planes Seen, 9. Enemy Planes Encountered, 7.
Time, 19h 45. Region, East of Oulchy-la-Château. 4000 meters.
Type, Six Fokker monoplace protecting one Fokker (?) Biplace.
Combats, 3. Number of rounds fired, 240.

Narrative: Lower patrol headed by Lt. Winslow and composed of Lts. Cates, Taylor, and Palmer piqued on the enemy formation. Lt. Cates dove on an E.A. and fired 200 rounds. He saw tracers enter the E.A. near the pilots seat. The Boche flopped into a slow spin and was last seen at 3000 meters going down. Lt. Cates was obliged to pull away to attack a second plane but both guns jammed. CONFIRMATION REQUESTED. (Sgd) R. Z. Cates, 1st Lt. ASUSR."

On that late patrol the squadron was dealt a tremendous blow by the loss of Alan Winslow, one of the most popular men in the squadron and the pilot who scored the squadron's first victory. He was seen diving on a Fokker, disappearing into the evening gloom. Winslow was badly wounded, losing an arm and was a prisoner until the end of the war.

So ended July, a month of great frustration, little accomplishment, but perhaps a month of maturing and learning: maturing in how to cope with seasoned enemy pilots flying the best planes they had to offer; learning how to get the most out of the new Spads, when to turn for home and when to understand the enemy tactics and when not to get a sucker punch for attacking decoys; flying in large patrols, but breaking them up for mutual protection, as well as for the most efficient position from which to attack. July, unfortunately, was a month when the leaders such as Rickenbacker and Campbell were not available to give their direction and support.

New and old flight leaders began to gain confidence from their experience which would temper them and carry many of them through the war: Coolidge, Chambers, Taylor, Green, and Meissner all were becoming pro's in the world of aerial combat.

The Spad XIII must have been a vast disappointment to the 94th who had held such great expectations of their new machine. At whose feet to lay the blame for the terrible showing of what was supposed to be the ultimate fighter, is an unanswerable question. Certainly the manufacturers, Kellner, Spad, Hispano-Suiza, the Solex Carburetor Company, the ammunition manufacturers, the Vickers Gun people, all must take part of the blame for this fiasco. The other squadrons of the 1st Pursuit Group shared these problems and without any question the unsung heroes of this whole terrible time in American aviation were the Engineering Divisions of the Pursuit squadrons and the individual mechanics assigned to each plane and its pilot who worked tirelessly to fix the many problems not of their making.

Reed Chambers and his Spad 4526 number 11 which he flew from July 14 to September 25, 1918 when it was condemned. Saints. Late summer 1918.

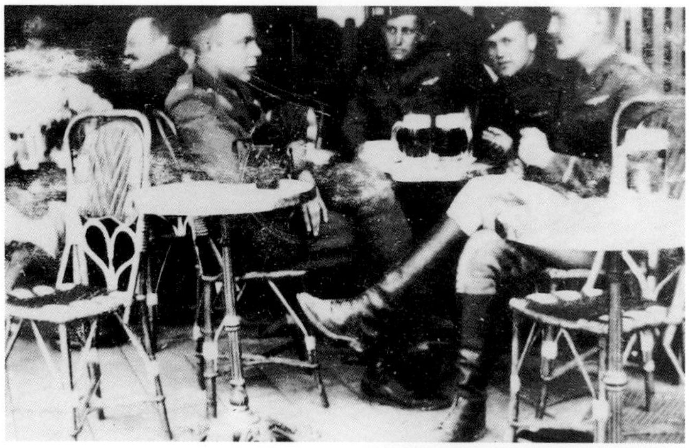

Off-duty with cold beers finds Pat Maloney, Alex Bruce, who was killed in a collision with Walt Smythe September 26, Weir Cook, and Alden Sherry. Summer 1918.

Below: Joe Eastman and his Spad 15006 number 19 with two of his mechanics whom he kept busy finding the many faults Joe perceived to be in his various planes.

6

August - Fine Tuning the Recalcitrant Spads

The weather was fair on the morning of August 1st and Headquarters French 6th Armée ordered three Breguets to mount a photographic mission in the region of Oulchy and Fère. The 94th was requested to form a protection patrol which departed at 9h 14 from Saints with ten planes in the formation. Shortly into the patrol, Lts. Green, Taylor, Wentworth and Maloney returned with a variety of motor troubles, with Lts. Loomis, Kaye, Cates, Palmer, Cook, and Rickenbacker continuing on to cover the Breguets. Rickenbacker states that he took a position much higher than the rest of the patrol, which was by his estimate 5000 feet above the others, and was able to observe the following action.

Soon after the Breguets crossed into Germany, six Fokkers appeared and began to circle the three Frenchmen and their escorts, each group maintaining their respective positions. As the photographs were being taken over Fismes, the Fokkers began to attack causing Loomis, the Flight Commander, to engage the enemy. With a height advantage, Loomis and the others were in a good position, as the Fokkers were then below the Breguets. As a result, a whirling dogfight began, soon to find Spad on Fokker tail followed by Fokker on the Spad, and then another Spad and so on. Loomis got into trouble with several of the enemy on his tail. Rickenbacker at that point left the high patrol position and dove to Loomis' assistance. Loomis got off a few more bursts and headed for home with a damaged engine. He made it to the lines, but his landing was not a thing of beauty. Spad number 15135 was so badly damaged that Lt. Rankin, the Engineering Officer, condemned it that day with no effort of repair.

Lt. Loomis' narrative of this action is taken from his Combat Report:

> "Narrative: Lt. Loomis, Patrol Leader of the lower patrol composed of Lts. Cates, Loomis and Cook, dove on a formation of five Boche which were piquing on the Breguets. Lt. Loomis got on the tail of a Boche and fired 150 shots. He saw tracers entering the fuselage of the enemy plane. Enemy plane flopped over towards the ground. Lt. Loomis was unable to follow because of motor trouble and for the fact that he had four other Boche on his tail. He made a landing at the farm of Dreaux, north of Beauvardes. CONFIRMATION REQUESTED. (Sgd) Lt. Loomis, ASUSR."

To the plus side of the ledger, French Headquarters informed the squadron of a victory scored over one of the Fokkers. One narrative of this fight came from the report of Lt. Cook:

> "Narrative: Enemy planes seen 6. E.A. encountered, 6. Time 10h 10. Region, Bois de Dole. Altitude, 3300. Type, Fokker. Combats 2. Approximate number of rounds fired, 70.
>
> Lt. Cook was just above the Breguets. He was attacked by an E.A. In maneuvering for altitude he managed to get in twenty bursts while approaching E.A. head on. The Boche however swung around on Lt. Cook's tail and Lt. Cook dove. Apparently no results. (Sgd) Lt. Cook."

The confirmed victory was shared by Lts. Cook and Cates, although no combat report by Cates has been found. Why Loomis was not included in the victory share with the others, is a mystery.

August 2 saw no squadron activity, but the *Report of Operations* showed sixteen out of twenty-three of the temperamental Spads were in service. This report did not quite match that of the Engineering Division which stated thirteen out of twenty-four were in commission. Two were ready to test; two were having new engines installed; one was having the engine overhauled; three with "carberator" troubles; one with a gun cam problem; one with a bum magneto and 15003 Squadron number 15 suffering from a forced landing by Lt. Crocker.

Only test flights were flown on August 3 which gave Ham Coolidge the opportunity for a brief letter to his father.

> "(Saints) August 3
> Dear P. A.,
>
> I hasten to correct an account of my adventures which gives me considerable pain! The *Herald* obviously had my name confused with that of an observer in one of the biplace observation groups. I do not drive a *big* French biplane, but a small one. It is not equipped with four guns. I did not turn upon seven attackers and send one down in flames … only a biplace Salmson observation machine fulfills the described conditions. The *Globe* account is correct. It is true that I have official credit for downing a biplace Rumpler. It is nothing but pure luck that my bullets happened to be the ones to bring out the flames, for certainly the other two boys deserve exactly as much credit for downing it as I do. Also it is the sort of thing that happens every day and they shouldn't have stuck in my picture and written all that junk. It's a pity.
>
> Lately we have had some close calls in the air. Once at least it was due to bad judgment on our part...the other time a patrol of Fokker biplanes came "out of the sun" on us … we were very lucky to get away alive. Those canny Boches play their cards well, and I think we have learned much from them. We are always ready to accept a battle when conditions are equally favorable to both sides. They won't as a rule."

August 4 was also a non-flying day, giving time for another Coolidge letter to his mother:

> "Aug. 4, 1918
> Dear Mother,
>
> You speak about Joe's doping the end of this mess … well, developments do seem to indicate that Germany's offensive power is about over, and without offensive ability has Germany got any hold on her people? I am hoping to go up to Chamery where Quentin is reported to have been buried.
>
> Last Monday we got mixed up in another horrid "dog-fight" with a large flock of those little Fokker monoplace biplanes. We were practically engaged in the combat before we realized that there were two of them to every one of us. They seemed to come from nowhere. Two of our boys had hair-breadth escapes, but the rest of us managed to clear out without getting "shot up." Of course the one morning my machine was out of commission proved to be the only time in the week that our patrol had an advantage of position on a Boche patrol. Our boys claim two of them.
>
> They gave me official credit for the biplace Rumpler three of us brought down together, but why make a fuss about it? People are doing it every day, so if they would only report the facts without the trimmings it would be all right. More and more one sees that the whole thing is mostly luck. Some of our best pilots have never had the luck to be in a position where they could have shot a Boche down.
>
> We had a little fun working low over the infantry last week, and I think it is immensely satisfactory work even if a little risky. At times, we dove down on our sides close enough to see the expressions on the faces of our soldiers. They were apparently full of enthusiasm, and frequently on automobile trips to the front they have told us that it has a very good moral effect on our troops to see their own planes overhead, very close. We did not actually shoot up the Boche infantry as I should like to have done, as we were on purely protective missions, and few in number, but I hope they give us some offensive work. You ought to see the effect of the Allied advance on everyone's spirits, it would do your heart good.
>
> Today we had lunch with an American aviator in the French flying corps, who recently escaped from Germany after ten months' imprisonment on his third attempt! You could have heard a crumb fall on the floor as we sat listening to him talk, reticently enough, about his escape. Working on the roads one noon, he made a break for the woods under a volley of bullets from the sentries. He stayed in the Black Forest travelling only at night, and gradually made his way to the Swiss border, suffering hideously from hunger and thirst. He ate raw potatoes only. The last kilometer was the whole thing because of the triple sentry line. He succeeded in slipping by the first one, then killed the next two with a knife, whereupon a hail of bullets came flying all around. The night was inky black, however, so they were all wild. And he walked to a Swiss village, weak from starvation and minus his trousers which he had lost in swimming a river before reaching the border.

Goodnight, Mammy,
Your Ham."

1st Lt. John Wentworth left the squadron on August 4 to become a Flight Commander for Captain George Fisher, ex-95th Aero, now C.O. of the new 49th Aero, 2nd Pursuit Group.

No flying on August 5 because of continuing bad weather and another opportunity for Coolidge to write a letter containing some interesting information on patrol philosophy and implementation:

"Aug. 5th, 1918
Dearest Lu,

I fear you have given me up for a bad job – at least I should fear it, were it not that your dear letters continue to arrive regularly. Thank goodness you're that kind of a feller.

We are just beginning to fatten up into normal looking humans again. You see some fool paymaster went and lost our pay checks for two months and the whole crowd soon became penniless – pardon me, centimeless is more correct. The result was that our mess became poorer and poorer as our credit at the local butcher shops waned, till finally the food was such that we could hardly eat it. Now, however, one of the two missing month's pay has arrived and we are all getting fat again.

Jove how those guns are pounding away! I'm sitting here on the floor of our rotten little farmhouse room, and writing on my trunk at the window. The ceiling hangs very low and we aren't flying; perhaps the low ceiling accounts for the way the sound carries. The front has been running away so fast we can hardly find it!

Each evening they post up on a door (bulletin board) the "service" for the following day. It might read like this: "High Patrol, 17.30 - 19.15 o'clock, all available pilots." An hour or so beforehand we all get together to dope out what formations we will fly in, what flight leaders we will follow, and what the tactics will be. Frequently we fly not all together in one mass, but in two or perhaps even three separate groups working together. This is very good dope if you have enough men. One evening I remember we "jumped" a patrol of six Boches below us only to have eighteen more sail down on us from above a ledge of cloud, and we had a hot time pulling out of it. They almost always work that way. Time and again we have been in the act of attacking a tempting morsel when intuition prompted us to look back of us and far above – *la, la*! – two patrols of seven, or perhaps one there and another way off to one side. It's almost like a game of checkers at times. Every movement of one unit produces a certain move from the other units that may be in the sky at the time – this maneuvering coming to a climax when a general combat develops or one or the other gang clears out in a hurry. Curiously enough a "dog-fight," or general engagement, almost always splits even as far as losses are concerned. We do not have many of them. Often our job is to act as a protecting escort to photography or reconnaissance planes. Then we often get into scraps.

P.A. just sent me some clippings from Boston papers in which they have some painful junk about me and worst of all a big picture. L., I hope you'll do your best to squelch all that 'rah, 'rah stuff, because they always get things twisted or exaggerate disgustingly. It is true that I and two other boys shot down a biplace Rumpler in flames, but under perfectly ordinary circumstances, under which the most romantic mind could never paint us as "heroes." We had a fairly exciting scrap for five minutes or so as they held us off with their rear guns. Once we closed in, it was all over but the cheering, except that a bunch of Fokkers dropped down and chased us back home. It does give you a thrill to see one of those heathens burst into flames under your fire! You know, Lu, you can actually see your bullets because one in every five is a "tracer" which leaves a streak of smoke, and naturally these come in rapid succession. In a hot combat these smoky streaks can be seen for a long distance, going in every direction.

The village where Q. is reported to have been buried is now in Allied hands, so I am going to try and get up there in an auto the first chance. You never saw such a mess as the whole country is in up there.

Affectionately, Ham."

Fourteen trial flights were made over the next three days, but on August 9 the weather cleared and the aerial activity increased accordingly. One protection patrol was flown to cover two Spads, which were in all probability Spad XII two-seaters who were photographing the region of Fismes. Two combat reports of the action were filed, a joint report by Chambers and Smythe, and an individual report by Rickenbacker. There are a few discrepancies between the two reports, the *Report of Operations* and Rickenbacker's book which in error stated the patrol was on the eighth as well as a few other details. We will let the combat report of Lts. Chambers and Smythe set the stage:

"Date – August 9, 1918. Visibility near lines, Very good. Mission, Protection for two French Spads. Route, Braine. Names of Pilots, Lts. Jeffers, Cook, Palmer, Sparks,

Loomis, Eastman, Cates, Maloney, Snow, Green, Coolidge. (The report left out the names of Rickenbacker, Chambers, Kaye, Bruce, Smythe, Sherry and Clark, which was in all probability an omission when the report was typed and which did appear in the *Report of Operations*.)
Hour of Departure, 13.30. Hour of Return, 17.30. Alt. 2000 mts.
Enemy planes seen, 6. Enemy planes encountered, 4.
Time, 16h 40. Region, Bazoches. Alt. 1400 mts. Type, Fokker.
Combats, 2. Number of rounds fired, 180.

Narrative: Patrol landed at Coincy. Left Coincy at 16h 00 to protect two French Spads. We protected the Spads successfully while they made three tours along the lines between Braine and Fismes, entering three or four kilometers into Germany and back again into France. Lt. Chambers was leading the patrol. During the protection he noticed six enemy planes hovering around about 800 meters above the patrol. On the second tour when the patrol entered Germany he only noticed two enemy planes where six had been. Immediately afterwards four enemy planes came piquing down thru clouds above the patrol but missed the patrol and passed in front of them. Lt. Chambers and Lt. Smythe pulled up on one of the E.As. Lt. Chambers fired about 150 shots and Lt. Smythe fired 30. Both saw their tracers enter the fuselage of the enemy plane. The enemy plane slid slowly off on one wing, then flopped off slowly in a pique and out of control in the region of north of Bazoches. Lt. Chambers and Lt. Smythe were unable to follow it down because of the necessity of staying with the protection. The combat took place at an altitude of 1400 meters. Lts. Eastman, Cates, and Maloney have not as yet returned. Lt. Chambers states that he saw a Spad being attacked during the same combat by a Fokker, but the Fokker was at least 300 meters behind the Spad. CONFIRMATION REQUESTED. (Sgd) Lt. Chambers and Lt. Smythe."

Rickenbacker's combat report lists all the above-mentioned pilots with the exception of Coolidge who probably was not present, and also claims he saw nine enemy planes, and nine were encountered north of Bazoches.

His narrative states that he saw five Huns in one formation at about 2000 meters altitude and in front of him and four in another at an altitude about 2000 meters behind him:

"Three of the first formation piqued on the Spads which we were protecting. I pulled up on one enemy plane and fired 75 rounds to two good bursts into him, but was unable to see if he crashed. When last seen he was in a steep dive an apparently out of control. I again joined the protection and we were not again attacked. This combat took place at 2000 meters in the region north of Bazoches. CONFIRMATION REQUESTED. (Sgd) E. V. Rickenbacker, 1st Lt. ASUSR."

No confirmations were given on either of these two requests which Rickenbacker attributes to the fast moving advance of the Americans which made it impossible to locate witnesses. Another problem caused by the fluid changes in the lines was the distance required for the 94th to complete their protection patrols which now required a refueling stop at Coincy and which also stretched the flying time out to over four hours. The additional take-offs and landings added to the maintenance woes, as the Coincy field was pockmarked with repaired shell holes that caused blown tires and undercarriage troubles aplenty, with our friend Eastman doing his share of damage there to poor old 15006 which bore the Squadron number 15.

With the heavy movement of men and material to cover the Allied advance, the air above had to be kept clear of prying enemy aerial eyes in order that some degree of secrecy could be maintained.

On August 10 one of these protection/barrage patrols departed at 15h 27 to cover the region – Foret de Nesles and Fère-en-Tardenois. Rickenbacker, now somewhat recuperated from some painful ear problems, and Chambers were the patrol leaders, with Captain Marr, Lts. Clark, Zacharias, Kaye, Bruce, Sherry, Snow, Loomis, Jeffers, Eastman, Maloney, Palmer, Green and Cook making up the entire patrol. This patrol achieved the necessary success and ended at Coincy at about 17h 00. The 1st Aero Squadron was ordered to take their Salmsons on a photo mission at 18h 00. The 94th had been reduced in numbers by the losses of Captain Marr who panned at Frenchville with motor trouble, Lts. Bruce, Zacharias, and Green, who had sat down at various fields with similar problems. Lt. Green returned to the group from Fère-en-Tardenois before the second patrol departed. The protection was accomplished with no loss to the 1st Aero, but Green panned again joined by Cook near La Ferté, both with motor trouble.

Reed Chambers filed his narrative report of both patrols:

"We patrolled the region of the Foret de Nesles and Fère-en-Tardenois, but saw no signs of hostile aircraft. Captain Marr landed with motor trouble at Frenchville. Lt. Zacharias panned Coulommiers with motor trouble. Lt. Bruce landed with motor trouble at Saacy.

After finishing this barrage patrol, we landed at Coincy. At 18h 00 we left Coincy on a protection patrol for the 1st Aero Squadron. We saw about eleven Boche and witnessed a combat at about 18h 30 at about 3000 meters, in the region west of Fismes between French and Boche planes, but were not attacked ourselves. We escorted the Salmsons back to the lines of balloons. Protection Accomplished. Lt. Cook had motor trouble and panned. Lt. Green panned at Fère-en-Tardenois. Signed: Reed Chambers, 1st Lt. Patrol Leader."

Rickenbacker saw it a little differently as his narrative relates:

"I noticed eleven Boche around us while on our protection. About 18h 30 three of the enemy planes started piquing on the Salmsons which we were protecting. I warned the Salmson and it turned back towards the lines escorted by our lower patrol. I then joined an upper patrol which was fighting with some Boche. I had thought that this was our own upper patrol, but upon arriving found it to be a French patrol. I got on the tail of a Boche and got two bursts of 75 shots into him and he fell off into a spiral. I could not watch him because I was kept busy by other enemy planes. I received a ball in one of my wings. ONE CONFIRMATION REQUESTED. (Sgd) Lt. E. V. Rickenbacker, Patrol Leader."

From all that can be learned about the activity of August 10, the patrol missions which were extremely important, were successful, but the combats that won fame and glory bore no results or confirmations. The same applied for August 11 and 12.

Ham Coolidge was experiencing Spad troubles in the same way as the others, which he describes in part in his letter of August 11:

"(Saints) August 11, 1918
Dear Nonie,

... I have been terribly busy in my letter writing time because of having to take care of both Bill Chalmers' and Quentin Roosevelt's affairs ... making inventories and writing letters, and attending to all their mail, etc. Then we have had a little flying thrown in on the side! Just at present I'm a hard luck kiddo. My first Spad was no good. My second one went beautifully for a while till one day a valve broke and tore my motor to pieces. They put in a new motor and we spent days getting it to run right. Yesterday we finally thought we had it *au point* so I started cheerfully out for the lines. A few minutes later I felt a drizzle of water in my face and suspected it was raining but no, the water was hot. Then a pipe burst and the cockpit was flooded with boiling water from the cooling system. Luckily I was able to land at a French field where they fixed up the pipe and I gaily started out a second time. Again a drizzle of water, this time from a different place, a plug had come out of the water jacket and let it all out again. My temperature began to rise and before I finally made a good landing field the poor old motor was almost *grillé*. A wooden plug in the hole held the water sufficiently for me to limp back home the most disgusted man you ever saw.

This morning I flew up to a little field near the lines where I took to a motorcycle to look for Quentin's grave. Well, what do you know ... in passing through a small village all shot to pieces, I suddenly saw Rose Peabody walking down the street! You can imagine the surprise of meeting her. Gosh it was swell! It turned out that her mobile hospital was located there. Then on to look for poor Q.'s grave which had been reported but never officially confirmed, to be at Chamery. I can say that, as it was published in all the papers. After scouting around for a while we finally found it near the town. The Americans had fixed up his grave decently. It had a plain wooden cross, but there was a little fence around the grave and some wild flowers upon it. Nearby were a few charred remains of his machine where it fell, and a hole some three feet deep which it had dug into the ground where it had crashed. Nonie, that's what makes an impression on one in this war. Bursting shrapnel, onion rockets, machine gun bullets and Boche planes give you a start at first, but you get used to all that. What you can never get used to, though, is to have your very best friends "go West."

From there we could hear all around us the pound, pound of big guns, and of a sudden a sort of shallower whang, whang, as the black Boche anti-aircraft shrapnel clustered around a group of our planes in the distance. All you can actually see of the lines from a place like that is the sausage balloons here and there along the lines....and the question on the lips of all the "dough-boys" is "What do you think of the liberty planes?"

Day before yesterday I went to Paris for a few hours of pleasure. I saw Quentin's sister-in-law and his brothers, Archie and Ted, both wounded as I suppose you heard. Arch is leaving shortly for home, and he says that he will go to see Mother which would be great. Also you knew that Douglas Campbell, the first American training "Ace" is on the water. We are very good friends and he, too, promised to drop in at 10 West Hill Place if he could work it...

Ham."

Joe Eastman, continuing with a black cloud of trouble over his head, blows out a tire landing at Coincy on August 10 and has to return to the field without rejoining the patrol. He completes a patrol on August 11, but doesn't fly August 12, and drops out of the patrol of August 13 with motor trouble, which he describes in his diary:

"My plane developed trouble on the patrol of yesterday morning – immediately on the heels of a combat between our lower formation and five Boches, and just at the moment I had lost track of where we were. The motor was knocking; and the oil no longer passed thru the gauge. And being entirely lost, I must naturally believe myself miles in Germany, and entirely surrounded by Huns, like a boche pretzel shop. Since returning I learn that the others were also lost, as we strayed down by Rheims. Save for the frequency of these occasions, I have no right to complain, for at the instant that there was the gentle rap of a broken connecting rod on its way thru the casing and I could go no further. I was able to glide onto the most beautiful aviation field in Europe, and the mechanics who came out spoke French..." The engineering report for August 14 shows, "15006 – installing new motor," August 15 "15006 – changing motor," the same on August 16, and finally on August 17 "15006 – changing the gas tank," August 18 "15006 – Broken valve, new radiator," August 19 "15006 – changing motor," August 21 "15006 – trying out motor," August 22 "15006 – Adjusting motor, new oil gauge," August 26 "15006 – New air pump," August 28 " 15006 – Changing magneto," August 30 "15006 – Knock in motor."

This one Spad, since July 18, soon after delivery, had been unavailable on twenty-six occasions. Bettering Eastman's down time record was Spad 15004, which was down twenty-nine days. Number 15004 was not assigned to a particular pilot and carried the Squadron number 10. In contrast to these apparent duds, Rickenbacker's Spad 4523 had only one down day to change guns. The question must be posed: were there airplanes which were always complete duds; were there pilots who abused their planes; were there others, like Eastman, who were timid and with each missed beat returned their planes to the Engineering people for solutions?

The good weather of August 14 allowed Rickenbacker to lead a morning patrol of twelve on a Route Courcelles – Fismes – Magneaux at 2500 meters. Eddie Green reported seeing at least twelve enemy aircraft, both Fokkers and two-seaters, and he fired at long range about 100 rounds at a biplace who was nearly 500 meters above him, with no results.

The other Eddie, as in Rickenbacker, filed his report:

"There was a great deal of aerial activity. At 8.40 I saw two enemy Fokker planes, well within our lines, south of Fismes and at an altitude of 6000 meters. At 9.15 I met a biplace photo machine coming towards our lines. When the E.A. saw me he turned towards Germany and I gave chase for about six kilometers, firing at the E.A. in bursts. When I turned away, E.A. slipped back to our lines again. I gave chase for the second time and fired. Again when I turned away he slipped back to the lines. I chased the E.A. back again, firing, and this time the E.A. did not attempt to slip back, but continued on into Germany. We hovered around for about 15 minutes, but did not see this E.A. again. No apparent results. This combat took place south of Fismes and at an altitude of 200 meters."

Four combats were fought on August 15 with Lt. Kaye requesting a confirmation for a Fokker destroyed near Jonchery at 15h 42. This was never confirmed. Eight minutes later in the same region, Rickenbacker, the patrol leader, spotted seven E.A. in formation, four above and three below which were chased back into Germany by the patrol. He reported:

"On our way back to the lines at 15h 50 in the vicinity of Jonchery at an altitude of 5000 meters we encountered four E.A. We maneuvered for height and when we were about 100 meters above them I attacked, followed by Lts. Coolidge, Cook and Bruce. We pursued the E.A. 6 kms. into Germany. I fired about 50 rounds, Lt. Coolidge 150 rounds, Lt. Bruce 100 rounds, and Lt. Cook 60 rounds, but the E.A. continued into Germany. No apparent results."

Two patrols were flown on August 16, one over the region of Courcelles-Fisme-Magneaux, eleven planes being involved with Lt. Sparks panning at Coincy. The other was a joint patrol with the 27th Aero to protect a Salmson of the 88th Aero Squadron. Three pilots from the 94th participated, Lts. Coolidge, Chambers and Sparks who, in spite of the Salmson developing motor trouble and scrubbing the mission, had a brief scrap with six Fokkers east of Fismes. Lts. Smythe and Chambers were in the upper echelon of the patrol and were jumped by the Fokkers who were positioned above them. One fixed himself on Walt Smythe's tail and only by the quick reaction of Chambers the German was attacked and forced to 2000 meters at which point both of Chambers' guns jammed. Thus the affair ended as quickly as it began. Smythe and Chambers had fired a total of 75 rounds, but Chambers' combat report held the too often used phrase, "No Apparent Results."

Good weather continued on August 17, but the results of the morning protection patrol were anything but good. The patrol consisting of Lt. Eddie Green as patrol leader, accompanied by Lts. Sherry, Taylor, Sparks, Smythe, Bruce, Clark, Snow, Cates and Coolidge, departed at 9h 00 on a route to Courcelles-Fismes-Magneaux at an altitude of 4000 meters. At 11.14 they ran into seven Fokkers of Jasta 15 at 350 meters east of Fismes with devastating consequences. There were three combat reports filed which give some of the detail. Green's narrative stated:

> "We made a patrol in conjunction with the 95th Aero Squadron. No planes were sighted until we started home from the lines. We were gliding down at about 4 kilometers this side of the lines, south of Fismes, when I saw 7 E.A. at 11.10, 1000 meters above us. At 11.14 E.A. attacked, one firing at formation from long range. Two of our machines, Lts. Bruce and Smythe, while maneuvering, crashed together. One fell, with the two wings on one side completely gone, spinning around in slow jerks. The other went down in a vrille, with the end of one wing gone. The other wings were apparently uninjured. I saw this last plane apparently in control but still going in a nosedive about a thousand meters below me. I judged these planes crashed southeast of Fismes." Lt. Clark reported "At 11.14 at 3000 meters several Boche attacked the upper formation and fired several bursts into me at long range. I piqued in a straight nosedive. Then I looked for the rest of the formation. One Spad had both wings off on one side and was spinning down. Another went down in a vrille, with a wing tip crushed. This was in the region 10 kilometers south of Fismes. I did not fire any shots."

The 95th patrol which accompanied the 94th began with six planes, led by Lt. John Mitchell, but it was reduced to three when Lt. Bailey landed at Coincy with a bad motor, and Lts. Gill and Avery had to leave the patrol with motor trouble. Lt. Mitchell reported sighting six Fokkers, and as he turned for home, one dived on the tail of the 94th formation. He observed two 94th planes crashing into each other, but did not see them hit the ground.

On August 17, Vizefeldwebel Gustav Klaudet of Jasta 15 was credited with a victory over a 94th Aero Squadron Spad XIII near Beauraignes at 17.10 German time. Klaudet began the war in a Ulan regiment and later joined the Imperial German Air Service and was assigned to Jasta 15 in early 1918. His Fokker D VII bore the Jasta colors of a red nose and blue tail, plus his own personal marking of a Ulan lance bearing a black and white swallow-tailed pennant. Leutnant Joseph Veltjens, the C. O. of Jasta 15, was also credited with a victory over a 94th Spad XIII near Roye at 17.20 German time. This victory is quoted as over a Spad XIII of "Spa. 94." Is it possible that these two claims by Jasta 15 could have been the unfortunate Bruce and Smythe? Was the time of these crashes 11.14 French time or 12.14 German time? Could a handwritten "2" in script have been mistakenly typed as a "7" as quoted in German records as 17.10 or 17.20?

If these two claims by the Germans were indeed Smythe and Bruce, the victories were rather easily obtained. The bravery of the attacking Fokker pilots is without question, as the odds were 13 to 6 or 7 in spite of the height advantage.

Ham Coolidge in his Sunday letter home speaks of this and earlier events of the week:

> "(Coincy) Sunday, Aug. 18, 1918
> Dearest Mother,
>
> The nice gray letters keep reaching me even on days when there is no mail for the rest of the squadron! They all howl with rage when that happens. Our little operations office is a tent out at the flying field. It serves not only as a shelter for the stenographer and clerks who do the paper work, but also as a general loafing place for lazy pilots, and it is there between patrols or while awaiting special calls that our letters come....
>
> Our work has been continuing but not too satisfactorily. Last Wednesday I think it was, we were coming out of Germany and saw a formation coming towards us out of France. We took it for granted for some reason that they were Spads – and likewise they apparently concluded that we were friendly Fokkers! Only when we were abreast of each other did we each suddenly realize that we were enemies. We swung around like a flash and pointed our planes down in a mad dive after the fleeing Fokkers, shooting angry streams of smoking tracers after them, but they had the start and we could not get close enough to do any damage. It was exasperating because it was a rare chance. Yes-

terday a very sad thing happened. As our formation was flying towards the lines they spotted a group of Huns "in the sun" above, and started to dive down away from them. As our boys dove they were naturally looking back over their shoulders watching the enemy, when suddenly two of our very best pilots collided. The wings were stripped cleanly from one machine which fell like a stone. The other had the wings on one side badly damaged. He was seen to go down in a slow spiral under more or less control. Everybody hoped that he might have landed safely, but later investigation proved that they were both smashed to pulp. It's such a hideous way to lose men....

Yesterday, however, there was one bright spot in a rather gloomy week. I walked over from our auxiliary field to the nearby hospital and found Rose Peabody. I spoke of meeting her just for a second once before, but this time I stayed for lunch, and a good old chat. It was delightful seeing such a nice person again. She looks bright and very cheerful, but also very thin I thought. She admitted that they have had some pretty hectic experiences with: shells, gas, a flood, bombs, and quantities of patients! No wonder she looked thin.

Mammy, why didn't you tell them to build some Liberty *chasse* planes? All these beautiful new Liberty biplace machines don't help us poor combat pilots any. We ride only single seater (monoplace) machines.

Monday. I have just come back from an auto trip close up to the lines to visit the graves of those poor boys who collided. The shells were bursting close at times. A few hundred yards away they were shelling a battery furiously.

Goodnight dearest Mother,
Your H."

Coolidge's letter is addressed "Coincy" which would indicate that the 94th was spending ground time there, possibly to be closer to the front than Saints.

Nothing occurred on August 18. A thirteen-plane patrol was reduced to five due to various continuing mechanical problems with the Spads; the same on August 19, and nothing further occurring on August 20 or 21. Reed Chambers filed an interesting but hard to understand Reconnaissance Report for August 22. He, as patrol leader, Sherry, Kaye, Clark, Jeffers, Sparks, Coolidge, Cook, Zacharias, Cates, Maloney, Snow, Green, and Taylor flew in the morning to Villa Coubray in a "Patrol formation" at 3000 meters. The narrative in his report tells that they flew to Paris in formation where they landed and "looked over new planes"; what new planes was not spelled out. Upon return they could not fly back in formation as they could only get one plane off at a time as there was no one "to crank props." A Lt. Pierce could not be found, so they did not report to anyone. Lts. Sparks and Kaye were unable to start their planes and remained at Orly awaiting repairs.

A one-hour "Offensive Patrol" was flown on August 23 with the plan to rendezvous with a formation of the 27th Aero Squadron. The patrol was led by Lt. Green who "thought he saw the supposed planes of the 27th Squadron about 10 kilometers north of La Ferté at 16.40, but lost them in the haze." The formation held together until they regained the field, but five planes, including Eastman, landed with motor trouble, a 40% plus rate of dropouts. The Engineering Department reported thirteen out of twenty-two planes as being available at the end of the day.

Lt. Green leading another patrol late in the afternoon of August 25, reported seeing nine Fokkers west of Fismes about 500 meters higher than his formation. He was unable to climb above them as they climbed also and refused to attack. He also reported meeting a *red* Spad at 4500 meters south of Fismes. What or who that was remains a mystery.

In a letter home on August 25, Coolidge, who was on a three-day "permission", talks about living in a "dreary monotonous place" where the "food is so infested with filthy flies that our tummies have gone back on us." A place where "all our regular operations have been suspended" and where "we have been doing mock battle manoeuvres to while away the time" which no other squadron did, and where "our motors are continually breaking down and causing trouble and keeping willing pilots from accompanying their companions on patrols over the lines."

Morale was obviously slipping to an all time low. Bad machines, loss of friends and no victories to offset the gloom were taking their toll, and the next six days of total inactivity did nothing to improve matters. The *Report of Operations* for August 31 tells the story: one trial flight by Lt. Palmer; no patrols; no protection patrols; no alerts; no combats; 16 pilots present and 21 out of 22 planes available.

Lt. Arthur L. Cunningham, the squadron Operations Officer, prepared the "Monthly Report, 94th Aero Squadron" for August in which he provides some rather telling statistics:

1. Total planes, average per day 23
2. Available planes, average per day 15
3. Available pilots, average per day 18
4. Total flights 279
5. Combat patrols (involving 176 planes) 17
6. Total trial flights 99

7. Total combats 20
8. Total enemy planes claimed 5
9. Total enemy planes confirmed 1
10. Total casualties 2
11. Total combat hours .... 329h 52 min.
12. Total Trial Flight Hours 55h 33
13. Total Flying Hours 385h 25
14. Percentage of Planes Avail. Per Day .... 65 %
15. Percentage of Casualties 10%
16. Planes Dropped 4
17. Planes Received 2

Unfortunately we don't know the number of days in which weather prevented flying, but seventeen patrols in thirty-one days seems to be a rather low statistic. The bottom line results of twenty combats netting five claims and one confirmation also seems to be rather low, but Rickenbacker's absences with flu and ear problems could have had some effect. It would be interesting to compare the 65% plane availability to the statistics of a World War II fighter squadron. Fighter groups of the 8th Air Force in 1943 were able to achieve a good victory to loss ratio of 6 to 1 in August of that year. They, too, were struggling with aircraft, P-38s, P-47s, and P-51s, trying to find the best plane for their missions with individuals preferring one type over another, as did the 94th with their Nieuports and Spads. It is said that history repeats itself.

Eddie Rickenbacker in his number 1 at Saints. August 1918.

Opposite
Top: Willie Palmer, two of his mechanics and Spad 4570 number 20. August 1918.
Bottom: Reed Chambers and Spad 4526 number 11. Saints. August 1918.

7

September - The Push Begins

For the past few weeks of August, the rumor mill was grinding out all manner of misinformation, but indeed something was in the works and the first real indication was a move to the west to the field at Rembercourt. Security was at the highest level and every effort was being made to keep the locations of the American squadrons from the Germans. No patrols were to be flown over the lines and constant protection patrols were being flown over the field to drive away any nosey Boche airman. All this was the build-up to the first real American drive to eliminate the St. Mihiel salient and straighten out the lines before attacking the Hindenberg Line.

The first two days of September were involved in the finalization of the move to Rembercourt and no missions were flown. On September 3, Lt. Thorne Taylor led a patrol consisting of himself and Lts. Cates and Coolidge on a balloon-strafing mission up to St. Mihiel and Fleury. The purpose of the mission was to keep the enemy observation to a minimum as the build-up for the attack was in progress. Lt. Taylor reported at 18h 30, sighting two Spads attacking "an enemy sausage" near Heudicourt. "The enemy pulled down the sausage. I am absolutely certain that no balloon is stationed at Montsec." The 95th had a patrol out consisting of Lts. Ted Curtis, Sumner Sewall and Walt Avery, to attack balloons at Montsec and Vigneulles. Lt. Curtis dove on one and it was drawn down. The 95th also put up a single plane to patrol over the field from 18h 30 to 19h 30. The operations order stated, "Mission to prevent enemy observation machines which are in the habit of flying over this field (Rembercourt) at 5000 meters from successfully performing their mission."

The 94th sent up Eddie Green at 17h 30 for the same purpose and he reported, "I picked up an enemy plane; type unknown, about 18h 25 headed toward Bar-le-Duc and coming from St. Mihiel. I followed him while he circled and turned back to the lines, but was unable to get to his height. He was at 5500 meters. I left him crossing the lines." This was probably a Rumpler which was able to fly higher than the other German two-seaters, as well as Spads, and has been noted before.

Lt. Chambers did the solo patrol over the field at 6h 05 to 6h 40 on September 4, followed by Lt. Cates at 9h 55 who had an overheating motor which set him down at Souilly at 11h 30. Prior to that problem, he saw two Rumplers in the region of Neuville. One was about 1000 meters ahead of the second. He attacked the first coming down out of the sun firing 50 rounds before his guns jammed and the E. A. turned back.

Lts. Taylor and Cook did a protection patrol over the field 14h 19 to 15h 45, while Lt. Green led Coolidge, Sparks, Kaye and Clark to Watronville (southeast of Verdun) to St. Mihiel at 4000 meters. They could not locate any enemy machines and returned home at 16h 46. These patrols from southeast of Verdun to St. Mihiel were conducted by the entire First Pursuit Group, alternating one squadron after another so as to have coverage at all times.

Two new pilots, Lts. Emery Samson and Charles Crocker, joined the squadron on September 4, with Samson flying patrols as early as September 6. On that day the weather was terrible, with rain, clouds and gusty wind, but in spite of it, Thorne Taylor led his patrol of Lts. Cook, Coolidge, Sparks and Eastman to a low altitude from where they machine gunned "the cantonments" at St. Mihiel. Lt. Samson, after returning from his first flight over Watronville and St. Mihiel, took the high patrol over the field.

To protect against photo planes, Ham Coolidge was on the high patrol over the field at 5700 meters from 11h 15 to 13h 00 when:

"At 12h 15 while flying at 5700 meters I saw two E.A. biplace Rumplers headed towards Bar-le-Duc. I got between them and the lines and dove under the rear plane. The E.A. saw me coming and turned off to Germany. I continued on to the leading plane. This E.A. also saw me before I could get close enough to shoot and headed gradually towards the lines. My motor was missing and very hot, however I pursued him exchanging shots at frequent intervals. When I last saw E.A. he was gliding down towards Thiaucourt with frequent puffs of black smoke coming from his engine. Perhaps my shots had injured his motor. My motor got steadily hotter and headed for the nearest field I could find and just made Toul Field before it stopped. CONFIRMATION REQUESTED."

No confirmation was ever received for this claim.

Lt. Thorne Taylor led the patrol from which Coolidge met the Rumplers and his combat report states:

"Attacked two Fokkers over St. Mihiel and kept them back of lines; they tried three times to cross by climbing. They held about 300 meters altitude on me steadily. Fired about160 rounds at intervals about 11h 45. Attacked E.A. balloon on way back near Vigneulles down to 1500 meters; it was pulled down and E.A. observer jumped, no other results, one balloon on each side of it; both on ground. Anti-aircraft active."

Lt. Joe Eastman took the high patrol over the field from 11h 15 to 12h 55 with Lt. Kaye taking the duty later in the day. Lt. Reed Chambers, patrolling with Lts. Sherry, Samson and Kay, twice chased 6 E.A. back into Germany.

With this activity, the 94th successfully completed their mission of the day, keeping the Germans at bay behind their own lines.

The only flying event of significance that took place from September 8 through September 11 was a trial flight on September 9 from 15h 03 to 15h 45 by Lt. E. V. Rickenbacker. He was back! Four new pilots were assigned to the squadron, Lts. Eugene Scroggie and Mandell Hopkins on September 9 and Lts. William Fowler and Edward Garnsey on September 10. The squadron was being built to full strength for the push to St. Mihiel which began in the early hours of September 12.

From September 4 to September 8, Ham Coolidge found time to get off three letters to his mother, the letter of September 8 telling of his attack on the two Rumplers:

"September 4, 1918
Dearest Mother,

Your letters come in precious profusion – but often with the dates all twisted. Just a few days ago I got letters of about the last of June – since getting several dating well into August....

If we have been for some weeks living a very dull life of almost complete and discouraging idleness, we are now very much in the war again. That is all I can tell you now, but you will surely know more soon. Last evening it was very calm and clear and we were sent "over" to try and bring down a certain enemy observation balloon. All was going beautifully – but when we approached the place we saw that it wasn't up – much to our disgust. Shooting down balloons is pretty risky work – a good deal more so than combat with enemy planes. You see they send up a fierce barrage of machine gun fire, Archies, flaming "onion" rockets, etc., in a circle around the old sausage. Today we patrolled nearly two hours, lying in wait for some of the photographic planes that come over quite often, and which we expected today – nothing turned up. That condition won't last long, as other patrols have encountered all kinds of Boche aircraft. Supper time – nice camp-like food in a tent – and not so many flies on account of the cooler weather.

Your loving,
H."

"(No Date)
Dearest Mother,

By good luck I am able to slip in a between-times letter to you to tell you that all goes well. I never felt better in my life, am a little thinner perhaps, but still as keen as ever about the work.

They speak of making me a squadron commander when I have a little more experience – I dread the day – because a squadron commander has so much paper work, etc., that he can hardly ever fly. Many of them are glad, but I want to keep flying above all else and do not care for advancement except for your sake.

Our machines are very fast, solid, and fairly dependable, far different from those awful firetraps we were using before, one of which Q. was shot down.

The Liberty looks *good* and I predict that very soon it will have become a counting factor in Allied aviation."

"Sunday, Sept. 8, 1918
Dearest Mother,

Our afternoon patrol has just been called off on account of rain, so I retire to our little barrack to write in comfort. The barrack is only temporary as we are to move into tents tomorrow. The tents don't particularly appeal at this time of year, but they have the one great advantage of being in a little pine wood and pine woods always smack of Squam and home. Anyway, it is a thousand per cent better than being billeted, to my way of thinking.

We are fairly close to the lines and it's great to be able to get there in a few minutes. We can see the sights and hear the sounds – day and night – that make you feel really in the war. In fact, one of our chief amusements in the evening is to stand outside looking off towards the lines where intermittent flashes light the sky for a brief second and low thunder follows soon after. Occasionally a searchlight beam roams the sky like a lost pilot looking for home. Then at clocklike intervals from Bocheland a string of fiery balls sails slowly upwards and fades out. These are variously interpreted, but they surely are signals of some kind. Less frequently than these signal lights, parachute flares go up, burst out in a brilliant flood of light, and sink slowly down to earth.

But that isn't flying, is it? On the whole flying is what preoccupies us most. Each night about nine o'clock the schedule for the next day comes in. From one corner of the dark barrack comes a cheer from the second flight who learn that their first patrol is not until 11 A.M. – while a dismal groan from the other side reveals the fact the first and third flights go on a daybreak! Inwardly, though, they are glad because that's a good time of day to fly. The early bird is pretty apt to catch the worm.

Well, yesterday I had a little excitement. My flight was on patrol but it was my turn to stay behind alone and patrol this side of the lines for enemy photography planes who take advantage of every opportunity to sneak over and snap some pictures. For an hour and a quarter I had been up very high (5700 meters) and was about to come home when some white Archie puffs below caught my attention. I stared hard, and there sure enough were two biplane machines headed towards ——— in our lines. I doped out my plan of attack and moved over between them and the lines – still far above them. Once directly behind them, I throttled down slightly and took a headlong dive of nearly a mile. The wires and struts of my plane simply screeched from the wind pressure but I wanted to get behind and below as quickly as possible so as not to be seen. About halfway down, however, the back man saw me coming and he swung off instantly into his lines. That shot spoiled, I kept on going for the front man who evidently had not yet seen me. My attack had been calculated for the back man so it naturally was not right for the front one who saw me before I could reach his "blind spot." He swung towards home in a big circle under full power with me trailing along behind trying desperately to get under his tail. Mine was a borrowed plane and the old motor suddenly began to splutter. I was mad as a hatter, but chased on, getting slightly closer. He decided it was too close so he banked over his machine and the gunner opened up on me. I swung behind his elusive tail and blazed away at him. The old tracers flew back and forth that way for some minutes but my misbehaving motor would not pull hard enough to give me a close range shot. Then it suddenly occurred to me that I was several kilometers in Bocheland and alone – with a failing motor! Obviously I could not make home but I knew of another field nearer to that place. My Boche had evidently decided it was dinner time for I last saw him gliding down towards his aerodrome; I, too, had an empty feeling in my tummy which a sudden burst of Archie shots only accentuated. The old motor got worse and worse as I sunk down and down – but now I was safely across the lines and well on the way to the aerodrome which I barely made with the dying gasp from an almost red-hot motor. The C.O. brought me home after lunch in his smooth running Cadillac. Another reminder of happy days!

It was a fierce disappointment not to have nailed one of those Rumplers. Perhaps my own plane (temporarily out for repairs) would have given me the chance – but then, it's all luck."

On the day of the opening of the great offensive, September 12, the weather was terrible; rain, low overcast down to 300 meters, and gusty wind continued throughout the day.

The first patrol got off at 7h 35, several hours after the attack began, with the express purpose to search out the location of enemy troops. Thorne Taylor was the patrol leader, with Lts. Eastman, Cook, Jeffers, and Sparks following at an altitude of 200 meters. Taylor reported his observations: "Three towns in flames; Lavignéville, Chaillon and Creué. Barrage very heavy over Vigneulles and Creué. Infantry seen advancing through valley as far as Châtillon. Boche still in St. Mihiel. No Boche balloons seen at Vigneulles. Our balloons at Troyon and Meuse up 250 meters."

Lt. Cook brought back further intelligence: "In region of Deuxnouds-aux-Bois saw grey colored Biplace with red, white and dark cocards at 8h 15. Explosion in region of Creué. American Infantry with very few French intermingled advancing in columns toward Vigneulles-les-Hattonchatel at 8h 25. Enemy balloon up for a few minutes in region of Heudicourt." It must have been extremely helpful to Headquarters to receive these up-to-date reconnaissance reports giving them situation data on a most fresh and timely basis. With this information the artillery fire could be more accurately placed when enemy as well as friendly troop locations were known.

The second patrol of the day was led by Lt. Cates and consisted of Lt. Snow, Zacharias, and Palmer. Departing at 12h 30, their mission was "Reconnaissance-Barrage Patrol;" an altitude of 1500 meters was attained due to slightly improving visibility. The reports of the pilots included the following information: Lt. Cates: "A very large column of black and white smoke was seen in the region of Chaillon, filling the entire valley north of St. Mihiel. A machine was seen on the ground in the region of La Croix-sur-Meuse." Zacharias quoted: "Large fire observed in the region of Chaillon. Several minor fires noted at points north of Chaillon. Enemy anti-aircraft activity in the region of Heudicourt." Lt. Snow added, "I saw one Spad; No. 22, down with two or three diagonal stripes in white in the region of Croix-sur-Meuse. Artillery activity all along the line. Received three bullets in plane when flying over region of the Hattonchatel Creué. These bullets were fired from the ground."

Joe Eastman, a member of Ham Coolidge's small Reconnaissance Patrol which included Harvey Weir Cook, filed one of his rare reports.

> "Patrol formed by Lieuts. Coolidge, Cook and myself. Early in patrol became coupled alone with Lt. Coolidge. Noted number of fires in the region east of Watronville, meeting considerable enemy anti-aircraft fire in that vicinity. One fire of a large hangar, apparently an enemy munitions dump, was out of control near Woël. Our artillery appeared to be taking great effect on the ridge southwest of Vigneulles-les-Hattonchatel. Received attention from enemy anti-aircraft around St. Mihiel, where we passed one of our Salmsons several times. At end of patrol, Lieut. Coolidge went 'en panne' in our lines without injury. Two kilometers east of Fresnes-au-Mont, identified plane No. 22 of 95th Squadron *en panne*, just in our lines. A single Spad, apparently separated from its patrol and continuing alone, was near us at times, possibly Lt. Cook. Lieut. Cook has not returned."

The Spad of the 95th, Bleriot built No. 15123 Squadron number 22, belonged to Denny Holden who later became renowned for his balloon busting. This Spad was written off and Holden was assigned a new plane. The final flying of the day was done in a heavy rainstorm by Chambers, Sherry and Kaye who observed numerous fires in the regions of Vigneulles, Montsec, Fresnes and Doncourt. The American artillery with their French 75s were advancing from Lavignéville along the road to Chaillon and no German planes were to be seen. Rickenbacker, now back in action, paired up with his favorite companion, Reed Chambers, and took off on a voluntary patrol from Verdun to St. Mihiel. The time was 12h 26 and the weather had lifted enough for fair observation.

In his book, Rick describes the flight:

> "Flying straight east to Saint-Mihiel, we crossed the river Meuse and turned down its valley toward Verdun. Many fires were burning under us as we flew, most of them well on the German side of the river. Villages, haystacks, ammunition dumps, and supplies were being set ablaze by the retreating Huns.
>
> We proceeded as far as Verdun. Then turning east we continued flying at our low altitude and passed over Fresnes and Vigneulles. Vigneulles was the objective point of the American forces. It lies east of Verdun some fifteen miles and about the same distance north of St. Mihiel. One American army was pushing toward it from a point just south of Verdun while the other attack was made from the opposite side of the salient."

As Rickenbacker and Chambers turned south from Vigneulles, they saw the road to Metz running north was crowded with retreating Germans, as was the road from St. Mihiel to Vigneulles. They chose the most suitable targets and began to strafe the horsedrawn artillery, causing considerable delay and confusion to the retreat.

Rickenbacker and Chambers continued to team up on September 13, flying two voluntary patrols, one at 9h 50 and the other at 12h 26. On the first patrol, which was flown at 300 meters, the weather continued to be poor as they flew the route Vigneulles to Fresnes. Along the way they noted American and French advance troops at Wadonville, Avillers and St. Benoit. These troops were supported by camions along the main roads and some 500 prisoners were being marched along the road to the rear. On the 12h 26 patrol the weather and the visibility was very good which enabled them to fly to Verdun and St. Mihiel encountering no enemy aerial activity. West of Vigneulles, they saw eight 155 mm German field guns each being drawn by six horses. Rickenbacker fired 20-25 rounds at them when his guns jammed beyond repair. Rickenbacker and Chambers noticed fires from baled hay and munition dumps and observed the American barrage shells landing on the crest of the hills just west of St. Mauriceville and Hattonchatel. On the way home they saw Holden's Spad, Number 22, under a French guard.

Rickenbacker set out again on a solo patrol at 15h 17 to Jaulny-Haumont-Woël-Harville-Maizeray-Riaville for a reconnaissance of the region. He was fired on by ground machine guns from the town of Riaville, located French infantry advancing single file from Fresnes towards Marchéville, and on the return could find no signs of the enemy. He noted a badly wrecked Allied Salmson or Breguet two kilometers south of Spada, but sighted no enemy balloons or aircraft. Chambers and Kaye met with poor weather on the late patrol of the day, flying at 300 meters. They saw the American troops dug in on the west side of the Fresnes-Beney road with a few small patrols to the east in contact with the enemy. In the region of Jonville-Haddonville-les-Lachaussee, they were fired upon by Germans on the ground.

On September 14 German aerial activity stepped up as well as that of the Allies, including the 94th, which conducted four patrols, three voluntary patrols, and one alert for a total of thirty-one sorties.

On the scheduled patrols, flights of three, four, five, and six aircraft were used, while only one or two were used in those of a voluntary nature.

Rickenbacker flew two solo voluntary patrols; on the first he departed at 7h 30 in good weather to fly to Verdun, Villecey, and Lachaussee at 4000 meters. His combat report narrative describes the events of this flight:

> "Lt. Rickenbacker reports: Left at 7h 30 AM. Met one enemy biplace over Verdun. Looked like an L.V.G. Followed him about seven (7) kilometers, but it was too high to reach. Then returned from the lines at 4000 meters. Met four (4) enemy Fokkers with red wings, light grey fuselage and striped tails over the towns of Villecey and Waville. They were flying at about 3000 meters. I piqued on the upper man of the formation, fired apparently 200 rounds and saw him go down, apparently out of control. Was unable to follow him on account of the other three, who showed excellent fighting spirits. This took place at 8h 10 and 8h 15. I then returned over Lachaussee, where at 8h 25, I noticed five (5) Fokkers with their regular camouflage and crosses on the tail, apparently new men. I started to pique, but they immediately turned for home. Fired about 50 rounds without result. Confirmation Requested."

This request was answered in G. O. Number 8, Sept. 22, 1918 –:

> "Par. 4. 1st Lieutenant EDWARD V. RICKENBACKER 94th Aero Squadron, First Pursuit Group, is hereby credited with the destruction, in combat, of an enemy Fokker in the region of Villecey-Waville at 3000 meters altitude on September 14th at 8:15 o'clock."

Rickenbacker stated later that the four Fokkers were following an American formation of Liberty-engined DH 4s returning from a raid on Metz. He climbed above them with his back to the sun, and then descended on the last man in their formation firing straight into the pilot's seat. The other three swung into a climbing *virage* and came about flying directly at him with guns blazing. Rickenbacker evaded his attackers by diving away with full power. By the skill of the pilots and the color of their machines, he was convinced they were from "the famous Richthofen Circus."

The other patrols all reported seeing enemy Fokkers in formations of seven, but no contact was made by either party. Reed Chambers led the final patrol of the day up to Conflans and Etang where they noticed five or six very large fires between the two towns. They then flew low in search of enemy balloons, finding two which were very low and some distance behind the German lines.

1st Lt. Hamilton Coolidge was one of only three 94th pilots who did not take to the air on September 14 which gave him time to write his brother Roger who was attending Groton, the same prep school from which he had graduated in 1915.

> "France, Sept. 14th, 1918
> Dear Roger,
>
> This is about the first time I've had a chance to answer all those swell letters you wrote me from Squam[1] trying to make me jealous! Well, I have to admit you succeeded pretty well, you monkey. No, when I cussed you out for not writing, those letters were not lost at all. A big bunch of them were delayed somewhere, probably on account of moving around (which we naturally have to do a good deal), so when I arrived here I found a whole fistful of your letters waiting. Pretty nice!

Dear old Mister – I wish I could take you with me on one of our trips "over" these days. I guarantee it would be the most interesting hour and forty-five minutes you every spent. At least it hits me that way. The other day we patrolled not three miles high as we often do, but just above the tops of the trees! We could see everything that went on below, only it was a little like trying to distinguish objects by the roadside when you go by in an auto at 130 miles an hour. A brief glimpse of something and you are past – then something else, and so on. In one place we saw an American battery of 75s right out in the open field banging away to beat the band. The American uniforms, however, are *very* hard to see against the ground. You don't see many men actually. What you do see are flashes of flame, puffs of smoke and great geysers of mud and rocks where shells hit and explode. Then we passed over Bocheland. We weren't sure it was Bocheland till we suddenly heard ra, ta, ta – ra, ta, ta, ta, ta! Then there was no question about it. They were shooting at us from the woods, but darn it, we couldn't see those machine gun nests. You'd be surprised what good acrobacy you can do when machine gun bullets and shrapnel begin to fly about you! The fellow behind me got seven bullets in his plane and said he saw a shrapnel burst right on top of me. I didn't realize it came that close, but later I found a few places where splinters had torn the linen. The other fellow was not hurt. When we come home we write a detailed report of every single thing we noticed on the ground, stating just where and when and how, etc….

One rather nice stunt was inaugurated a few days ago. They issue us packages of cigarettes all bundled up in padded cloth with a note attached. We fly right down over our attacking troops and chuck them overboard. The infantry boys get the cigarettes and read the note which makes them feel fine. It says that they are advancing wonderfully – that the air service is right with them, and to keep going like Hell or something after that order. Anyway, it helps keep up their spirits.

Get husky and wise at Groton this year, old boy – and remember that even if your old brother isn't there to cuss you out all the time, he's thinking of you often.

Love,
Ham."

The action continued the following day, September 15, with 24 sorties flown, made up from one voluntary, one protection and two regular patrols. Rickenbacker conducted the solo voluntary patrol up to Etain, Haddonville and Pagny, departing at 7h 16 with good weather at 4000 meters. In his combat report he reported:

> "Encountered six (6) E.A. with regular camouflage at 8h 10 in the region of Bois de Waville and the Bois de Bayonville after having flown up and down the sector with them parallel with the lines at about the same altitude. Then returning over the above-mentioned region this patrol piqued on our Spads, one of which I noticed to go down in a vrille. I saw my opportunity to pique on the last man of the E.A. patrol, which was a Fokker type. I got several good bursts into the cockpit and noticed the E.A. to go down flopping from side to side out of control. The encounter started at 4500 meters and ended at 2000 meters. At the time that I piqued I noticed nine (9) E.A. flying from the direction of Metz over Arz-sur-Mosel. Confirmation Requested."

The 95th Aero Squadron had a twelve-plane patrol flying in the region at this time and Lt. Bob Eoff had to break off due to motor trouble and return to the field, which may have been what Rickenbacker noticed. Confirmation was received on September 17 in General Order Number 6, paragraph 4, for an enemy Fokker near Bois de Waville at 8:10 o'clock. This was Rickenbacker's victory number 8.

The protection patrol of nine planes which departed at 8h 49, consisting of Lieut. Jeffers, Patrol Leader, Lieuts. Palmer Eastman, Cates, Cook, Sparks, Zacharias, Sherry and Chambers, soon lost Sherry and Chambers to motor troubles. For the patrol this was only the beginning of things to come as Lt. Jeffers' report and others bear out:

> "Patrol left field at 8h 50 to 9h 05. One plane (Salmson) taxied out, but none left field. Patrol then went to Lake Lachaussee and waited from 9h 20 to 9h 35, but saw no Salmsons. Patrol then continued on regular route and was attacked in region of Jonville-St. Helaire by nine (9) Fokkers at 9h 55 from an altitude of 5000 meters. Patrol at this time was at 4200 meters. Five (5) Fokkers attacked and four stayed above patrol to protect. The rear of the patrol was attacked and I turned, climbing above attackers, into the sun. The attackers pulled off after falling about 400 meters and shooting at a distance from 300 meters. They then turned under their own protection, which left the region of the lines. Patrol then continued and returned at 10h 20. No Salmsons were observed doing observation in sector of Patrol. Three (3) Allied planes were

doing observation in the region of Villers-en-Woëvre-Grinaucourt sector."

Lt. Willie Palmer added the facts that Woël was burning as well as other fires in the region of Chambley and that he was unable to engage the five attacking Fokkers as they maintained a height advantage and turned back into Germany after piquing only once. Lt. Sparks was attacked at a distance of 300 meters, received no hits and was followed for about 500 meters. Poor Joe Eastman who always seemed to be having one problem or another reported:

> "Was straggling behind our formation on account of low R.P.M. of motor, when over the region of Jonville and St. Hilaire, at 3800 meters, four enemy Fokkers approached us from above in the rear. Unable to maintain position in our formation and the enemy planes bearing down on my airplane, I immediately piqued sharply with four enemy airplanes in pursuit and firing to about 1500 meters. The enemy withdrew. Noticing a number of bullet holes in my elevator and elsewhere, I returned to the home field."

Later that day Eastman wrote a long entry in his diary concerning the attack commencing September 12, as well as the patrol of September 15:

> "Sunday, Sept. 15th. There has been much, much indeed of local entertainment since the first day of the attack. The line seems to rest now after having spread across the St. Mihiel salient. What is to come next no one knows, though on our patrol this morning I observed heavy barrage fire No. East of Verdun where it is believed the French combined with our troops are to strike. Reports give that 15,000 prisoners have been counted, and many more are being rounded up in the woods now within our lines. Secty. Of War Baker congratulates the khaki lads in St. Mihiel, while the papers are congested as usual with epistles of felicitation between the people who write such.
>
> The unusual strain on our apparatae has kept a goodly number of them on the sidelines. Consequently, maintenance of patrols through the days has kept those with flyable machines considerably on the go. My motor has been going beautifully save that my ceiling is 3600 meters and both yesterday and today I have straggled behind and under my formations. Thus, this morning when straining to keep up with the most disgracefully *milling* formation one ever saw, I saw four planes descending and gaining on us from the rear. At first – as a fool does who has a distaste for bad news, true or false, I tried to believe them British. They kept coming, and still wishing to behave honorably, I struggled for our formation. My friendliness for them ceased when within one hundred metres of me, I saw that in earnest or silly jest, each and every one of them was aiming exactly at the small of my back. Acting with the characteristic cleverness of my decisions once reached, I prayerfully poked my nose as vertically towards the earth as six months at the front had taught me to do. How one stills the mind against bad news! I actually – among other sensations – felt a little surprised to see them, all four, come tight on my heels crackling as they came. Like one in a tepid shower bath who awaits in anticipation for the ice wake just turned on, I curiously watched and listened to the tracers splashing around. As much as seemed provident, I twisted my rudder to give some slight irregularity to my course. They kept shooting. Still perfectly whole, I waited for the strange sensation. En route I had thought to switch on to the spare tank – and of a sudden this uncertain friend went over to the enemy – the motor ceased firing, my speed slackened. Convinced that now the thread of hope had snapped, I nevertheless tried switching onto the hand pump gas feed – and worked at it to beat Sam Hill. It caught more speed. Still crack! Crack! And at about 1500 meters the miraculous happened. The four Fokkers drew up and disappeared in the sun. But, in the name of caution, I continued for awhile straight down, finally at 800 m. pulling with great gentleness into normal 'ligne de vol'. Continued home. Found about eight holes in the wings, one nicking the elevator bar and another buried in the felt binding of the cockpit having grazed my shoulders at the good as a mile distance of three inches. –Where upon does my plane go to the doctor for new wing and tail assembly – to be ready tomorrow."

Ham Coolidge gives his side of the previous week's adventures in a long letter to his mother dated September 15, 1918:

> "[Rembercourt] September 15th, 1918
>
> Dear Mother,
>
> To try and describe the events of the past week in any sort of a complete way would be impossible and unpermissible. Do look back at your newspaper clippings of about this date and you will know the general history of events. Perhaps I can add some details to help out a little,

though it is only from the point of view of a pilot who can see but little of all that takes place. It's a little like trying to recall all that one sees from an express train window after the journey is over, only we have the added difficulty of having to pay considerable attention to our little express train itself. We are the engineers as well as the passengers.

Thursday morning we went out in groups of threes or fours, flying at a height of perhaps two hundred feet. Our object was to see everything possible on the ground and to try and establish the location of the lines. I headed a group of four, one on either side a little in back of me, and one a few hundred meters above and behind. Well, you never saw such a sight or heard such sounds. We started down our lines just at their edge and every second came flashes and white puffs from our batteries. We were so close that every explosion rocked us about frantically and often threatened to dash us into the tree tops. In fact sometimes our little ships were almost unmanageable. Just below us in the open field was an American battery firing madly at an objective we knew well. We could see very few men actually. The color of our uniforms is very hard to distinguish against the ground, and we were tossing about madly in the writhing air currents. By this time we were quite far in Bocheland. Burning villages, dumps and storehouses stood out sharply. On we went, but now over woods again – Boche or Allied?

I could see horses mounted by officers rushing to and fro on the roads, and trucks, wagons and men moving madly along, but dared not fire on them for fear of their being Americans. You simply couldn't distinguish their uniforms. Then the party began for us. The Archies opened up full blast, hanging hideously close, when suddenly, sharp and distinct through the noise of our motor came the unmistakable ra ta ta ta ta of machine gun bullets. I thought a Boche might be on my tail and began to squirm wildly about, looking back all the time. No one was there except the other three boys who were also squirming. Of course they were shooting at us from those machine gun nests in the woods, but as they used no tracer bullets I could not see where they came from. One man (on my left) got seven bullets in his plane and had to leave. It was really pretty hot work patrolling so low – but it was intensely interesting. The air was filled with Allied aircraft of all types and strange to say not a Boche appeared. Since then, however, they have come out in large numbers. One of our four had left already, another had a *panne de moteur*, and just squeaked over the lines. The last two of us then started back against a heavy wind with Archies breaking all around us and occasional ra ta ta ta's from the ground. No sooner had we crossed the lines than my motor groaned and died! Down I went into a little valley and had a nasty time worming my way into a tiny patch of good ground past telegraph wires, barbed wire entanglements, and shell holes. I came to rest not four feet from one of the last named. A Spad is heavy and lands fast at best, so it's no fun to have forced landings. From here I walked to a French divisional headquarters where I found the other boy who had *panned* previously. We tried desperately to communicate with home but the wires were too busy, so by supper time we were still there. At this point the General emerged from his holy of holies, greeted us most cordially and invited us to mess with him and his staff – and at the threshold of the mess-hall insisted that we go in first! These Frenchmen certainly beat the world for politeness. At dinner the conversation was entirely military and most interesting. Also, we were able to tell the General several interesting things we had noticed on our patrol that afternoon. The feeling between French and Americans is wonderful. Apparently they can work together in perfect harmony on any kind of a job. In fact I'm not sure that they don't often make a point of mixing them up in military operations.

At ten o'clock we had not succeeded in getting in touch with our squadron, so the adjutant sent us home in the General's limousine! You can imagine what fun it was comparing notes with all the others next morning. It was then that we learned of the beautiful little *coup de main* made by Lieut. K. (Jim Knowles, 95th Aero) of one of the other squadrons (there are four of them) in our group. Patrolling low over some woods he saw a convoy of Boches on the road below. He dove down with both guns blazing, and saw horses and men in mad confusion. Several horses dropped, others jumped up against wagons and trucks, stopping the whole convoy. He then raced home, told his news and a bombing squadron was immediately sent to the spot where a few well-placed shots effectively stopped the whole outfit, most of which was soon after captured by the advancing infantry.

I've been kicking myself ever since for not realizing that much of what I saw was Boche – but our primary object was visual reconnaissance and it's a hideous thing to fire on one's own troops. You see it isn't like hanging above the show in a balloon. At that low altitude one's field of vision is so restricted that it changes every second. You travel a hundred and thirty miles an hour, rocking and tossing about and squirming around to avoid the deadly shrapnel and sputtering bullets – so it's very hard to see things clearly!

Since Thursday the drive has been going splendidly as you know. Our boys have accounted for several Boches and done some fine protective and defensive work. They have been meeting more and more hostile planes, but – etc.! The words "liberty plane" are often heard these days. But I can best tell of things that I myself have seen, and yesterday I saw things I shall never forget.

The Captain invited me to go with him in his car to X – where Tom Crocker was *en panne*. Now this place had been in Allied hands for just a day and a half. The plane landed among the hills back of the town which for four long years the Boche had occupied. When we finally got to the plane by walking about a mile from the car, we found it would take an hour or so to fix it. We left the mechanics at work on it and started out to look around. The hills were just riddled with German trenches and battery positions. Every step through the woods revealed dugouts, "pill boxes," trenches and gun emplacements. We had to be terribly careful because the Boche leave every conceivable kind of infernal machines, mines, time bombs, etc., when they get a chance. The day before, eight Frenchmen had been killed by touching a hidden wire or picking up an interesting object to which was attached a wire communicating with a bomb of some kind. The place was just thick with wires on the ground – on trees, in fact everywhere. Of course most of them were telephone wires. In one concrete dugout the walls were three feet thick, a partition separated it into two small rooms in one of which was a switchboard with hundreds of wires. In the next room a stool and desk were placed in front of a narrow slit which looked out down a slope and off for many miles into our territory. It was a splendid observation post for artillery *réglage*. In other dugouts were comfortable bunks with stoves. The whole thing impressed one by its solidity and permanence. We dared not go down deep into any of the countless subterranean passages, but even on the surface we found some very interesting things – some of which might help along your precious scrap-book. There was any quantity of ammunition of all kinds, and countless other things.

Remember we only covered a few hundred yards in those miles of unexploited wonders, and it was interesting that we were the first Allies in some of those spots, or at least I think we were (and have good reasons). When Tom's plane had been fixed and he was safely off for home, we started back in the car. Our way lay through X – , the town just reoccupied by the French. Two thousand civilians had stayed there all those years of Boche occupancy, and only the day before had the French soldiers come marching in. They told us that when the women saw their soldiers coming they rushed out into the streets and threw their arms around their necks. From every window flew French flags. All the civilians dressed in their Sunday best walked around with happiness in their faces, drawn thin and haggard from all they had been through. In the Square *place* were many French soldiers and civilians and a brass band was playing. It pleased me that in spite of the fact that there were no Americans present and they hadn't seen us, they played the *Stars and Stripes Forever* as one of their tunes. Then followed the Marseillaise and we went home with lumps in our throats and little shivers up our spines. The spirit of these people is so wonderful.

It's supper time, dear Mammy.

Your,
Ham"

Patrols and pannes were the orders of the day on September 16. Lts. Sherry, Crocker, Hopkins, Scroggie, Palmer, Zacharias and Sparks all encountered troubles with their Spads and could not complete their patrols and, as a result, two more planes were written off. Thorne Taylor, while leading a protection patrol for two Salmsons, encountered an L.V.G. biplace at 4000 meters near Fresnes. Taylor, with the sun at his back dove from 5100 meters, came up under the two-seater's tail, firing 100 rounds. He then turned and attacked from the right side pouring out another 150 rounds into the L.V.G. which sideslipped and then piqued, starting to smoke badly and seemingly was out of control. Taylor then beat a hasty retreat as he was attacked by thirteen angry Fokkers. He did not request a confirmation, and none was given. Reed Chambers and Sam Kaye met a Rumpler on a later patrol, chasing him for forty-five minutes as far as the German lines, both expending all their ammunition and all but a little of their gas before returning to the field. They reported the Rumpler had lower wings with the usual camouflage, but with distinctive markings of white circles on the tips. The center of the circle was unpainted, the regular camouflage showing, but with a narrow white cross inside the circle. Rickenbacker continued his practice of flying solo patrols with one at 8 AM and another from 1600 to 1800 in the afternoon. He encountered three Fokkers over Haddonville, firing 50 rounds at long range, but achieved no results.

Poor visibility over the next few days kept aerial activities at a low level both actually and figuratively, with absolutely nothing on September 20th but test flights over the field. The weather was fair on September 21 and a flight was patrolling the main roads from Chaumont-sur-Aire to Nixéville then to Clermont-en-Argonne and then returning via the main road from Clermont to Chaumont, this being a triangle from the field north towards Verdun to Nixéville, then west to Clermont-en-Argonne, and south to the field. Lts. Palmer and Snow of the patrol reported trucks going in both directions with one large convoy north of Souilly and another north of Lemmes on the road to Nixéville. Lots of cavalry troops and wagon trains were also reported moving north. It is doubtful there actually were cavalry troops on horseback as the enemy had reduced their cavalry to fighting on foot although horses were still being used for much of the transport of goods.

Lt. Rickenbacker on a solo patrol September 22 reported two formations of German fighters of about six each behind their lines which made an attack impossible. While on another solo patrol on September 24, he met five Fokkers over Etang de Lachaussee, which, because of its shape, was called *three fingered lake* by the Americans. He took long range shots at them. Later three Fokkers dove on him without success; even later he saw five more Fokkers 6 kilometers in their lines north of Verdun. Also on September 24, Captain Ken Marr was relieved of his command of the 94th and sent home to the United States. The following day Rickenbacker was officially made C.O., while at the same time Ham Coolidge was made a flight leader. That night before the official announcement was made, Rick had a pep talk with the pilots and then spent an hour talking to the mechanics about their importance in making the contributions needed to give the 94th the leading position in the American Air Service.

On the morning of September 25 to celebrate his new command, dauntless Eddie took off on a 7h 40 voluntary patrol from Verdun to Lake Lachaussee at 4500 meters. The weather was good and as the story unfolds, so was his luck. The story comes in two versions, the first from his official combat report and the second as described in Chapter XXVII of his book.

The Combat Report:

"Patrolled the line from Verdun to the Lake Lachaussee. At 8h 15 I noticed twelve (12) monoplace Fokkers in the region of Mars-la-Tour. After staying on the line for about ten (10) minutes, they returned toward Metz. At 8h 40 I noticed our anti-aircraft shells bursting in the region of Billy. Saw five (5) Fokkers protecting two (2) biplace planes coming toward our lines. I was flying at 4500 meters and they were approximately 3000 meters. Dove out of the sun onto rear man. Then last seen he was going down out of control. Fired about 100 rounds at close range. Continued my dive thru the formation and fired about 100 rounds at a Halberstadt biplace from about 50 to 70 meters. This combat lasted about three minutes and when last seen, from an altitude of two hundred meters, he was going down in a very steep nosedive. His protection then returned from a greater altitude than I had, forcing me to retire. Two Confirmations Requested."

The book:

"Early in the forenoon I started for the lines alone, flew over Verdun and Douaumont, then turned east toward Etain. Almost immediately I picked up a pair of L.V.G. two-seater machines below me. They were coming out of Germany and were certainly bent upon an expedition over our lines. Five Fokker machines were above them and somewhat behind, acting as protection for the photographers until the lines were reached.

Climbing for the sun for all I was worth, I soon had the satisfaction of realizing that I had escaped their notice and was now well in their rear. I shut down my engine, put down my nose and made a bee line for the nearest Fokker.

I was not observed by the enemy until it was too late for him to escape. I had him exactly in my sights when I pressed both triggers for a long burst. He made a sudden attempt to pull away, but my bullets were already ripping through his fuselage and he must have been killed instantly. His machine fell away and crashed just south of Etain.

It had been my intention to zoom upward and protect myself against the expected attack from the four remaining Fokkers as soon as I had finished the first man. But when I saw the effect of my attack upon the four dumbfounded Boches, I instantly changed my tactics and plunged straight on through their formation to attack the photographing L.V.G.s ahead. The Heinies were so surprised by finding a Spad in their midst and seeing one of their number suddenly drop that the remaining three banked to right and left. Their one idea was to escape and save their own skins. Though they did not actually dive for home, they cleared a space large enough for me to slip through and continue my dive on the two-seaters before they could regain their formation.

The two-seaters had seen my attack and had already put down their heads to escape. I plunged after them, getting the rear machine in my sights as I drew nearer to him. A glance back over my shoulder showed me that the four Fokkers had not re-formed their line and were even now circling about with the purpose of again solidifying their flight. I had a few seconds yet before they could begin their attack.

The two L.V.G. machines began to draw apart. Both observers in the rear seats were firing at me, although the range was still too long for accurate shooting. I dove more steeply, passed out of the gunner's view under the nearest machine and zoomed quickly up at him from below. But the victory was not to be an easy one. The pilot suddenly kicked his tail around, giving the gunner another good shot at me. I had to postpone shooting until I had more time for my own aiming. And in the meantime the second photographing machine had stolen up behind me and I saw tracer bullets go whizzing and streaking past my face. I zoomed diagonally out of range, made a *renversement* and came directly back at my first target.

Several times we repeated these maneuvers, the four Fokkers still wrangling among themselves about their formation. And all the time we were getting farther and farther back into Germany. I decided upon one bold attack and if this failed I would get back to my own lines before it was too late.

Watching my two adversaries closely, I suddenly found an opening between them. They were flying parallel to each other and not fifty yards apart. Dropping down in a sideslip until I had one machine between me and the other I straightened out smartly, leveled my Spad and began firing. The nearest Boche passed directly through my line of fire and just as I ceased firing I had the satisfaction of seeing him burst into flames. Turning over and over as he fell the L.V.G. started a blazing path to earth just as the Fokker escort came tearing up to the rescue. I put on the gas and headed for my own lines." This was great prose written about a spectacular fight that brought well-earned confirmations and recognition.

General Orders 10, September 27, 1918, para. 4 gave Rickenbacker credit for a Halberstadt in the region of Foret de Spincourt, 2000 meters on September 25, 1918 at 8:50 o'clock.

The second confirmation was not received until the issuance of General Order 26, November 15th, 1918, para 1, which credits Rick with a Fokker in the region of Billy at 8:40 o'clock, 3000 meters, September 25, 1918.

On November 6, 1930, President Hoover presented Rickenbacker with the Congressional Medal of Honor at Bolling Field, Washington, DC. The citation read: "For conspicuous gallantry and intrepidity above and beyond the call of duty in action against the enemy near Billy, France, September 25, 1918. While on a voluntary patrol over the lines, the then Lieutenant Rickenbacker attacked seven enemy planes (five type Fokker protecting two type Halberstadt). Disregarding the odds against him, he dived on them and shot down one of the Fokkers, out of control. He then attacked one of the Halberstadts and sent it down also."

In a letter to his mother, Ham Coolidge tells of his appointment as a 'Flight Leader' and his frustration in the lack of victories:

"September 25, 1918

Dearest Mother,

Nothing particularly exciting of late. We have had a run of rainy weather which has kept us on the ground. Even on the ground we are busy. Gun sights to line up at frequent intervals, machine guns to keep limbered up, countless little adjustments on the plane which need one's attention, and pistol practice, etc., if one wants. I want to, because I have not got a string of Boches to be proud of or satisfied with, and every little way in which one can train oneself in spare time is pure gain.

I am a "flight leader" now. A squadron contains three flights of six to eight planes and pilots each. These flights usually operate individually, following the daily operation schedule, and sometimes we even split up our flight, working in two groups of three or one of four and one of two at different altitudes. Last week the only time we met Boches at all was when we outnumbered them so that they turned tail. You'd be surprised how hard it is to get Boches. Conditions are so very seldom right for a good combat at equal odds. I go out alone on voluntary patrols whenever I get a chance, but unless one is an "ace" he is not allowed to cross the lines alone. My chance of course is the venturesome photographic who tries to sneak across the lines unnoticed. I told you about attacking two, but not, or probably not, succeeding in shooting either one down. This morning I had a lone photographic all picked out, but my plane simply could not climb up to anywhere near his level. He must have been between six and seven thousand meters up! Then I carefully maneuvered into the sun over another plane which looked Boche-y and a steep dive brought me right upon him in a few seconds all in position to fire, and unseen. But it turned out to be a French Spad of a smaller size than ours. He had not seen me approach, and noticed me only when I was right on his tail. He was so surprised that he did about three turns of *vrille* before collecting his wits enough to recognize my plane!

Your loving,
Ham"

With the continuing Allied advances, it became more important to blind the eyes of the enemy, particularly through the destruction of their observation balloons. With this in mind, the pursuit squadrons were given this responsibility. As mentioned before, balloon busting was not an easy task, but there were those pilots like Frank Luke of the 27th Aero Squadron who became pros at the job. The 94th mounted two balloon straffing patrols on September 26, the first departing at 5h 10 with a heavy mist on the ground. Coolidge reported that due to the heavy mist it was impossible to locate the balloons in their nests, nor were any in ascension. They did encounter heavy ground machine gun fire after which he descended to tree top height locating a German wagon train going south. He straffed it on four passes, firing some 200 rounds and causing a great confusion and probably casualties. Rickenbacker departed 10 minutes later and upon returning filed the following report of his actions:

> "Left ground at 5h 20 o'clock. Arrived at the enemy balloons in our sector at about 12 minutes of six, was unable to locate either one, so I flew east about five kilometers in their lines. Noticed one balloon go down in the region of Damvillers at approximately seven minutes of six o'clock. This balloon I found later was shot down by Lieut. Vasconcelles of the 27th Aero Squadron. At the same time I noticed what I thought to be another balloon go down in the region of Montfauçon. Continued to fly in the region of Damvillers, when I met up with a Fokker at 1500 meters, at who I fired about 100 rounds and noticed him go down apparently out of control. During the combat my propellor was shot up badly, forcing me to retire and land on the auxiliary field at Verdun. Was just about to land when I noticed a large flare in the region of Stain but was unable to state what it was. After changing propellor's and refilling, I returned to the lines. Flew up to the Argonne Wood, back over the Fresnes and only noticed one enemy balloon and that was to the south of the Lachaussee. Confirmation Requested on Fokker Plane."

The confirmation came from G.O. 10, September 27, 1918, stating "Destruction in combat, of an enemy Fokker, in the region of Damvillers, 1500 meters September 26, 1918, at 5:55 – 6;00 o'clock." Over Nantillois Reed Chambers attacked a balloon on three different passes noting during the first pass that the observer jumped and the balloon started down. During the action he fired about 300 rounds and actually saw them going through the balloon. At the time it was so dark he could not clearly see through his sights and the balloon was pulled down below the mist. He circled for thirty minutes, but there were no further ascensions during that time. He requested a confirmation which was not made. Willie Palmer attacked the balloon near Cuisy at 7h 15 firing about 250 rounds. He stated it did not burst into flames, but was drawn down immediately. He, too, requested a confirmation which was not made. Lt. Sparks shot about 100 rounds into a balloon in the region of Gercourt encountering very little ground fire, but proceeded in causing the balloon to be pulled down.

At 16h 15 Rickenbacker went on another solitary patrol out to the lines where he saw American anti-aircraft bursting very low near Malancourt. He dove to 800 meters where he saw three Fokkers at about 200 meters making for the Allied balloons. On seeing him, they reversed direction toward their own lines. The 50 rounds he fired at long range had no effect on the Fokkers, the action taking place at 16h 40. Lt. Weir Cook went out on a 16h 30 balloon straffing patrol and eighteen minutes later he flamed one in the region of Grand-Ham at an altitude of 75 meters. He requested and received confirmation of its destruction for his first official aerial victory. The last patrol out for balloon work consisted of Lts. Sherry, the patrol leader, followed by Kaye, Crocker and Alan Nutt who had joined the 94th ten days earlier. This patrol was to meet up with two Spads from the 27th Aero Squadron, which six minutes after the ordered take-off failed to materialize. Sherry then led the patrol toward Verdun with Lt. Crocker soon dropping out due to motor trouble. Nutt and Sherry passed over the town of Forges headed for Dun when they were jumped by eight Fokkers, five of whom drove Sherry to the ground between Brabant and Forges, with a bullet riddled engine. Lt. Nutt fought the other three, bringing one down in flames before he was brought down and killed near Drillancourt.

Leutnant Franz Büchner of Jasta 13 was credited with his 34th victory over a Spad, serial #4505, which was Nutt's airplane, on September 26 near Charpentry. His total score was to be forty, seventeen of which were scored in the month of September alone.

Thorne Taylor flew an interesting mission on September 27 when he dropped a carton of cigarettes to a group of American Infantrymen near Gercourt near where 94th Aero Squadron plane Number 4 had crashed. Number 4 was Nutt's Spad 4505. While he was performing this drop, five Spads drove an enemy biplace down directly over him. Taylor pulled up over him and then dove down and under him, both guns jamming after only 30 rounds. Taylor was sure he had hit the two-seater, but not well enough as the observer continued shooting wildly in all directions. This occurred around 5:00 in the afternoon. Lt. Eugene Scroggie was in the air at the same time and ran into an enemy formation at an altitude of 700 – 750 meters, coming from the east. Scroggie was high man over the other two in his group, so he swung around and shot at the leading German plane while he was occupied diving on the second man of the 94th flight. This attack was followed by two more enemy planes with two more behind them. Scroggie's guns jammed after 10-12 rounds which caused him to break away. After clearing the jams he turned back on the last German. He was only able to get away two or three shots as his guns jammed again. He then pulled off to the southwest seeing one German plane fall out of control. He lingered for a short while watching what he thought to be another Fokker fall out of control. With jammed guns he withdrew as an E.A. headed his way. He requested and received a confirmation for one enemy Fokker, 600 meters, in the region of Montfauçon for his first official victory.

Balloon straffing and low patrols were the duty on September 28 with 40 sorties being flown, five patrols and five combats. The squadron received three new Spads this day to cover recent losses, due both to enemy action, as well as accidents.

Early in the morning at 5h 20, Rickenbacker flew up to the region of Sivry-sur-Meuse in search of a balloon in ascension. He flew up the Meuse River to Milly, about 8 kilometers. From there on the west side he crossed and turned down the main road on the east side of the river at an altitude of about 200 to 300 meters. As he flew along the road he noticed a balloon at about 100 meters high being hauled down the road by truck to be put into a new position between Vilosnes-sur-Meuse and Sivry-sur-Meuse. He fired 100 rounds at close range and saw it erupt into flames, the time being between 6h 00 and 6h 05. He was fired on and hit by a machine gun on the ground which struck the main strut in the tail section. The sound of the hit was so loud that he landed at the advance field at Verdun to inspect the damage. He found the damage to be slight, refueled and continued back to the 94th's field at Rembercourt. He requested and received confirmation of the kill, making it victory number 12. While Rickenbacker was up at Sivry-sur-Meuse, Weir Cook was in the region of Clery-le-Petit and Clery-le-Grand where he was attacking another balloon. He made a half circle around the one at Clery-le-Grand which was up at 50 meters, approaching it from the side firing 25 rounds as he piqued over it. These shots missed and he turned coming at the balloon from its end flying just off the ground firing another 150 rounds which this time caused it to burst into flames at about 6h 00. As he was leaving the scene, he saw another in flames near Bantheville with a Spad departing the area. This well could have been Rickenbacker's victim. Cook requested and received confirmation for his second victory.

Reed Chambers, flying a low patrol, had a running fight with a two-seater L.V.G. in which he chased the enemy to the ground and 5 kilometers into Germany. He fired some 200 rounds from fairly long range, but as they were close to the ground, he could not get a good position on him. The L.V.G. fired a good many rounds at Chambers without results and did not return to the Allied side of the lines.

Ham Coolidge, as ever the good correspondent, wrote a long letter home on Sunday, September 29, telling about his activity earlier in the week:

"Sunday, Sept. 29, 1918

Dear Lu,

Last Wednesday night our program for the next morning was announced. Our squadron would take off at 5:15 A.M. (by flares), proceed to the lines, and, precisely, at 5:45 attack simultaneously the enemy observation balloons in a certain sector. Those down in flames, we might finish out the patrol protecting our own balloons or doing such work as might demand attention. Now, Lu, you'll understand why I tell everything hereafter in the first person. It is because of the darkness at that hour which made concerted action impossible. We couldn't even see the planes when we started. Also you are alone in a *chasse* machine even though you generally operate in groups.

At eleven o'clock P.M. the barrage started – a barrage that few of us will ever forget – surely it was one of the heaviest in the history of the war. You can imagine the effect on one's dreams! We did manage to sleep though, until the orderly woke us all sharp at four. We tucked away a good hot breakfast amid the time honored remarks about "better make a meal of it, because it will probably be our last" and that sort of junk. At 5:05 we were sitting in our Spads, all groomed up for the occasion, with our motors warming up lazily. It was pitch dark save for the row of searchlights which illuminated the take-off. One by one we taxied down to the path of light and took off into the blackness beyond. I had a hideous second just as I left the ground, when I missed a collision by inches. That was soon forgotten in the anticipation of our work. Once above the field I looked around. The mist hung heavily below particularly in the valleys. For just a brief second "Is it worthwhile to go on; I won't be able to see a thing and besides," then a loud "Hell, let's go!" came from somewhere else within, and off we went for the lines. In spite of the mist there wasn't a shadow of doubt in which general direction to sail. In about five minutes I had reached the barrage and vainly sought Verdun, which was shrouded in mist below. My mind just swam with the enormity of what went on.

As far as I could see to the west and southeast thousands of flashes glared out of the mist below in alternate glows and twinkles. It seemed almost a colossal band of flame about a kilometer wide. I circled round to get my bearings before passing through that magnificent extended eruption of thousands of volcanoes. The river was unmistakable because of the barrage. With this dope well digested, I took a big breath and plunged in. An airplane motor makes a roar, but it was as nothing compared to the boom of the guns immediately below. My little ship rocked and shivered in the blast, and at times I could actually see shells fly by. A faint, sudden streak or thread of pink against the darkness was all I could see but I knew it must be a shell passing. I marveled that in such a rain of flying shells a plane could escape being hit; only one man in all of our aviation did get hit by our own shells that day. Now I knew that our balloon positions must lie beyond where those shells were landing. Below I could see a dark stretch of ground, while ahead the flashed appeared again. No Man's Land was quickly passed and I was over their lines. The flashes were clearer and the air was full of strange manifestations entirely new to me. Several green flaming balls would slowly ascend in one place, while red or blue rockets glowed at another. Then funny whistling masses of flame would glow out. I kept on but could make out almost nothing distinct which would guide me.

The East was just beginning to light up a little and I saw a patch of woods where I knew one of their balloons ought to be. I circled round behind them and came down fairly low to look. Nothing was there in the shape of a sausage balloon. All right, let's look for the next one. But no, not so easy. The Boches had been willing to let me come over their wood, but they didn't want to let me go back. Suddenly a line of green dots whizzed up in front of me. Then another and still more. They looked like streams of scintillating ghostly fire and waved gracefully back and forth in a semicircle ahead as does the water from a battery of powerful fire hose. Obviously I would have to pass through that impressive pyrotechnic display. They were using all incendiary bullets in their old machine guns. Most of the streams seemed to issue from one spot in the woods, so I thought I would at least show them I had some fireworks on my ship too. I pointed her nose straight at the spot and let drive a stream of incendiaries from my balloon gun. Instantly their old barrage stopped and I lost no time in beating it! Looking back I saw them again but they all went behind me.

After looking all around I simply could not find a single Boche balloon. It was getting lighter now and I could just begin to distinguish towns and roads and forests below. As long as I was over there anyway, I decided to have my money's worth out of the occasion. I could see occasionally dark objects sail by me and sometimes with streams of fire shooting out ahead and down. They were my friends. I dropped down very low to look around, and immediately noticed a long line of dark objects on the road below. It was a *supply train.* I thought it must be Boche, but wouldn't it be hideous to shoot up an Allied train? How my old heart just hammered with excitement as I dove down beside that road, not fifty feet high, and recognized those Boche helmets! In a twinkling I was past them, gained a little height to turn in safety, and came diving down upon them from the rear. I just held both triggers down hard while the fiery bullets flew streaming out of the two guns. Little glimpses were all I could catch before I was by. Another turn and down the line again. I had a vague confused picture of streaming fire, of rearing horses, falling men, running men, general mess. Turn again and back upon them. This time I clearly saw two men shot off the seat of a wagon, then more awful mess. A fourth time I turned and came back. One gun stuck but the incendiaries still blazed on. Horses rearing on fallen men; wagons crosswise in the road; men again dashing for the gutter. I craned my neck to see more and to be sure not to run into trees or houses beyond. Suddenly a ra-ta-ta-ta and a series of whacks like the crack of a whip broke loose. I knew only too well that the bullets were coming very close to crack that way! I *rocked* and swung and turned and the rattle died away behind. I found myself trembling with excitement and overawed at being a cold-blooded murderer, but a sense of keen satisfaction came too. It was only the sort of thing our poor doughboys have suffered so often.

It was now respectably light at last; light enough to see plainly the machines which swarmed the air. Now watch out for Huns – but none could I see. Spads, Breguets, Salmsons, Liberties, Letords – were recognized as I passed fairly close. Archie bursts now dotted the glowing skies in a vain endeavor to reach the Allied planes. I sailed back very low until I found our doughboys. In one place they were packed in solid ranks, in another I could see them dotted along the trenches, but it was impossible to see them out in the open. They take advantage of every bit of natural cover, are just the color of the ground, and our own speed is very great. I circled by close to a crowd and waved. Not a motion in return. They either thought I was Boche or were thinking hard of other things! Usually they are very responsive. We often chuck them cigarettes or newspapers which are always received with great enthusiasm! Honestly, those boys are wonderful. There is so much to tell about them that I can't do it! But in dull times I shall certainly tell you some of the remarkable stories which I know are true. In one place that morning our doughboys came on a stove with breakfast cooking. They replenished the fire and eagerly devoured the hot Boche food which they said wasn't half bad! A queer sort of compressed malt bread effect and some hot soup.

As I passed our front lines, our balloons loomed up, great gawky sausages, with the first gleams of the sun reflected on their wet sides. They were so close together I didn't dare pass beneath for fear of hitting an unseen cable. It did my heart good to realize that in each of those uncouth craft sat one or two observers regulating our barrage fire and watching the movements of the troops. The homeward trip through our barrage was as stormy as the first, but it was quickly over. All the way home formations of planes kept passing me on the way out. I felt as if we had just won a Yale game! At last it really looks as if we had the supremacy of the air – a statement which we certainly could not make on the Château Thierry front.

Since that memorable morning we have been constantly busy. Many of our crowd have Boche planes and balloons to their credit. I seem to have no luck at all that way. Every time I miss a patrol because of motor trouble the crowd seem to meet Boches, and if I make a dozen successive patrols nothing at all turns up. A man is judged by the results he shows, not by intentions in the game. My score stands pretty painfully low, and it gives me a pain. I do feel though, that my turn will surely come if I stick to it.

Jove, it's fun to sit round and listen to the stories which the pilots tell at mess time; men who landed in No Man's Land; others just behind the lines, and one who landed in German territory was captured by the Boches only to be retaken an hour later by the advancing Yanks! It's almost like a strange and thrilling dream.

Lu, for goodness' sake be a sport and don't talk about the junk I write in these letters. Just as you say, there are a few thousand other men in the air service all doing the same thing, but a man's family is rather apt to lose sight of that fact!

Good bye, you old sport, with loads of love to Dickie and the kiddoes – Ham."

A low patrol of thirteen Spads went out mid-afternoon of September 29 from which Kaye and Chambers got into a heated scrap with six Fokkers. Chambers reported:

> "Arrived over Epinonville at 16h 30 at 600 meters and saw the other Spad formations. We spread out over the sector and about 15 minutes later I saw a formation of six (6) Fokkers coming out of Germany at about 1500 m. There were several formations of Spads above them and I expected the Spads to attack, but they did not. I started climbing and met Lieut. Kaye. Together we got under the Hun formation which at that time were within our lines. We got within about 500 meters of them and opened fire. They evidently thought they were being attacked from above as they all started doing acrobatics and one went into a vrille and zig-zagged thru the mist (abut 600 meters) out of control. He was apparently hit. The rest dove for their lines and also went under the mist about two (2) kilometers further into their lines. Confirmation Requested."

The confirmation was forthcoming and Chambers and Kaye shared the victory, the first for Kaye and the second for Chambers.

A morning and afternoon patrol ended the Squadron's activity for September, both flown at an altitude of 200 to 450 meters. Each encountered shrapnel, shells, and machine gun bullets for their troubles, and saw no enemy aircraft, but due to the large amount of machine gun fire encountered between Sommerance and Gesne, it was assumed that a large body of Germans was in that area.

The Squadron monthly report for September showed 429 sorties flown, 32 combats fought, 3 special missions, 6 attacks on enemy balloons, 4 E.A. confirmed, 17 E.A. unconfirmed, 1 killed in action – Lt. Nutt; 1 injured in an accident – Lt. Samson; 4 crashes, 8 protection patrols, 36 test flights, 58 patrols along the lines, 2 alerts, for a grand total of 294 hours and 14 minutes of flying time.

---

[1] Squam – Squam Lake, New Hampshire, a summer colony for families from Boston, New York and Philadelphia. Coolidge's father, Joseph Randolph Coolidge, II, was a Boston architect who had a home on Squam Lake. He designed homes for families who summered there and nearby.

Dudley "Red" Outcault on the left, joined the 94th in September 1918.

Eddie Rickenbacker and his flight crew who did a masterful job of keeping this Spad in the air from July 7, 1918 to March 1919.

After an attack by a German fighter, the observer of this balloon has taken to his parachute and was photographed making a safe descent. *U. S. National Archives, RG 111, SC 24874.*

8

October - The Heaviest Fighting

The month of October was to be the most active period for the 94th during its entire time at the front. The Allied armies on the ground and in the air were on the offense. The Germans, therefore, were throwing everything they had into the air battle in an effort to slow the offense and attempt to protect their balloons that were supplying them with intelligence of the utmost importance. They, the Germans, were flying in larger numbers and were keeping close to their own lines, their mission being one of a defensive rather than offensive nature. Balloon attacks by the 94th became more dangerous as the importance of German balloon intelligence became greater and their defense was made even stiffer. Orders were given the 94th which directed them to flying low level patrols not to exceed 2000 feet and usually much lower along the lines.

October 1st was a clear day in which a five plane low patrol led by Ham Coolidge flew along the lines with no results other than that both Lts. Cook and Coolidge encountered motor trouble which left Lts. Palmer, Eastman and Hopkins to complete the job. Two hours later Lt. Reed Chambers led a "Concentrated Patrol" of fourteen planes up to Cierges and then eastward to circle at an altitude of 600 meters. Chambers reported that the formation stayed at about 600 meters over Montfauçon, which was north and west of Verdun, for "quite some time." They sighted eight Fokkers about 400 meters higher than they were and rose to meet them. Chambers got on the tail of one, firing 150 rounds at 200 meters. The enemy maneuvered and escaped; Chambers returned to his patrol. A great many enemy aircraft were seen in the area, but most of the time they were observed they were on the defensive staying over their balloons. Rickenbacker went out at 18h 40 on a balloon straffing run up to Puxieux which was south of Mars-le-Tour where he located a balloon on the ground. He piqued on it firing 75 rounds which were enough. The balloon burst into an explosion of bright flames that looked to him like an ammunition dump going up; this was because the balloon was so close to the ground. Rickenbacker requested a confirmation which was received on October 8 for his thirteenth victory.

The following day, October 2, was an active one for the Squadron with twenty-two sorties being flown, four confirmed and one unconfirmed victories the result of 40 hours and 30 minutes of total service hours in the air. Sam Kaye and Weir Cook went out on an early volunteer high patrol at 6h 15 when they ran into four Fokkers flying east above Cierges. Both groups climbed to get a height advantage, but Cook was crippled by a bad motor leaving Kaye to climb alone. The Fokkers turned for home allowing Kaye to get off 100 rounds with no effect.

At about 10 AM, seven Spads took off on a low patrol led by Thorne Taylor. They were to fly the route of Brieulles to Apremont at 600 meters. Apremont was northwest of Verdun and near there they ran into two formations of six Fokkers flying at 3000 meters. The twelve Fokkers did not attack and as the visibility was very poor near the ground, they may not have seen Taylor's patrol. Two pilots, Lts. Hopkins and DeWitt, both panned before the patrol ended. The 2nd Pursuit Group had high patrols flying at the same time, possibly accounting for the lack of enemy aggressiveness, although Taylor reported a heavy artillery barrage in Argonne and to the west of the forest.

Rickenbacker on the first of two solo patrols reported poor weather north of Montfauçon located west and north of Verdun. In that area he had the chance to warm his guns as his combat report will attest:

"Met one Halberstadt north of Montfauçon at 17h 30. Fired about 100 rounds. No apparent results. About 17h 40 met 7 or 8 Fokkers at 1000 meters in the region of Vilosnes. Fired about 250 rounds when I noticed one (1) Fokker go down out of control. Was forced to leave for home on account of the enemy's advantage. Confirmation Requested."

This confirmation was forthcoming on October 14.

At about the same time, a patrol of eight with two leaders, Coolidge and Chambers, were to fly at 600 meters direct to Epinonville which lay slightly southwest of Montfauçon. From there Chambers flew east to the Meuse River to Vilosnes-sur-Meuse where the following action took place:

"Lieut. Chambers reports: When I first arrived at the lines there wasn't an enemy plane in sight. At about 17h 30 two (2) formations of Fokkers came over the lines, protecting a Halberstadt two-seater. When the Fokkers saw the Spads they got back over their lines. I couldn't get close to the Halberstadt but fired about fifty shots from long range and he went back into Germany. I saw several Fokkers attacking a Spad in the region of Vilosnes-sur-Meuse. I pulled up on one and got about 200 shots into him when the gas ran out of my small tank and the propellor stopped. I dove and the Fokker was on my tail. I caught the propellor and got out of the fight. When I left there was a general mixup taking place. Saw no planes go down. Confirmation Requested."

This confirmation was given on October 8, 1918, G. O. Number 14, par.10.

Unless there was an error in Chambers' combat report when he states, "I dove and *the* Fokker was on my tail," the word "the" is the confusing and questionable word. He does request confirmation, but of what, and was it for the Fokker he attacked which was one of those after the Spad? The confirmed plane, nonetheless, was a Fokker and made Chambers' third victory.

Ham Coolidge, the other patrol leader, was leading his group over Septsarges southwest of where Chambers was having his fight, and ran into five (5) Fokkers. Two from his patrol and several other Spads chased them back into Germany where they disappeared in the clouds, none being seen to fall. He wrote in his report:

"Encountered two (2) Halberstadts over Avocourt at about 17h 40. Attacked one alone at first, firing about 50 rounds when both guns stuck. Just before seeing Halberstadt biplace, Lieut. Garnsey, my companion, disappeared. After an exchange of shots for a few minutes, about eight (8) other Spads joined the combat. We drove him towards the south and just over Bois-de-Ville he caught fire and crashed in flames, into the woods. He fell about 18h 00 or slightly after."

Coolidge's missing companion, Ed Garnsey, filed a most interesting report which explains his disappearance and the rest of the story on the downed Halberstadt. While in the company of Coolidge, he developed motor problems and was returning from the lines when he saw two biplace Halberstadt's being shot at with black archie fire in the area of Malancourt which was near a heavily wooded region. Even though his engine was not 100%, he fired at the first Halberstadt until his gun jammed. The jams he was able to clear only in his left gun with which he got about five more bursts into the two-seater. At this point the enemy had been driven down to 50 meters near Bois-de-Ville. He then fired another burst of about ten rounds, and the tracers were seen entering the fuselage. There were two other Spads shooting at the time when the Halberstadt burst into flames and crashed in the woods. In his report he stated that he, "landed and found that the two Germans were taken prisoner by the Americans. I talked to the German pilot who told me that the machine was a Halberstadt. Confirmation Requested." From this report the site of Garnsey's landing spot is unclear. Did he land near the crash scene, or at a nearby airfield? G.O. Number 17, October 19, 1918, par. 17, credits First Lieutenants Hamilton Coolidge and E. G. Garnsey, 94th Aero Squadron and Second Lieutenants A. H. Jones and F. M. Simonds, 147th Aero Squadron with the destruction of an enemy Halberstadt in the region of Bois-de-Ville, at 50 meters on October 2, 1918, at 18:15 o'clock.

Later that day at 17:30, Chambers and Rickenbacker were credited with another Halberstadt which in reality was a Hannover, in the region of Montfauçon from a height of 600 meters. They also were given credit for a Fokker near Vilosnes at 17:40, brought down from 1000 meters. Rickenbacker's victory list now stood at fifteen; Chambers at four. The Hannover landed in Allied lines with little damage, was repaired and flown by the 94th until the end of the war.

Eight victories were confirmed on October 3 to six pilots. Weir Cook got two balloons; Ham Coolidge got two balloons, a Fokker, and shared with Rickenbacker and Ted Curtis of the 95th, an L.V.G; Rickenbacker, a Rumpler and the aforementioned L.V.G.; finally Lts. Sparks, Palmer and Taylor shared a Fokker.

Cook went out with Lt. Crocker at 5h 50 to balloon strafe in the region of Sivry-sur-Meuse to Grand Pré. At 6h 08, Cook sighted the balloon he was sent to find slightly west of Grand Pré and about one kilometer north of the Dire River. Sivry-sur-Meuse lay about 20 kilometers north up the Meuse fromVerdun, while Grand Pré was 30 kilometers to the west from there. The balloon was on the ground when Cook dove at it from the north side firing 50 rounds which did not hit. He dove again from the south, firing another 50 shots with no results. Finally, in exasperation, he dove on the end of the balloon firing 50 rounds and as he passed over it, he saw three small flames appear on the top of the bag which were soon joined in one large sheet of flame. The nest of the balloon was between two small hills causing Cook to have to make three passes through heavy anti-aircraft machine gun fire. American military authorities confirmed the destruction of two enemy balloons by Cook at Grand Pré on the ground, but gave the time in error as 16h 15, not 6h 08 as stated by Cook in his report.

The second patrol of the day of ten planes departed at 6h 10 led by Coolidge and Rickenbacker, which was a low patrol flying at 400 meters. At about 7h 25 they encountered eight Fokkers coming from the northwest over the Meuse River at 1000 meters. Sam Kaye reported that the patrol climbed to meet them at which point the Germans saw the Spads and disappeared into the clouds and as the patrol was close to the end of their flight, no pursuit was undertaken.

The afternoon mission was a combination protection-balloon strafing patrol led by Ham Coolidge with Rickenbacker in a solo role above the other eleven. The route was Dun-sur-Meuse, 40 kilometers northwest of Verdun, to Bantheville, 12 kilometers west, to Cunel a few kilometers south in a triangle. At 16h 42 the visibility was good to 1000 meters; the patrol was flying at 600 meters and Lt. Willie Palmer reported, "I attacked with Lts. Taylor and Sparks one Fokker who was on a Spad's tail. Shot 50 rounds into him and the bullets appeared to be entering the fuselage. He attempted to pull up but slipped off on a wing and went down out of control. He went down just north of Doulcon at 16h 42. I saw a balloon go down in flames at 16h 37. I also saw a Fokker go down a little north of Dun, with a Spad on his tail. The Fokker never did pull up but went to the ground nose on. This was about 16h 39. Confirmation requested." As the action became more intense, Lt. Snow reported that his formation consisting of Taylor, Sparks, Palmer and himself came out of the clouds over Clery and saw about seven Fokkers at the same time a Spad was going down on a Fokker's tail, with another Fokker on the Spad's tail. He fired about 100 rounds at the pursuing Fokker causing him to break off the chase on the Spad. He spied two Fokkers above him leaving the area. He then joined a formation of Spads which patrolled in the region of Montfauçon. He observed a machine go down in flames, burn brightly for a few seconds near Dannevoux, the time being 17h 07. This was the L.V.G. which was brought down by Rickenbacker, Coolidge and Ted Curtis of the 95th Aero Squadron. This shared victory was confirmed on October 8 by G.O. Number 14, par. 14.

Lt. Sparks who was flying with Taylor and Palmer reported his view of the action with the Fokker, stating "At 16h 42 I attacked a Fokker in the region north of Doulcon with Lieuts. Taylor and Palmer, firing about 100 rounds into him, some of which I saw enter the fuselage, after which the Fokker fired about 100 rounds at me, three of them hitting my plane. I turned and fired 125 shots at him. He turned and headed back into Germany. Balloon burst into flames at 16h 37, shot down by Lieut. Coolidge. Confirmation Requested." Thorne Taylor in his report confirms the balloon victory of Coolidge, plus a Fokker, also by Coolidge, shot down west of Dun-sur-Meuse at 16h 39. Rickenbacker he credits with a biplace at 16h 40 near Clery and another at 17h 07 west of Dannevoux.

Rickenbacker's combat report covers both victories:

> "Was alone ahead of our protection at 16h 37, saw balloon go down in flames. Attacked (1) one biplace Rumpler just over Clery-le-Essand at 16h 40. Fired about 100 rounds when he was seen to go down by Lieut. Crocker (94th). Returned to our lines, was patrolling same when I noticed two (2) L.V.G. planes in our lines. Attacked one, fired about 150 rounds when he went down in flames. Lieuts. Coolidge and Curtis (95th) also attacked the same plane and should share in the victory. This plane fell in flames just west of Dannevoux. Confirmations requested: 1 Rumpler and 1 L.V.G."

The final combat report of the day was filed by Ham Coolidge:

> "Attacked and brought down in flames one enemy balloon, in the region of Clery-le-Grand at 16h 37. Another balloon straffer ahead of me crossed the river to attack a balloon when about seven Fokkers dove on him. I dove steeply on the nearest Fokker, getting a heavy burst into him at close range at 16h 39. I saw him wobble and others said they saw him crash, but I had to turn as several Fokkers were on my tail shooting. The protection joined in at this moment. A general mixup for many minutes of fighting.

At 17h 06 I saw a German biplace with Lieuts. Rickenbacker and Curtis shooting at him from a fairly long range. I joined in by a steep dive from the side and together we got close up on his tail. Fired heavy bursts of incendiaries. He burst into flames and crashed to the ground just west of Dannevoux at 17h 07. Confirmation requested."

All three of Coolidge's victories were confirmed by American military authorities on October 8, 1918.

The only loss by the 94th on October 3 was 1st Lt. E. R. Scroggie who was wounded in the foot, shot down and captured while participating in the last patrol. Leutnant Hermann Becker of Jasta 12 was credited with shooting down a Spad for his nineteenth victory near Aincreville at 16h 30, which must have been Scroggie. Becker went on to gain four additional victories over Spads, the final when he and his squadron mates shot down five Spads in five minutes. The unfortunate 23rd victim of his and the Jasta's 150 kill was from the 22nd Aero Squadron. Germans reported losses which could match up with the 94th claims would be two-seater of Schsta 26b flown by Unteroffizier Ludwig Pflüger with Gefrieter August Thäder listed as gunner. The casualties occurred at Cierges which is within 10 kilometers of Dannevoux. FA 227 (A) lost Ltn. d. R. Friedrich Hummel, observer and Gefr. Otto Weissbach in the region of Grandleys which does not show up on the map of the area, but well could have been one of the loops in the Meuse River in the locale of Dannevoux.

On October 5, two more victories were scored by the 94th, one by John Jeffers in the region of Romagne, a Fokker and the other by Sam Kaye, also a Fokker in the Bantheville area. Ham Coolidge reported, as Flight Leader, the action in which Jeffers scored his first victory:

"At 15h 40 while patrolling over Romagne at 600 meters, ten (10) Fokkers dove on us and another stray Spad. The patrol consisted of Coolidge, Garnsey, Fowler, Snow, DeWitt and Jeffers. Our upper echelon of three was able to fight them on their level, but the lower two had a narrow escape to get out from under. No protection whatever was offered from above, although one formation of six Spads and another of three had been seen in the vicinity a minute or so before. Just after the combat, three German biplaces over Montfauçon at 3000 meters crossed the lines without molestation other than the usual archie fire. The ten Fokkers resumed formation and proceeded parallel to the lines high above us during the rest of the patrol."

From the tone of his report Coolidge seemed more than a little annoyed at the lack of assistance from the other Spad formations. Lts. Mather and Willard of the 147th Aero Squadron were patrolling the area at that time and reported seven Spads and ten Fokkers in a fight over Romagne. Mather dove on one, but his guns jammed and Willard was attacked from the rear and withdrew. The 95th Aero Squadron had ten planes aloft at the time, one group of seven planes, one of three. The three plane voluntary patrol made up of Lts. Knowles, Gravat and Sewall were out dropping newspapers to the frontline troops did sight ten Fokkers north of Montfauçon, but did not engage; the other group of seven had "nothing to report." It would seem that there was a real lack of communication between squadrons as to the overall effort when patrolling a specific region. Headquarters 1st Pursuit Group was responsible for the coordination of the four squadrons of the group, the 27th, 94th, 95th, and 147th Aero Squadrons and in this instance did not accomplish the job particularly well.

As stated earlier, the day was not without successes. John Jeffers in his first confirmed victorious fight describes his part:

"We were at 600 meters when ten (10) Fokkers engaged in combat with several Allied planes at 2000 meters. The combat was taking place nearly over our heads and the only other Allied aircraft above us was a formation of nine (9) Spads, who paid no attention to combat.

I climbed with my patrol to 1500 meters, which was about the height of the center of combat. I encountered one Fokker and piqued on him. I fired about 100 rounds into him. He went down in a wiggling dive and continued in the same dive when I pulled off with both guns jammed. Confirmation Requested – 1 Fokker."

Lt. Sam Kaye scored his second victory and reported:

"Saw a combat between nine (9) E.A. (Fokkers), and some Spads over Cierges at about 16h 25, at 3000 meters. No results. This formation of E.A. went into Germany and later seven (7) more E.A. came into sight much lower and kept around Romagne at about 2000 meters. Three of these dived and shot at me from above, following me almost to Montfauçon. Here I turned and climbed at them opening fire, and shot about 150 rounds at one E.A. Saw tracers enter his fuselage, and he went down in a fast glide towards Germany. I think he landed or fell in the region of BANTHEVILLE, but I lost sight of him while locating the other two, which had gone back into their territory. These six played to the north of and above my patrol for some time afterwards. There was a formation of (7) or (8) Spads patrolling back of our balloons at about 2500 meters. Numerous combats took place higher up, but I could not see the results. At about 17h 10 two (2) Fokkers dived on a Salmson in the region of LANDRES; I piqued for the Fokkers. One pulled up and turned back. I shot at the other from a very long range and he left. The Salmsons returned O.K."

Kaye requested and received confirmation for one Fokker in G.O. Number 17, October 19, 1918. Par. 30.

Ham Coolidge found time on October 5 to write his mother a long letter describing his experiences since the launching of the Meuse – Argonne Offensive on September 26. In this letter he speaks the loss of his favorite Spad number 15034 which was condemned due to battle damage earlier in the week. His reference to "poor dear Spad" and comparing it to a "trusted horse" shows how attached the pilots would become to their aircraft after the long period of working out the "bugs" which usually came with a fresh from the factory airplane:

"[Rembercourt] Oct. 5, 1918

Blessed Mother,

This is the first instant I have had to write in for a long time. I wrote my usual Sunday letter to Lu this time because I hadn't written her for ages and she has written me constantly. In it I tried to describe a little my impression of the morning of Sept. 26 attack! We have been frightfully busy since then trying to do our utmost to help in the good work. Our group, the first pursuit group (four squadrons), has actually many more victories and fewer casualties than the whole first Wing composed of *three groups!* Which is a record we are all proud of.

I must write fast and briefly I am sorry to say, but I know you understand, Mammy. On October 2 I picked up a Halberstadt biplace fighter over the lines. My guns jammed after about fifty rounds, but I kept maneuvering with him to keep him occupied until help arrived. Help *did* arrive in the form of seven more of my companions! We cut the old boy off from his lines and started driving him home. We wanted to drive him back to our aerodrome, but he persisted in trying to escape, and one of the boys growing impatient, put a few incendiaries into him and brought him down in flames. All this was *way* back in our lines and I could look down on the roads as we passed over and could see autos stop and people gape open-mouthed as the Boche passed not fifty feet over their heads with eight Spads around, above, and behind him! Strange to say both pilot and observer were practically unhurt in spite of the flames, but naturally they were both taken prisoners immediately.

The next day, Oct. 3, was the most thrilling day of my life so far, and it came within a hair of being my last one. Two of us attacked enemy balloons ten kilometers behind their lines at 4:35 P.M. I hardly had time to think of Archie fire and streams of machine gun bullets that flew by as I dove on my balloon. I could see my incendiaries pour into the old gas bag, and the observer jump out in his parachute. A few seconds later the flames burst out and down it went. My companion, a boy from another squadron, was ahead of me and about to attack another balloon, when I suddenly saw a formation of seven Fokkers above. My heart stood still. He never saw them, Mammy; it was hideous. My shriek of "Look out Walter!" (Walter Avery, 95th Aero) never got beyond my mouth because of the roaring exhaust. In a second they were upon him. Just a glimpse of the poor boy in the midst of those devils was all I could catch before the whole mess went circling to the ground. When I reached the spot they were careening around like a flock of buzzards over a freshly killed prey. I was so mad I saw red, and dove upon the nearest of them. He didn't see, so I waited till I was close upon him, then just riddled him with bullets. At this very second I heard that awful whip cracking sound and saw the bullets were also flying by my head. I was completely surrounded, but my situation was so futile that I was strangely cool. I tried to keep head on to my attackers. In a few more seconds they would have had me in such an unequal combat, and I was wondering what sort of a funeral they would give me, when a Spad flashed down from the sky above, and another and another! The protection, six Spads, had arrived. I almost wept for joy – but suddenly realized that the fireworks weren't over yet. For fifteen minutes we milled together, rolling and tumbling – Spad, Fokker, Fokker, Spad – in the wildest, most confused whirling mass I ever hope to see. The air was just streaked in every direction with the smoke of the tracer bullets. We all have little photographic impressions of different moments in that fight. I remember looking back once only to see one Fokker on my tail and another from the side shooting streams of bullets at me. A second later it might be entirely different. Things happened too fast and changed too often to enable any of us to retain anything but a confused impression of that awful combat. Gradually we edged towards our lines and finally crossed them with the Fokkers in hot pursuit. They turned back together, however, when we finally did reach the lines. It is unhealthy for them to come over our side of the fence.

Once on our side we drew breath easily again and took count each within himself of the "score." One poor boy, a new pilot in our squadron, was missing and the poor balloon strafer ahead of me was gone. Our leader had got one biplace in flames, I had got a balloon and one of the other boys in the protecting patrol confirmed the fact that the Fokker I had attacked had crashed to the ground.

The day was not over yet, however. After the main bunch had gone home a few of us were still out on the lines. The Boches evidently thought we had *all* gone for they sent an observation plane sneaking over to do some quick reconnaissance work. Three of us spotted him almost simultaneously a few kilometers in our lines. We raced at him together and ten seconds later he was in flames. He sailed on a little, about two hundred feet above the ground, then tottered and crashed in a final burst of flames! We all three got credit for his destruction. If all my victories are officially confirmed I shall be an "ace" (5 victories), but *please* don't talk about it, as *official* victories are the only ones that really count and even then there are a few millions of other men in the war all doing just as hard and dangerous work, much of which is never known about or "noised abroad." It's much nicer just to sit tight and be humble and thankful to the Almighty for His great goodness; don't you think so? The feeling I have on looking back on three victories in an hour is not one of triumphant power. It is rather a feeling, stronger than ever, that we mortals are mere specks of dust in the wind, blown about at His pleasure, and I realize as never before, that it was due to no cleverness or bravado on my part that I scored these victories; it was simply His will that I should live through it, and mere chance brought me the successes.

My poor dear Spad No. 22 is so badly shot up that it will have to be replaced by a horrid new one. It's strange what affection you can develop for an inanimate object, but my old Spad stained with oil and smoke and even cold sweat from my brow was like a trusted horse to me. I have cut off from its side our squadron insignia "Uncle Sam's Hat in the Ring" and the No. 22 just as it was, all dirty and weather beaten, as a revered souvenir of a plane which performed steadily and faithfully for a long time unrewarded, and finally came to a glorious end on the day of victory! I am also sending several pieces of its wing-covering, pierced by Boche bullets, and some of them with remarks written on them. Do keep them carefully, because they will always be interesting to look back upon....

I simply am swamped these days and am utterly unable to write letters. It is a question of just sticking on the job till the nerves go bad or the bad weather brings a needed rest. The work is so thrilling that it is actually sustaining and tiring at the same time!

I got a sudden shock at lunch the other day, and for a minute couldn't think why Then it suddenly dawned on me that I was eating soup from a little bowl with ears just like ours at home, *except* that it had horrid polka dots instead of the yellow chickens and the lucky one with the house!

Your lovingest
Ham."

Protection patrols and balloon straffing continued on October 6 with Ham Coolidge exploding a balloon at 10h 59 in the vicinity of St. Juvin near Grand Pré which was confirmed on October 8 by American military authorities. It would appear that Coolidge's new Spad, number 7743, was not a total "horrid new one" as he had predicted in his letter of the previous day.

One high patrol and two low patrols were flown on October 9, with John Jeffers reporting some action near St. Mihiel. He was a member of the high patrol which was flying the route Rembercourt, Watronville to St. Mihiel which was unusual as the action was all taking place up along the upper Meuse and the Argonne. The patrol consisted of Lt. Thorne Taylor as leader and Lts. Joe Eastman, Ham Coolidge, John Jeffers and Weir Cook. Jeffers reported:

> "On patrol at 5000 meters I noticed French archies at 2500 meters, near St. Mihiel. I dropped down to 2500 meters in pursuit of a plane, when I discovered another plane 250 meters directly below me. I piqued vertically on him and shot two long bursts. He piqued vertically. The other biplace maneuvered around to assist the E.A. I was attacking and left when I pulled up from this plane, and kept straight into Germany. When I turned back toward our lines he followed part way. The encounter took place near a German balloon which was hauled to the ground at a promontory near Buxieres."

This location was some 20 kilometers northeast of St. Mihiel.

The low patrols accomplished little due to poor weather, losing Reed Chambers who had to panne near the Foret de Hesse and Lt. Crocker went down with motor trouble.

At this time the Germans were aggressively attacking the Allied balloons for the same reasons that we were attacking theirs, causing a new dimension to duties of the patrols of the 94th. Chalmers, Palmer and DeWitt were on such a patrol on October 8, Chambers reporting:

> "Altitude 600 meters. Time 17h 45. Meuse to Charny. On arriving at lines, saw 5 E.A. Got in the sun on them but they went out of sight in Germany. The flaming onions were going up east of the Meuse and went towards them. A Spad patrol was coming west, and behind them two Fokkers. They were out to get our balloon just west of the Meuse River. The enemy archies would signal them (about the approach of Allied planes) and they would go back into Germany. They did this three times and I stayed close to the balloon. The last time they started an attack on the balloon they saw us and left."

The use of archie fire both by the Germans and the Allies was an effective alarm and spotting system to alert planes in the air of other aerial activity. Allied bursts were white while the Germans were black or in the chain-like flaming onion pattern.

On a daily basis Eddie Rickenbacker as Squadron Commander flew solo voluntary patrols, sometimes flying high cover for the low flying straffing assignments and often the reverse flying at 600 meters looking for balloons. On one such mission on the 9th of October between Dun and Murvaux, he reported this action:

> "Saw two (2) reglage machines on their side of the lines, I returned to Montfauçon until they disappeared, which was about 17h 25. Then started up the river (Meuse) at 17h 30. I went a few kilometers beyond Dun, returning, found the balloon on the edge of the woods, (between Dun and Murvaux) on the ground. Attacked it about 17h 52. I fired about 150 rounds when it caught fire, making quite a blaze. I then returned to the airdrome at 18h 05. Confirmation Requested – one (1) Balloon."

The confirmation for this claim came in S.O. Number 21, October 27, 1918. Par. 26. and again in S.O. Number 22, November 2, 1918. Par. 4.

On October 10 attacks on enemy balloons continued as well as protection and voluntary patrols giving more than satisfactory results. Action for the day began at 8h 45 with a low patrol led by Reed Chambers with Lts. Crocker, Coolidge, Smith, Norris, Collins and Sherry as company. They were flying between 400-600 meters when they spotted fifteen enemy aircraft in two formations, one of five and one of ten planes. These formations kept their distance taking no offensive moves at all. They were at 1000 meters just above an enemy balloon at Brandeville which they appeared to be protecting. Heavily outnumbered, Chambers decided that attacking at that point would not be prudent. Lt. Crocker was forced to leave the patrol with a bad motor, landing safely.

The scheduled protection patrol which followed consisted of eleven planes and departed at 14h 55 for the region of Doulcon. Lt. Willie Palmer, one of the members of the patrol, reported firing 100 rounds during his attack:

> "Followed Lt. Coolidge down on a Fokker which was after a Spad. Piqued vertically on him for about 600 meters, firing about 100 rounds into him. Saw tracers entering the wings and fuselage. He went down in a tight right hand spiral, apparently out of control. Time 15h 51. Region: North of Doulcon.
>
> Information Item: One E.A. seen to have gone down in flames east of Doulcon about 15h 50. Confirmation Requested – 1 Fokker."

Coolidge's report of the incident was:

> "Arrived at Doulcon exactly 15h 46 as pre-arranged. Five (5) Fokkers piqued at our rear man. Made two half-turns to face them, but they did not attack, and later turned off. Just then I noticed two (2) Fokkers below. Turned and dove sharply followed by Lt. Palmer. Opened fire at 50 meters. The other then got on my tail. I saw the first one wheel sharply on its side, but could not stay as I had the second on my tail. Lt. Palmer attacked just after I did.
>
> Information Item: A minute after above combat, I saw a man over Dun descending in a white parachute, but had seen no balloon. Confirmation Requested – 1 Fokker (with Lt. Palmer)."

The parachute seen could have been the pilot from one of the downed Fokkers as the Germans were equipping their flyers with parachutes at this time.

Coolidge and Palmer shared this victory, confirmed for their seventh and second victories respectively.

Occuring at about the same time Reed Chambers reports his combat:

"Our formation started into Germany in fine shape. Found no balloons. Was attacked by five (5) Fokkers from above. I fired about 100 shots into one from below at about 150 meters and I fell off in a vrille. On coming out I couldn't see him, and there were only three (3) Fokkers in sight. This was at 15h 48. Region, southeast of Doulcon.

Information Item: After I pulled out of above combat, I saw one plane falling with another behind, which may have been a Fokker. Both planes crashed in the region of the Bois de Sartelle. About two minutes later, a Fokker shot past me in flames and continued to burn after hitting the ground, in the region of Bois de Sartelle. About 16h 05 saw 30 Fokkers very high in three formations over the lines. Confirmation Requested: 1 Fokker."

This was confirmed on October 23, 1918 for Chambers fifth victory and his entry into the ranks of "Aces."

Rickenbacker, continuing his routine, was flying a voluntary mission over this patrol at about 1000 meters. He reported:

"Followed formation to Doulcon when five (5) Fokkers came down on the formation from the southeast. I piqued on one in the region of Clery le Petit and fired about 150 rounds at close range when I was forced to leave on account of the other Fokkers behind. Did not follow him down. This combat took place about 15h 52 at which time Lieut. Chambers claims a Fokker fell in flames. I then noticed a Spad below being chased by a Fokker. I piqued on him and fired about 100 rounds into him. When last seen he was in a steep bank. Confirmation Requested – Two (2) Fokkers."

Both of these victories were confirmed, one on October 23 and one on October 27, which brought Rickenbacker's score to twenty.

Poor visibility set in for the next two days, but late on October 13 Ham Coolidge was sent out alone on a balloon straffing mission in the region of Andevanne which was west of Dun. He reported:

"Attacked balloon north of Andevanne somewhere about 400 meters. It burst into flames at 16h 07. Started to attack Biplace Rumpler on way back, northeast of St. Juvin, but was pursued by eight (8) Fokkers all the way to the lines. Saw about five (5) Biplace Reglage Planes during the trip. Saw balloons also in region BOULT AUX BOIS at 600 meters and at MONTIGNY – DEVANT – SASSEY. The former was regulating; as heavy artillery fire was falling on ST. JUVIN and GRAND PRÉ. Average ceiling at lines was about 1000 meters. Our archie fire was excellent in directing me towards E.A. CONFIRMATION REQUESTED – ONE BALLOON."

This request was confirmed by: "Special Order Number 20, October 23, 1918. Par. 37. Captain HAMILTON COOLIDGE, 94th Aero Squadron, First Pursuit Group, is hereby credited with the destruction of an enemy balloon, in the region north of Andevanne, at 400 meters altitude on October 13, 1918, at 16:07 o'clock.

Earlier in the day, Coolidge wrote to his mother describing the fight of October 10 when he and Palmer got a Fokker and after the above balloon victory he wrote of it to his younger brother:

"Sunday, Oct. 13th, 1918

Dearest Mother:

This is the first Sunday in ages which has seemed like Sunday, and the reason is that a drizzle set in at an early hour this morning, so that when the second flight began the painful process of getting up to make a seven o'clock patrol, they soon discovered that it was unnecessary, and went back to bed for another snooze. Breakfast took place at an "easy nine" as on the best-regulated peace-time Sundays!

I wrote you a short mid-week letter just before we set out on a balloon raid. I might do well to continue where I left off, for the raid, like most of its predecessors, was somewhat eventful. It was a carefully planned affair. Three "strafers" would arrive over the enemy balloon position at a certain minute. Thirty seconds later three groups of about eight planes each would meet over the spot from different points of the compass to protect the strafers who should have just shot down their balloons. All worked out quite perfectly except that when we arrived on the scene not a single balloon was in sight. I was leading a protective formation this time, and, true to form, the Fokkers came piling down on us a few minutes later. A general "dog-fight" ensued. One of the best pilots in the group found himself face to face with a Fokker. Each opened fire simultaneously and each thought the other would be the one to turn at the last second, but neither did. They crashed head-on and dropped wingless to the ground. It was one of the few times when the Boche didn't yield in a tight place when he was working alone.[1] Another Boche went down in flames and another of our pilots also took the count. My duty was to get my formation home since we were ten kilometers in Heinie's territory where he naturally fought to a great advantage. Gradually we edged towards our lines while the Fokkers, one by one abandoned the fight. Soon we were well on our way to the lines with no Fokkers in pursuit, but suddenly below and behind us I saw a lone Spad with two of them hot "on his tail." I turned so quickly that only one man of our formation saw me. The rest continued on while we two circled around, then down, full motor, down on the Fokkers. I noticed that the lone Spad had made good his escape and that the Boches had throttled their motors and turned towards home. All this was at not more than a few thousand feet up. The great speed of the dive carried me quickly up on one of the Huns. I saw that he had not seen me, so I waited till I was only 50 meters away, then opened both guns at his cockpit. In a flash I was past him, but Willie P – (Palmer) behind me saw him careen over on his side and start rapidly down. Then he opened fire and added what finishing touches might have been necessary. The next thing I knew the Boche's companion was "on my tail" shooting madly. I realized that there were more Fokkers around and that I was still in Boche-land so I didn't stop to give battle, but headed for home, motor wide open, and squirming from side to side to give him as difficult a target as possible. Gradually he fell behind and once more I breathed easily, especially when I saw Willie pull up beside me unhurt likewise. One of our balloon observers is said to have seen the Hun crash, so we stand a good chance of getting confirmation.

This and one other confirmation are pending. If they come through I will have seven official – and at this second Tom Crocker comes bursting in with the news that the "Kaiser accepts everything," that he is sending a delegation to decide how he can retreat without getting beaten up in the process! What next, dear Mammy? This peace talk is awfully bad for a fighter, because when a man starts to get "careful" of himself, he stands the best chance of getting killed, or at least of not accomplishing results. So Hammy will forget about it and join those who take the attitude, "Yes, I'll begin to think about peace when the order comes through to stop fighting." All I say is that I pity the Boches when our soldiers cut loose in their territory. Mammy, the American doughboy is one of the hardest most relentless specimens in the war, and the Boches have a wholesome respect for them.

By some queer arrangement I have become a Captain! Here's the way it strikes me. I don't know any conceivable reason why I should have been made a Captain while our Commanding Officer, a man with eighteen official Boches (the leading American Ace) and admittedly one of the best C.O.'s on the front, remains a lieutenant. That puts me in an awkward position to say the least. Also I don't want any position higher than the one I now hold, that of a flight-commander, where I lead in person my little band of six or eight on their stunts. I'm afraid they will make me a squadron commander or something where I will have to *tell* my men to do things instead of being able to lead them personally. I *don't want* a position of "authority or responsibility" where one sits in a chair. If they will leave me alone a simple pilot and flight leader I won't mind being a captain – *voilà!*

From all over the barracks are coming remarks: "Are you all packed yet, John?" or "I'm glad I didn't buy that new uniform after all!" It seems so unbelievable and we all know how treacherous those fiends are, that nobody really takes things seriously though the news came in an *official* report.

Well, Mammy, if it *should* be true don't forget to tell dear old Anna to have my tuxedo pressed, my citizen clothes taken out of camphor, and the sewing machine removed from my room!

More anon – I'm thrilled, but dare not really expect anything.

Your loving
Ham."

"Sunday, Oct. 13, 1918

Dear Dickie,

Lu has been writing such good letters all summer, and from them I have gleaned an idea of your experiences in shipbuilding. I gotta hand it to you, that's all. They tell me, however, that you were marked as an aristocrat and hopeless "swell guy" when you inadvertently disclosed the fact that you frequented Mooney's (is that the right name?) – a restaurant which you described to Lu as comparing favorably with the Ayer Station lunch counter! It honestly must have been a mighty satisfactory experience. Do drop me a line some time or add a P.S. to one of Lu's letters.

Gosh, one doesn't know what to think these days with all this peace scare flying around; in fact they told me this afternoon that orders had been received in the trenches to stop firing. I was able emphatically to contradict that rumor this evening however.

I had counted on a peaceful Sunday at last as a steady drizzle had set in, but no peace for the wicked. At three o'clock they sent down word that someone was needed right away to go out and knock down an enemy balloon which was directly embarrassing artillery fire. I found the weather better over the lines and finally located my old sausage. A tricky approach put me in position and as I dove on it I inwardly speculated on whether I was putting more shots in the balloon than they were putting in my plane! From the flickering dots of incendiaries that cracked around me I decided the odds were well in their favor until suddenly a little glow appeared in the top of the balloon and a moment later it burst into flames and descended gracefully to earth. I was still in the air doing my prettiest twisting to evade the various forms of Boche fireworks they were sending up in my honor. On the way home I took a shot at a passing German biplane, but managed things so unskillfully that I found I was the goat (being square in the observer's arc of fire). Uttering a loud "wrong again," I swung hastily away from him only to see at a short distance away and coming straight in my direction a group of eight Fokkers. The Boches had evidently decided that the fireworks were not a fitting mark of recognition for the occasion so they had sent a convoy of their prettiest little planes to escort me home. The speed of a Spad has been a matter of some discussion Dickie, but all I say is that I wish the doubters might have seen me on my way home this evening. Honestly it was a funny sensation. After opening the motor wide and holding the head south I knew there was nothing more I could do, so I sat there turned half around in my seat watching those boys and wondering whether or not they could catch me. For a while they gained steadily, because their greater altitude gave them increased speed on the down slope, but after they once got on my level my old ship pulled gradually away from them, and I couldn't resist putting my thumb to my nose when they turned and swung back *chez eux*. The balloon was pretty far in and rather low down so our observers may not have seen it go down, in which case official confirmation will be lacking, but it's one's own satisfaction that counts anyway.

Must get some sleep Dickie, but best luck and loads of love to you.

Ham."

On October 15, Major Maxwell Kirby was assigned to the squadron to gain combat experience.

Poor weather curtailed flying activities for the next few days, but October 16 was a red letter day for the Engineering Division as they had 100% of the twenty-three available Spads ready for flight. With the well-known difficulties of keeping Spads in flying condition, this was a major accomplishment and a tribute to the ground crews. A mixed bag of weather conditions was experienced on October 18 allowing two low and one voluntary patrols to be flown. On the second low patrol at 15h 35, Lts. Cook, Kaye, Outcault, Garnsey and Sherry attacked a Halberstadt near Exermont. The five Spads fired over 350 rounds into the hapless two-seater which piqued and dove for Germany. Lt. Outcault noticing the enemy returning to his own lines, piqued on him firing about 100 rounds which caused the German pilot to reverse direction and head for the Allied lines behind which he landed and turned up on his nose. Lts. Cook, Kaye, and Sherry were given the credit for this victory.

On October 19 Lts. Chambers and Outcault in the first morning low patrol met up with an enemy two-seater, the action described by Chambers: "Saw a Hannover about two kilometers in the enemy lines north of Brieulles at about 9h 30 at 400 meters. We kept playing around waiting for him to cross over, but he did not. We made several circles into Germany, but each time he would keep out of range. At about 10h 00 we went in after him and I got about 150 shots at him from 150 meters without apparent results, except that he went toward the ground and flew back into Germany. The combat took place over Doulcon at about 300 meters at about 10h 00. We were fired upon by machine guns from the ground all the way back." No other action took place worthy of mention during the other patrols which were plagued with poor weather and motor troubles which caused Lts. Hopkins, Snow and Crocker to have forced landings.

No flying was done on Sunday, October 20, due to poor weather, although all aircraft were airworthy and twenty-six out of twenty-seven pilots were on hand. Ham Coolidge, taking a well-deserved leave to Paris, found time for a letter to his mother:

"Sanger Hall, Sunday, October 20, 1918

Dearest Mother,

This Sunday's letter comes not from the front but from a station near Paris where I am on a 3-day leave. I was awfully glad to get away for a few days of rest and a chance to buy some much-needed clothes and shoes. I intend to skip down to Romorantin to see the dear Normants, but the train service is hopelessly bad and the weather is of the same quality so I cannot accept the kind offer of a plane to fly down in.

This is a huge reception park for planes coming from the factories and going from here to various points on the front. I might explain that "Sanger Hall" is to outward appearances a tar-papered barrack but inside! You see Capt. Sanger was killed here in an accident, and his wife gave this building in his memory. She worked out the interior arrangements with Paris interior decorators and the result is wonderful. There are two large rooms with a big open fireplace at the end of each. One room has a piano, phonograph, magazine table, and comfortable sofas and chairs covered with a kind of burlap in alternate light and dark blue stripes. The other room is a combined library and writing room also equipped with sumptuous lounge chairs and sofa. The paneling is a light yellow, the curtains emerald green, and at each of the dark stained writing tables are large quill pens in brilliant greens, blues and reds. Green shaded reading lamps at each table and large yellow shades are on the lamps of the center table. The floors are carpeted and all the fittings, such as desk pads, ink stands, lamp brackets, paper holders, are of the same kind you find in the Somerset Club. The whole is harmonious (even though my description might not convey that impression) and in good taste. It seems to strike a medium between the ordinary camp rest room and a rather swagger club.

I have run into many old friends, both pilots and men in the Paris office. They treat one *very* well, in fact Maj. – who just brought me out here in his car explained that hereafter pilots who had made a good record on the front might ask for about any kind of plane they wanted. Naturally we have strong preferences for a Spad equipped with certain kinds of motors, but in the ordinary distribution it's pure luck what you get. Also they will equip such a plane with any instruments or equipment the pilot may desire. I didn't have the nerve to ask whether he considered me eligible for this "special' arrangement, but that will probably take care of itself. I certainly should like to be able to say, "I want a K— Spad with a B— motor in it; two V— guns instead of the regular M— guns, a C— compass instead of the ordinary one, a B—carburetor with so many jets of such and such a size, etc."[2]

The day before I left we had another combat. I was leading our formation when I suddenly discovered we had "cut off" a lone German biplace from his lines. I started to attack him but both my guns jammed after a single shot from each. The other boys, however, made short work of the Boche. We followed him right down to the ground for he lit in our lines. Neither pilot nor observer seemed to be injured in the crash, but I won't guarantee that our doughboys didn't eat them alive!

This rest is wonderful. It is such a change to be able to step over to the A.R.C. canteen for hot drinks at tea time, then, once more at Paris, to sleep in a comfortable bed and bathe in hot water in a real tub!

Bestest love, dear Mother, and all the crowd,

Your loving,
H."

The early morning of October 21 came with poor visibility. Lt. Cook on an early balloon straffing mission reported even at 150 to 200 meters conditions were poor. The weather improved as the day progressed with five additional patrols being mounted with no results. The *Daily Squadron Report* noted that Lt. Rickenbacker conducted an "Exhibition Flight" in the afternoon. This may well have been a flight made in the Halberstadt captured on October 18.

In continued poor visibility on October 22, Lts. Cook and Crocker departed at 5h 25 for a balloon straffing mission up to Dun and Argonne. Lt. Crocker filed the following report:

> "I was flying at an altitude of 1000 meters, 5h 55 in the region of Tailly I noticed a brilliant flare which appeared to be a balloon in flames at about 200 meters from the ground. A few minutes later I saw a Spad returning from that vicinity headed for Verdun. Noticed a large fire west of Doulcon. At approximately 6h 05 I saw a balloon set on fire in the vicinity of Boult-aux-Bois, and the machine that apparently attacked it headed due west over the Argonne."

Weir Cook's report clears up who was flying the mystery Spad seen heading for Verdun:

> "Attacked one (1) balloon north-west of Dun-sur-Meuse in the region of Tailly at about 5h 54. Made two dives at the balloon, firing two bursts. The bullets of the second burst penetrated the bag, but just before I pulled away both guns jammed and account of the fire from the ground I did not wait to see if my shots had set fire to the balloon. Visibility was poor. Noticed large fire west of Dun-sur-Meuse."

Special Order Number 21, par. 21, "First Lieutenant H. Weir Cook, 94th Aero Squadron, First Pursuit Group, is hereby credited with the destruction of an enemy Balloon, in the region of Tailly, northwest of Dun-sur-Meuse, at 200 to 300 meters altitude, October 22nd, 1918, at 5:55 o'clock."

As the day progressed, two more low patrols and one voluntary patrol by Rickenbacker were flown without results. At 15h 00, a seven plane "Concentrated Patrol" was flown to Cunel – Beaumont – Champneuville at 600 meters which was to produce both good as well as sad results. The patrol had been in the air for 45 minutes when the action began. Lt. Jeffers' report gives some of the details:

> "On patrol over Brieulles we were attacked by three Fokkers who came from a formation of six. I piqued on one of the Fokkers at 600 meters and fired about 100 rounds into him at 75 and 40 meters. He went straight down in a half spin and at 300 meters another Spad started firing at him from the opposite direction. This forced me to pull up to keep from crashing with the Spad. At 250 meters the Fokker was still in a nosedive. The combat occurred almost directly over Brieulles at 15h 45. CONFIRMATION REQUESTED – One (1) Fokker."

Sam Kaye, one of the seven on patrol, reported:

> "While flying over Brieulles at 600 meters, six (6) Fokkers dived on our formation from about 2000 meters, leaving six more Fokkers at that altitude. I wiggled my wings and tried to signal that they were coming. Three E.A. opened fire on our formation and I turned and shot about 75 rounds at one of them. In the meantime I saw a Fokker go down apparently out of control. This was the one Lieut. Jeffers was shooting at. Information Item: Enemy aircraft were aggressive this afternoon, especially in attempting to cut off Allied planes returning to our lines."

Lt. John Jeffers received credit for the Fokker in S.O. Number 21, par. 22, for his second victory.

Lt. Raymond J. Saunders, who had joined the squadron on September 26, had been out on an earlier patrol on which he experienced motor trouble returning to the field for another plane and resuming that patrol. He later was part of the seven-man "Concentrated Patrol" and failed to return. Saunders, flying Spad number 7708 which had been delivered to the Squadron on October 3, fell victim to Ltn. Georg von Hantlemann of Jasta 15, for his 23rd victory. Von Hantlemann shot Saunders down at 17h 00 German time in the fight over Brieulles.

The final mission of the day was a voluntary one flown by Rickenbacker and Chambers up the Meuse River from Sivry to Liny to Cléry to Dun-sur-Meuse. Rickenbacker reported his part of the action:

> "Went up the east side of the Meuse River at 1200 meter. I noticed a Fokker pique on a Breguet, and I piqued on the Fokker, firing about 100 rounds into him at close range. This was in the region halfway between Cléry le Petit and Dun-sur-Meuse at about 15h 55. When I last saw him he was going down out of control at about 700 meters. Lt. Kaye reports seeing a plane go down in flames from about 400 meters at 15h 55 in the region of Liny. (Liny is close to Dun-sur-Meuse.)
>
> At about 16h 00 I noticed another Fokker pique on a Salmson. I fired 50 rounds at long range. When last seen he was piquing into Germany. Lieut. Chambers also fired at this same Fokker and the E.A. did not regain his formation. CONFIRMATION REQUESTED – One (1) Fokker."

While Rickenbacker was flying the east side of the Meuse, Chambers was on the west flying parallel to him. Reed reported:

> "I had one combat with a Fokker over Cunel (some few kilometers west of the Meuse) at 16h 02. He was piquing on a Salmson observation plane. I fired about 75 rounds and he went down in a spiral and then into a dive and pulled into Germany. I did not see him crash. At 16h 30 in the region of Bois-de-la-Côte Laimont, I saw five Fokkers diving, and went down on the last man firing about 150 rounds into him from close range, and he went down. Confirmation Requested – 1 Fokker. I then pulled away with the other four shooting at me. When they turned away I turned on them and emptied both guns into them. They were straffing our troops on the ground. I could see one crash into their lines. Confirmation requested – 1 Fokker. This fight took place south of Vilosnes-sur-Meuse over the Bois-de-la-Côte Laimont. Time 16h 30 – 16h 32. Alt. 300. CONFIRMATION REQUESTED – 2 (two) Fokkers."

G.O. Number 21, October 27, 1918, Par. 23, confirmed Rickenbacker's Fokker for his 21st and G.O. Number 22, November 2, 1918, Par. 9 confirmed Chambers' two Fokkers for his sixth and seventh victories.

Ham Coolidge in an October 22 letter to his father gives some insight into Rickenbacker's leadership qualities and also comments on the strange fact that his promotion from a 1st Lieutenant's rank to that of Captain or Major, which were ranks given to other much less deserving officers commanding U. S. Aero Squadrons, was so slow forthcoming. In his other letter to "Ollie", he makes mention of the night fighter, or pursuit planes, who at that time were total novices to flight and combat in the dark:

"Oct. 22, 1918

Dearest P.A.,

I am just back from a three days' leave quite profitably spent in Paris (buying clothes, shoes, etc., for the winter) and in Romorantin where I had the great pleasure of spending a night at the Normants where Q. and I used to spend such happy week-ends in days gone by....

Returning to my squadron this morning I was delighted to find that my C. O. (the leading American Ace, 19 official Boches) had at last been awarded the D.S.C. with four oak leaves in partial recognition of his work, although they have not yet condescended to give him his well-earned captaincy or majority. He is a remarkable C. O., accompanying his pilots on every mission of importance or danger, and his pilots are therefore willing workers.

This afternoon a disagreeable experience robbed me of what I feel quite sure would have been another victory. During my absence my plane had received harsh treatment at the hands of a rather clumsy friend who damaged it in landing. The mechanics assured me that the injured parts had been replaced with new ones. Foolishly taking their word for it I went out on patrol. We soon located a German two-seater and maneuvered unseen into a very favorable position, I dove to attack with my two comrades close behind me. Suddenly my machine gave a terrible lurch which snapped me against the safety belt. I knew something was wrong and swung off, followed by the other two, leaving the surprised Hun to a peaceful retreat. I babied my ship home and landed safely only to find that my stabilizer had been broken internally, and that the fierce air pressure incurred in the dive had twisted it almost off, making my plane unmanageable until the air pressure lessened. I did some healthy "bawling out" much as I hate to. My mechanics have been very hard and faithful workers, but this seemed a clear case of careless inspections. It was hateful to see that Boche sail home with impunity."

"Oct. 22, 1918

Dear Ollie,

We've just been outside watching a show, one of the kind that puts a thrill in things. What kind of a show do you think one would be looking at out of doors at 8:30 P.M.? *Je vais vous dire, mon vieux:* – I had just written the heading of this letter when suddenly someone yelled, "Lights out!" Out they went damn quickly. It was soon apparent what the row was all about for a barrage dotted the sky over X— not far away, and the roving beams of the searchlights swung slowly, inquisitively, around in a vain effort to pick up the raider. A few seconds later came a thundering whang! slam! bang! Far louder than a barrage, and we knew the old boy had dropped his eggs. Then a different tone of motor told us that our night *chasse* was on the trail. We all stood outside cheering them on. I know not how they could see each other unless the moon was sufficient or a stray searchlight beam accidentally reached the right spot, but anyway the old machine guns opened up. Little dots of fire flashed back and forth and a minute later came the ra ta ta ta. We were rooting hard for our boys but they couldn't seem to land their shots in the right spot. The fitting climax would have been for the Boche to burst into flames and drop – but we had to call the combat a draw, because no one came down. We could see in the far distance still another combat going on. There was some excitement when one of the raiders droned right over our field, but he must have been on his way home for he dropped no bombs on us. Our boys are new at this night *chasse* work, but I think soon they will begin knocking down the old Gothas. They certainly work before a good gallery and confirmation for a victory at night would be forthcoming from a few thousand different witnesses.

Best love,
Ham."

The *Daily Squadron Report* for October 23, 1918, mentions four "Sector Patrols" which was new nomenclature and used for the first time. These sector patrols were made up of three Spads each and were assigned a rather small area 25 to 30 kilometers west of Dun-sur-Meuse. They flew from 600 to 1200 meters and only two reports were made, one by Sam Kaye who was a member of the first patrol and one by Reed Chambers in the fourth patrol. Kaye reported: "At 13h 00, saw one of our balloons burn up; west of EXERMONT. We were close to it at the time, but could not find the machine that destroyed it. Saw a Biplace over the lines, north of SOMMERANCE, but could not attack because there were six (6) Fokkers above it. All seven E.A. left a few minutes after I sighted them." Chambers' report gave no further clue as to the new term of "Sector Patrol." "Saw several formations of Fokkers chasing our Bombers out of Germany, but did not venture very close. They would shoot from about 500 to 600 meters, and then go back. Saw no planes go down."

Later that day Rickenbacker left the field at 15h 25 on another solo voluntary flight to the region of Le Grande Carre Ferme and Montfauçon which was south of where the other patrols had been working. He reported:

> "While patrolling just north of Montfauçon I noticed one (1) of our balloons going down in flames west of Montfauçon. Saw the Fokker who attacked the balloon headed for the enemy lines. Started to cut him off and while watching him ran into four Fokkers, probably his protection. Fired about 100 rounds into one of them at close range. This took place at about 16h 55 in the region of Le Grande Carre Ferme. When last seen the Fokker was in a steep nosedive. I was unable to follow him any further as the three others began firing on me. Altitude of combat 600 meters. CONFIRMATION REQUESTED – one (1) Fokker."

American authorities confirmed this victory on October 27, 1918, for Rickenbacker's twenty-second.

No flights were flown on October 24. The next day the only patrol achieved no results due to poor visibility which continued on October 26, shutting down Squadron operations.

The morning of October 27 began with dense fog and a patrol of five led by Ham Coolidge went out at 6h 40 and returned in less than an hour due to the poor visibility. Rickenbacker went out on a solo patrol, at 9h 10, flying at 100 meters and achieved no results, this being followed by a low patrol of four which lost two members to motor trouble and saw Reed Chambers firing a few ineffective shots at a Halberstadt in the region of Champigneulle.

An eleven plane protection patrol was called at 14h 30 which was to have disasterous results for the squadron. Captains Coolidge and Rickenbacker were leading Lts. Hopkins, Smith, Garnsey, Outcault, Evitt, Crocker, Kaye, Sparks and DeWitt in two groups of a high and a low patrol. The mission was to protect Allied bombers coming out of Germany after a raid to the north. Twenty-five minutes into the mission, Ham Coolidge was blown out of the air. Sam Kaye reported the following:

> "In the region north of GRAND PRÉ just across the river, an anti-aircraft shell made a direct hit on Captain Coolidge's machine, blowing both right wings off and sending it down in flames. Time, about 14h 55. Altitude, about 550 meters. Captain Coolidge was leading the patrol at the time. I took the patrol and proceeded on. Saw several combats higher up but noticed no results. Nine Fokkers started diving on my formation in the region of Bantheville and I joined another formation nearby. The Fokkers pulled up before coming into range."

Rickenbacker in his book stated that Coolidge was hurrying to the assistance of American bombers which had been bombing Grand Pré and were being attacked by a large formation of Fokkers. The anti-aircraft barrage was intended for the bombers and a chance shell caught Coolidge's Spad as he was flying to their protection.

Joe Eastman speaks of Coolidge's loss in his diary entry of October 27:

> "We learned that during the patrol of this afternoon we lost our right good comrade Ham Coolidge. He was struck by a direct hit of a hun archie which carried away his wing and set him in flames. We like to believe that he was killed instantly by the explosive – beyond that, for one thing, I am reminded that he was the one man I've seen in the army who made an evening practice of kneeling by his cot in prayer. His scoreboard shows seven or eight confirmed victories – which he described to me in detail not so many evenings ago, always giving them as illustrations of the conviction that it's all a matter of 'pure chance happening'. I do believe that his 'chance' of today hurts the rest of us more than it did him. But it won't be long, just as Ham himself would have felt in the case of any other."

Coolidge was buried 300 yards northwest of Chevières, near Grand Pré. His grave was carefully marked and a map showing its location was sent to his mother.[3]

Minutes after Coolidge's loss Lt. Crocker, part of that fateful patrol, reported:

> "Just east of Grand Pré, a Fokker attacked me from above and from our side of the lines. While on a dive towards our balloon, I noticed two parachutes jump from our balloon and another Fokker leaving it. The balloon did not burn. As a Fokker was on my tail, I was unable to attack the Fokker which was leaving our balloon."

Lt. Red Outcault, also in the low patrol, further reported on the attacking Fokkers:

> "At 15h 38 I was with a formation of 8 Spads. Just northeast of Oling, 5 Fokkers piqued on formation and I piqued down under the leader. As we reached our lines and I saw 2 Fokkers begin to withdraw, I turned to regain my place in the formation and fired 50 rounds at E.A. I had to turn immediately to stay with formation, so cannot say that I saw E.A. go down, but my tracers seemed to be very close to him. Altitude of combat – 12 meters."

Rickenbacker flying solo above the low patrol was northwest of Grand Pré and did not see Coolidge go down, but managed to get into two eventful fights. The first:

> "While flying above, our low patrol was attacked by three Fokkers from above. After a short dive I pulled up and turned on the end Fokker, firing about 125 rounds at close range. When last seen he was going down out of control, about two kilometers northwest of Grand Pré. Time, about 14h 50. Altitude about 2000 meters."

The second took place at 15h 05 in the region of Bois de Money:

> "Engaged one Fokker firing at one of our bombers. Fired about 200 rounds and noticed his motor stop. I ceased firing and then started maneuvering him into our lines, but before he landed another Spad tried to shoot him down. I placed myself between the two and the Fokker landed safely in the region of the southern edge of Bois de Money, turning up on his nose. He had a blue fuselage with white circles on it and the usual crosses on the wings. Altitude 3000 meters to the ground. Confirmations Requested – Two (2) Fokkers."

This second victory was Ltn. Max Kliefoth of Jasta 19, who after being taken prisoner gave the American intelligence people a great deal of misinformation, in particular information regarding the colors of J G. II. While Rick was trying to steer the crippled Kliefoth back to the Exermont field which was about four miles behind the Allied front lines, another Spad came from nowhere and started firing at the Fokker. Kliefoth turned away from his attacker and the field, only to crash land nearby wrecking the aircraft which Rick had planned to fly as a well-gained prize. In consolation his Captaincy became official ending his long wait for his overdue promotion. Both of these victories were confirmed in S.O. Number 22, November 22, 1918, par. 15 and 16.

Poor weather on October 28 brought little results from four Sector and one Voluntary patrols. The following day saw an improvement in the weather and increased enemy activity. The first of four Sector Patrols flew from Beaumont to Champigneulle and consisted of six Spads led by Sam Kaye. Lt. "Madame" Sherry reported an attack by seven Fokkers east of Sommerance who dove on the patrol from 3000 meters and chased them to a point south of Exermont where they turned back into German lines. Lt. Kaye filed the following combat report:

> "Flying toward Champigneulle at 600 meters, seven (7) Fokkers (Altitude 3500 meters) dived on our formation from the north. I turned towards Exermont and they followed us all the way, two of them shooting at the end of my formation. I turned and opened fire, shooting 200 rounds at one E.A. and he went down towards Landres-St. George, apparently out of control. Time, about 8h 52; Altitude about 1000 meters; Confirmation Requested. All but one E.A. then turned back, seeing another formation of Spads approaching. The one E.A. stayed above and I shot 100 rounds at him. He then piqued for Germany. Confirmation Requested – 1 Fokker."

The 95th Aero Squadron had a patrol up in the same region at the same time which well could have been the Spads seen by the Germans.

Lt. Kaye was awarded his fourth confirmed victory for this action in S.O. Number 22, November 2, 1918, Par. 7.

Lt. "Willie" Palmer led an afternoon patrol to Gesnes-Romagne-St. George where he found low flying impossible due to the heavy haze. The Germans were out in numbers as his patrol was attacked by 12 Fokkers near Grand Pré, but from the statements in his Reconnaissance Report: "They did not get close enough to fire any shots." 1st Lt. Edward G. Garnsey of Grand Haven, Michigan was a member of Palmer's patrol and was shot down and killed by seven enemy planes just south of Hill 272 in the region of St. Juvin and was buried slightly west of Exermont. Strangely, there is no mention made by Palmer of this engagement which possibly may have gone unnoticed in the heavy haze. Rickenbacker simply states, "On the twenty-ninth Lieutenant Garnsey fell near Exermont after having fought a brilliant combat against greatly superior numbers."

Garnsey was shot down by Ltn. Max Näther of Jasta 62, this victory bringing his score to twenty-four. Later in the day he also shot down a DH9 and a DH4 which was from the 135th Aero Squadron, U. S. Air Service.

Näther was born in East Prussia in 1899 and was, therefore, one of the youngest German aces. At the age of 18 he was given the command of Jasta 62 and was nominated for the Pour-le-Mèrite on October 29, the day of his three victories. The collapse of Germany prevented the final approval of the award, and Näther, after the Armistice, flew against the Poles in that border war, being shot down and killed by ground fire just six months prior to his 21st birthday.

The loss of Garnsey, which was the squadron's last, was avenged on the following day, October 30, by Rickenbacker and Lt. Harvey Weir Cook. Cook on a morning sector patrol of five Spads reported as follows:

> "At about 8h 10 I encountered an enemy biplace in the region of Crépion at about 1000 meters and chased him further into enemy territory, firing about 100 rounds at long range. Returned to the lines and encountered a second biplace about 900 meters below me. I dove under him and fired about 75 rounds at close range. This occurred in the region of Crépion. Returned to the lines and sighted a third biplace about 200 meters directly above me. I climbed directly under him and fired about 75 rounds at a distance of 75 meters. He dove steeply as I fired and my guns jammed. As I turned away to fix the jam, the plane disappeared in the mist below apparently out of control. This happened in the region of Chaumont-devant-Damvillers. Confirmation Requested, L.V.G. biplace."

American S. O. Number 23, November 5, 1918, Par. 44 credited Lt. H. Weir Cook with the destruction of an enemy L.V.G. at 800-1200 meters at 8h 30 near Chaumont-devant-Damvillers on October 30, 1918.

Rickenbacker who was leading the patrol met a Halberstadt over Grand Pré at 800 meters, chased him north about 5 kilometers, fired 150 rounds with no results. The afternoon Sector Patrol departed at 14h 50 and was also joined by Captain Eddie with more dramatic results. Lt. Sam Kaye was leading the First flight on this patrol as Reed Chambers was in the hospital recovering from a serious infection. Rickenbacker was checking on Kaye's tactical leadership and remained above and behind the patrol. An hour and forty minutes into the patrol on the third circuit between Grand Pré and Brieulles, Rickenbacker reported:

> "Was following our formation when two (2) Fokkers with red fuselages and red noses piqued on the rear end of the formation. I fired about 50 rounds at long range without results. Went up the line towards the Meuse to Romagne and returned within enemy lines about two (2) kilometers. In the region north of St. Juvin I met the same two (2) Fokkers. Fired about 100 rounds at one of them at close range before I was seen. He went down out of control and his gas tank exploded when he crashed to the ground. The other Fokker disappeared into Germany. At this time I was about 200 meters high. This took place about 16h 35 in the region north of St. Juvin. Confirmation Requested."

On his way back to Rembercourt, near the village of Remonville which lay two miles inside the German lines, Rickenbacker spotted a balloon in its bed. He immediately dove and fired 150 rounds which caused it to burst into flames. The time was 16h 40 which gave Rick very little fuel for his final return which he completed with a dead stick landing as dusk was approaching.

American military authorities confirmed these two victories on November 2, 1918, making them his twenty-fifth, twenty-sixth, and last victories.

Three Sector Patrols were flown on October 31 in the same regions as the day before and heavy German fighter activity was encountered during all three. On the second patrol near Grand Pré, Lt. Willie Palmer engaged a Halberstadt at an altitude of 150 meters. Palmer maneuvered under his tail, fired 100 rounds at him seeing his tracers entering the fuselage. The Halberstadt went down in a slow pique and passed out of sight behind the Foret de Boult near Quartre-Champs. S.O. 24, November 7, 1918, Par. 5 credited Palmer with this victory, his third and the last for the month of October.

The Squadron summary report for October was indeed impressive with 418 sortees flown, 56 combats, 34 confirmed victories, 65 sector patrols and 10 special missions for a total of 557 hours and 48 minutes of flying time. The 94th was not without losses though; the deaths of Coolidge, Saunders and Garnsey and the wounding and capture of Scroggie, were sobering reminders of their hazardous fighting in the air.

---

[1] This pilot was Lt. Wilbert W. White, Jr. of the 147th Aero Squadron. White was credited with eight victories and this was to be his last patrol before returning to the United States.

[2] A Kelner built Spad with a Bleriot motor; two Vickers guns instead of the regular Marlin guns; a C ? compass instead of the ordinary one; a Bendix carburetor, etc.

[3] Memo to Commanding Officer, First Air Depot from Reed Chambers C/O 94th Aero, Feb. 13, 1918.

This first version of the Hannover CL III was similar to the plane brought down and captured by Rickenbacker and Chambers, October 2, 1918.

John Jeffers and crew stand by Spad 15052 number 8 which was also flown by "Madame" Sherry.

Willie Palmer stands by Spad 4573 number 20 with Spad 15056 number 23 in the background. Number 23 was not assigned to a specific pilot and was wrecked on August 23, 1918 when five planes from one patrol went down with a variety of mechanical problems.

Ham Coolidge sporting his Captain's bars and a silver "Hat in the Ring" pin just below his pilot's wings. These were made by Cartier, the jewelry firm in Paris.

Above: Harold Tittmann was wounded terribly in action on July 2, 1918. This photo was affixed to his pilot's identity card.

Above right: Alan Nutt, who joined the Squadron on September 16, was shot down and killed just ten days later, on September 26, by Ltn. Franz Bückner of Jasta 13. *Photo courtesy of Mike O'Neil.*

Right: Lt. Raymond J. Saunders joined the 94th on September 26, 1918 and was shot down and killed in action on October 22, 1918. Saunders was flying Spad 7708 when he was lost. *Dennis Gordon collection.*

Eddie Rickenbacker and "Madame" Sherry ham it up for the benefit of the 94th and some German POWs. Rick has chosen a pickelhaube for his hat of choice, while Sherry favors a steel helmet and mutze, or soft cap. The weapons seen include an M.96 Mauser pistol, Gew. 98 rifle, a Luger and a Colt .45 automatic. Why Sherry goes from raincoat to bathrobe will always remain a mystery, but we do know the POWs thought it all great fun.

Eddie Rickenbacker and "Ole Number One". Rembercourt. October 1918.

On October 2, 1918, Rickenbacker and Chambers forced this Hannover down. The plane landed at this spot, experiencing little or no serious damage. The pilot survived unhurt, but the observer was killed during the fight.

Another view of the Hannover crash site. The plane was a CL III, model number 3892/18.

A port side view of Halberstadt CL IV built by Roland, number 9470/18.

A starboard side view of another Halberstadt CL IV. These two-seaters were used in quantity along with Hannovers, Rumplers, DFWs, and LVGs in the German observation duties.

The Hannover was taken to the 94th hangars at Rembercourt where the propellor was repaired and the plane generally checked out.

Reed Chambers points to the bullet hole in the side of the Hannover, marking the entry of the round which killed the observer. *U. S. National Archives, RG III, SC 27150.*

A close-up of the rear section of the Hannover.

Jimmy Meissner, Eddie Rickenbacker, Alden Sherry, Reed Chambers, and Weir Cook pose with the propless Hannover. *U. S. Air Force Museum.*

The Hannover in the hands of the mechanics. Rembercourt.

Rickenbacker takes a moment to check out his new prize, while the mechanic adds liquids to the Hannover.

On October 27 while leading a patrol, Ham Coolidge suffered a direct hit by an anti-aircraft shell which destroyed his Spad in mid-air. This photo shows all that remained of Spad 7743. The crash site was 300 yards northwest of Chevières, near Grande Pré.

A mechanic gets his picture taken with the Hannover for the folks back home.

Weir Cook and his Spad 15169 number 24. Rembercourt. October 1918.

Two officers (the one on the right looks like Sherry) tending Coolidge's grave prior to erecting the cross.

The cross has been erected and part of a wing has been placed between the cross and the original square grave marker.

Another view of Coolidge's grave with a tire from his Spad resting on the original marker.

Chambers' Spad 15225 number 11 which he flew from September 1 until September 29. Rembercourt. *Reed Chambers album.*

The tail end of Joe Eastman's number 19 showing the rudder markings as applied by the factory.

Reed Chambers views the wreckage of a crashed plane. It is not known if this was the remains of Coolidge's Spad as the terrain does not look the same as that seen in other photos of the site.

Rickenbacker and number 1 ready for cold weather flying. Rembercourt. October 1918.

Rickenbacker and number 1. The photo clearly shows the wheel cover and landing gear strut decorations, as well as the white number 1 under the lower left wing and a diagonal stripe under the lower right. The radiator cowling was thought to be red.

Reed Chambers and his number 6. Rembercourt. October 1918.

A well-known picture of Eddie Rickenbacker in his Spad. Note the large ring-sight by the right hand gun and the adjustment, or alignment, bar connecting the two Vickers guns. *U. S. Signal Corps photo.*

Joe Eastman, Jimmy Meissner, Eddie Rickenbacker, Reed Chambers, and Thorne Taylor having a smoke by Rick's number 1. Rembercourt. October 18, 1918.

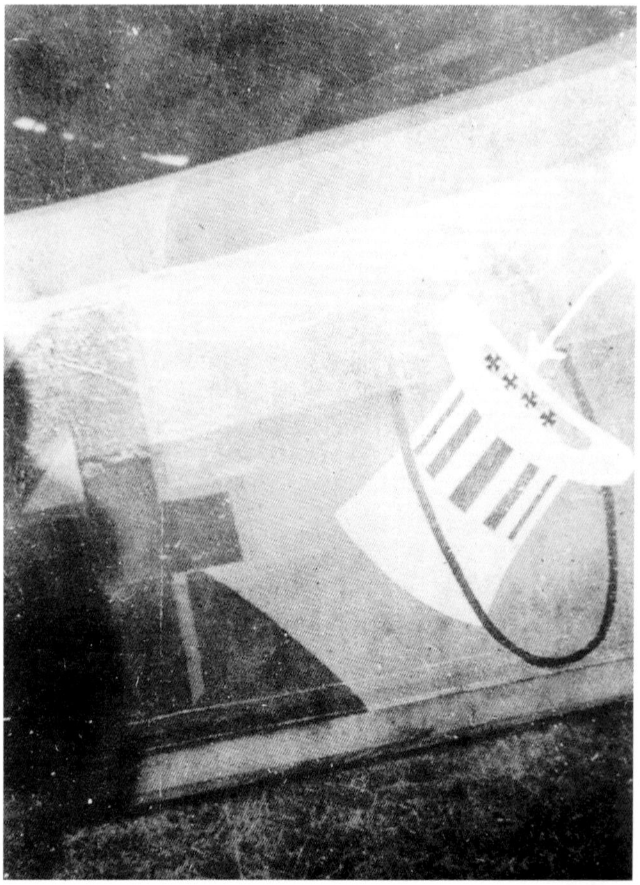

A close-up of the right side of Weir Cook's Spad 15169 number 24 showing his four victory crosses on the headband of the top hat. Rembercourt. October 1918.

Sam Kaye stands proudly by his SPAD 130 number 16. Rembercourt. October-November 1918.

A group of enlisted men and the Hannover. Rembercourt. November 1918.

About mid-October Rickenbacker as C.O. gave a pep talk to all members of the 94th in preparation for the last big push of the war. This took place at Rembercourt with the trophy Hannover in the background.

A group picture of the 94th which included Major Hartney, Commander of the 1st Pursuit Group, Major Geoffrey H. Bonnell, and other members of the 147th Aero. Note "Spad" the mascot made the picture standing on the Hannover.

The remains of Eugene Scroggie's Spad, brought down after his wounding on October 3, 1918. Scroggie was made a POW and the Spad became the victim of shell-fire and souvenir hunters. *Sid Bradd photo.*

Major Maxwell Kirby was assigned to the 94th on October 15 to gain combat experience before taking command of his own squadron. Rembercourt.

Right: The right side of Rick's Spad showing a bullet-hole patch on the left marked by a white dot and a black cross, plus 26 crosses for his confirmed victories spilling from Uncle Sam's hat.

Below: The classic photo of Eddie Rickenbacker and number 1. *U. S. National Archives, RG 111, SC 29655.*

Joe Eastman. Rembercourt. October 1918.

9

November-December - The Finalé

The first day of November brought low ceilings and poor visibility, Rickenbacker flying the only patrol, a voluntary one, for just forty minutes. The following day the weather did not improve greatly, but one Sector Patrol was flown reporting Allied troops advancing northeast of Grand Pré, truck trains as far as Remonville, troops advancing double file along the same route. No enemy aircraft were seen, but many Allied biplace and pursuit planes were noticed as well as heavy fires in the region of Buzancy. Rickenbacker, that same day while on a Voluntary Patrol, noted a German supply camp on fire, plus other bright fires in Bayonville, while German artillery with 77 mm guns were retreating between Boult-aux-Bois and Germont and American infantry were seen in shellholes and dugouts south of Verpel awaiting orders to advance. Rick also noticed truck trains in Aincreville and soldiers in Doulcon which meant the Germans were being rolled back towards Dun-sur-Meuse and the river.

Rickenbacker flying at 500 meters and slightly lower reported that the American infantrymen "seemed very jubilant over the sight of an American plane at this altitude." He went on to advise that possible future patrols fly low as an extra boost for moral.

Sector Patrols continued on November 3 with the weather following an unfriendly pattern. The first patrol, Grand Pré-Champigneulle-Imécourt, departed with nine Spads led by Sam Kaye and included Lts. Palmer, Hopkins, Evitt, Outcault, Crocker, McKenzie and Cates. Kaye returned to the field for five minutes to affect a repair and rejoined the group. Outcault and Cates both panned cutting the group to seven. During this flight an enemy aircraft was engaged, shot down, and confirmed, but no other details are known. Lt. Cook on the afternoon patrol attacked one of three enemy Fokkers over Fontaines and drove the others back over the Foret de Woëvre northeast of Dun-sur-Meuse.

Two Sector patrols on November 4 produced no results as was the case of three Sector and three Voluntary patrols flown on November 5, although improving weather was reported. The following day Captain Faunt Le Roy and Lt. Cook made a morning Voluntary Patrol up the east side of the Meuse. Captain Cedric Faunt Le Roy, who had flown with the French and then had been the Officer in Charge of the Acceptance and Inspection Division at Orly, supervised the American acceptance of over 2000 French planes and had personally made over 3500 test flights.

Finally, after much pleading to higher authorities at Orly, Faunt Le Roy on October 25 was assigned to the 94th to gain combat experience. During this patrol they observed eighteen enemy aircraft: seven Fokkers east of Dun-sur-Meuse, seven Fokkers in the region of Brandeville some ten kilometers east of Dun-sur-Meuse, and four biplace near Ecurey southeast of Brandeville. No contact was made with the enemy, but Fount Le Roy got a taste of the fact that the German Air Service was still alive and well. Low clouds and haze made operations impossible on November 7, but things improved slightly on November 8 permitting flying at low altitude throughout the day.

A balloon straffing mission and fifteen single plane Voluntary Patrols were flown from 8h 17 to 16h 15. Lt. John DeWitt, who had joined the Squadron on September 30, flew the balloon straffing mission departing at 9h 00 in very poor weather. He reported "I observed the balloon at an altitude of 50 meters in the region of Olley on my left while I was coming out of Germany. I turned and piqued on it firing 75 or 100 rounds into it, when both guns jammed. Because of machine gun and anti-aircraft fire, I zoomed up into the very low cloud, making it impossible to observe effects of fire. Time 10h 05.

Observed three balloons (including the one encountered) directly east of Verdun in the region of Conflans. One was deflated on the ground about one kilometer from the one encountered. Located a fourth balloon on the ground in the region of Etain. I observed movements of long transport trains moving out of Conflans on the road which lead southwest to Metz. Confirmation Requested. 1 Balloon."

The issuance of S.O. Number 26, November 15th, 1918, Par. 13 awarded 2nd Lt. John DeWitt with the destruction of an enemy balloon for his first and only victory. Poor weather persisted on November 9 and 10 allowing minimum activity with the exception of a Voluntary Patrol flown by Major Maxwell Kirby the morning of November 10. Kirby had been assigned to the 94th to gain front line combat experience which would prepare him for a squadron of his own. His description of the experience of his one combat is worthy of inclusion:

> "In the region of Maucourt at about 10h 50 when emerging from a low cloud bank I suddenly came upon a Fokker monoplace at an altitude of 50 meters. I fired a burst into him at very close range (15 meters) and pulled away. He went down in a steep dive into the side of a hill and crashed. Confirmation Requested – 1 Fokker."

Kirby's report was confirmed by Special Order 26. November 15th, 1918:

> "Par. 16. Major Maxwell Kirby, 94th Aero Squadron, 1st Pursuit Group, is credited with the destruction in combat, of an enemy Fokker, in the region of Maucourt, at 50 meters altitude, on November 10th, 1918, at 10:50 o'clock."

Major Kirby had scored the final victory for the 94th Aero squadron, 24 hours and ten minutes prior to the Armistice.

Joe Eastman recorded in his diary more of the events of November 10:

> "Sometime after dinner while in the act of rolling up my right spiral puttee[1], a great clamor outside draws us to the door. There is a parade of enlisted men – drumming a tin pan, tooting a bugle, mob cheers. Before we can make out the cause of the excitement, though it is possible to imagine, in runs Jimmy Meissner from the 147th barracks across the way, very much in a twitter. 'They've signed an Armistice, official wire up at operations from C.A.S. (Commander Air Service). All hostilities to cease tomorrow at 11:h 00.' He tells us – and: 'Everybody come on over to the 95th's bar.' Which sets the lot of us to hooting and floundering mudwise, one spiral on or less – over towards the Kicking Mules. By the time our advance contingent has skated to the field, all Halifax and its fireworks[2] has torn into celebration. From each of the black hangars surrounding us there shoot up all colors of landing – rockets, red and green flares – and a complete din gathered from the sentiment of a New Years and the arms of a battle. Someone in the direction of the 95th barracks, inspired by the cow-boy yells and revolver shots, captures a machine gun which he starts joyously rattling some few inches over our heads. Between whoops we yell at him to pop elsewhere yields the fruit of prayers to Confucius. So we hop from puddle to puddle with every instrument of din and illumination with the group egging us on. Cheers! many cheers! Don't you know the War is finally over?
>
> In that event let's see what the Kicking Mule has to put out. Why describe an orgy...for some inexplicable reason, I failed to make that madness of Peace that was attained by some yet, friends will be friendly – and I did at least greatly aid in the pollution of America's one and only Rickenbacker. At that point of jubilation when toasts became necessary a great diversion was created outside the tent by Captain Rankin's band. Out poured the crowd leaving a noted Nat. Geog. Mag. Writer clutching for a suitable word. With a machine gun again rattling, with the Captain's delirious band going – Eddie leads a swaying serpentine to threshing about in the dark. Shortly this becomes disorganized into a series of gentlemanly wresting bouts, and many do roll in the plentiful lather of mud thereabouts. Which I view with that content of one who knows much better, and am congratulating myself when I am unmanfully and cowardly attacked without warning by silly "Madame" Sherry – who is bent on revenging his own recent downfall. So that my fur-coat is quite ruined and until we have each pleasantly smeared the others face in mud there is little peace well into the evening."

On Armistice Day, November 11, 1918, there was but one flight made. At 11h 05, Captain E. V. Rickenbacker departed the field at Rembercourt on a solo flight returning to the field at 11h 25. There is no official record of what actions Rick took during that twenty minutes of flight, but one would have to imagine it was not spent in a level attitude. The war was officially over and the 94th Aero Squadron would have no more battles to fight in the War to end all Wars.

In December, in honor of its great contribution to the United States segment of war in the air, the 94th was given the assignment and ordered to be part of the Army of Occupation.

In the last month of 1918 some rather interesting occurances were noticed and unusual situations were revealed concerning the character of some of the 94th pilots and others with whom they came in contact. Well known are the character, bravery, and heroics of the likes of Lufbery, Campbell, Chambers, Coolidge, and Captain Eddie, but we do uncover some different characteristics of other members of the Squadron. As we read Joe Eastman's diary, we find him a pilot haunted with a lack of self-confidence and extreme timidity; other pilots fought the good fight, but were not terribly aggressive in their flying performances; and finally, the self-admitted downright cowardice of Oscar J. Gude. More of Gude will be heard. Somewhere in the mix we find John W. F. M. Huffer, who with Ken Marr are each shrouded with a little mystery and questionable attainments. Both had experience with the French, Marr with the Lafayette Escadrille and Huffer with three different French Escadrilles, both achieving the rank of Major, Huffer at the onset of his U.S.A.S. commissioning, Marr starting as a Captain who was later promoted to Major.

These ranks were given it would seem more for perceived experience rather than leadership skills. Both were to command the 94th, Huffer from March 7 through June 5, 1918, and Marr from June through September 25, 1918 when Rickenbacker took over. One gets the notion that Huffer was easy going and generally well-liked by the squadron, but probably officially met his Waterloo due to his non-performance when he and Gude were involved in Lufbery's last fight on May 19, 1918. Gude, as we recall, shot off all his ammuition from a safe distance and Huffer who was in the air at the time, took no reportable action during the fight. Huffer was assigned in June to Headquarters Air Service, 1st Army A.E.F. as Liaison Officer to the French, in all probability because he was born and raised in France and was fluent in the language. He served in Headquarters until July 25 when he was given command of the 93rd Pursuit Squadron of the 3rd Pursuit Group. Someone in Headquarters thought enough of the good Major to give him another command which he held to the end of hostilities.

Among those who were in the first drafts of pilots assigned to the 93rd was none other than Oscar J. Gude! He reported for duty on August 4, 1918, his whereabouts after the Lufbery disaster unknown, but because of his seniority as a pilot dating back to March when he joined the 94th, he was carried on the 93rd roles as Flight Commander. The squadron records of the 93rd show that his Spad #15219 was reported "out of commission" for weeks. He was assigned a new Spad #7977 which also became a casualty of one difficulty after another. After October 13 all Squadron Reports discontinued naming Gude a Flight Commander and he continued to drop out of more patrols than he flew with his ever present "motor trouble" excuse. Huffer in frustration on October 22 ordered Gude to participate in an offensive patrol, also ordering him to take his, Huffer's, Spad, as it was "working perfectly."

The Gorrell History of the 93rd contains the following report:

> "...On the 22nd a patrol of eight planes, under the command of Lt. Wright, (1st Lt. Chester E. Wright, DSC & OC, 9 victories) set out on a patrol over the east bank of the Meuse River in the region of Fontaine. The leader observed an enemy plane coming out of Germany which Lts. Follmer, Hartmann, and Wright engaged in combat. This fight took place in a teeming rainstorm and when they arrived back at the airdrome, wet and happy, Lt. Gude failed to return from this patrol. When last seen he was flying toward Germany."

Soon after the Armistice, John Jeffers of the 94th, while visiting the German field at Metz, was given photographs of Huffer's Spad in German hands, clearly showing the 93rd Indian head insignia, the white number "1" and the C.O.'s stripes on the rear of the fuselage. Jeffers was told that the American pilot claimed to have run out of gas, but upon inspection by the Germans, plenty of fuel was found in the tanks. This defection ended the strange saga of Gude, but not that of Huffer.

On November 24, 1918, a General court-martial was called at Headquarters, First Army Artillery, Souilly, France. The court-martial was to take place on December 2, 1918. The defendant was Major J. W. F. M. Huffer, Air Service, Signal R. C., U. S. Army. The charge was Violation of the 95th Article of War. The specification: "In that Major J. W. F. M. Huffer, A. S. Sig. R. C., did while in uniform at Gengoult Airdrome, France, on or about the twenty-second day of June, 1918, well knowing that a woman known as Marcelle Collas was a common prostitute, cause her to be present at a dance at which other officers of the U. S. Army and civilians were present; and in their presence did openly and publicly associate with her at said dance." The individual bringing charges was Davenport Johnson, at the time of the alleged offense, Major, U. S. S. C.

During the trial Johnson was the chief witness for the prosecution, while for the defense were Captain John Wentworth, ex-94th and then 1st Pursuit Wing, Captain E. V. Rickenbacker, U. S. R., Commanding Officer 94th Aero Sqdn, Major James A. Meissner, Air Service 94th, Captain J. Barrett H. Smith, Air

Service 24th Air Sqdn, 1st Lt. Arthur L. Cunningham, 94th Aero Sqdn, Captain Reed Chambers, 94th Aero Sqdn, and finally Brig. General William Mitchell, Air Service.

Under cross examination by the defense, Colonel Johnson was questioned on a particular point, the answer to which in all likelihood had a great bearing on the verdict:

Q. Have you known Major Huffer for a long time?
A. Yes, since last March.
Q. You brought up these charges?
A. Yes, as Commanding Officer of the First Pursuit Group.
Q. Was Major Huffer at any time your Commanding Officer?
A. Not that I know of.
Q. You were in command of a squadron at some airdrome?
A. Yes. (Johnson commanded the 95th Aero Sqdn).
Q. During that time was Major Huffer in charge?
A. He was in charge of operations.
Q. And while so acting you were virtually under him?
A. Yes.
Q. Did any unpleasantness occur between you and Major Huffer in that period?
A. I think at one time I was reported for not having something up which should have been in the line of duty. I was reported to Colonel Mitchell and corrected.
Q. He reported you for lack of duty?
A. He reported me but not for lack of duty.
Q. Was that previous to this dance?
A. Yes.

The questioning then went back to the night of the dance and how Johnson knew the woman to be of ill repute and if Huffer was fully aware that the woman was a prostitute and knowingly brought her to the dance. Huffer was defended by Major Harold E. Hartney, Commanding Officer 1st Pursuit Group, Laurence G. Driggs, civilian attorney, and Captain Henry G. Lyster, 1st Pursuit Group, all of whom did a supreme job in dealing with this apparent farce. Huffer was acquitted[3] and not heard of again, but more of Johnson's actions and reputation were to surface.

Many of the Air Service pilots who had been POWs were back from captivity and were not necessarily assigned back to their old squadrons or to new ones. This gave them the opportunity to visit other squadrons, catch up with old friends and swap tales of their various experiences. One of these returned POWs was one "Red" Miller who visited the 94th for several days. Miller had been shot down and captured in the early days of the Château Thierry show, so had spent considerable time as a guest of the Kaiser and recounted to Joe Eastman and others some of his experiences. He described that the first German Intelligence Officer to interview him volunteered to him the names of the Group's squadron commanders and then asked if Rick "had more plans" which was followed by the gloomy observation that "the war for Germany was lost." He went on to criticize the American fliers because "they never know when not to attack and were too scatter-brained to be anticipated in action."

From another source, "Red" picked up the information that when the American squadrons entered the sector near Saints, the Germans were completely disconcerted by the activities of the Nieuport 28s, and as a result lost so many pilots by their "unspeakable tactics" they concluded the 1st Pursuit Group was a band of British Aces. They thought these "British Aces" had been banded together to try to stop the best German circuses opposite them. It made a good story and Eastman entered it in his diary.

Miller went on to state that "Dusty" Rhodes of the 95th, another POW just released, was bringing back an official document signed by the German pilot who was credited in bringing down Captain Jim Miller, the first C. O. of the 95th. The following recount also comes from Eastman's diary entry of December 19. "The paper is a report on Jim's descent and his dying statement. It is remembered that when we first were organized at Villeneuve, "Jam" Johnson returned with the story that he and Jim were on a wildcat patrol wherein his (Johnson's) gun jammed causing him to retire – while Jim was shot down. The paper quotes Jim as saying (and the hun also) that Johnson alone seeing the distant hun formation – had immediately left without warning Miller. Jim's last words read '____ ____ Johnson, he's yellow son of a _____! You can tell him that, and I hope he's stuck up against a brick wall and shot.' We, who know Johnson, his vindictiveness and unscrupulous career can't help but derive satisfaction in hearing further proof of our convictions." From all of this one can only assume "if there's smoke, there's fire." Johnson survived the rumors, court decisions to the contrary, and later became an Air Corps General in World War II.

In December the Squadron moved to Noyers, closer to Germany and by April 1919 were at Ft. Alexander, Coblenz, taking part in the III Army Carnival held at that time. Many of the original pilots who had been with the squadron in the early days were rotated home. Rickenbacker had gone on a bond selling speaking tour of the United States, but those who stayed on in Germany had one more triumph. That triumph was to create the most gaudily painted Spad XIIIs that ever existed. John Jeffers, Pat Maloney, Joe Dawson, Reed Chambers, Willie

Palmer, Sam Kaye, Weir Cook and others designed paint schemes which can only be best described by the photos included within the text.

The actual colors were never officially recorded at the time, but there were a few entries regarding them in Eastman's diary. An interview with Pat Maloney in the 1970s regarding these colors was, in the writer's opinion, inconclusive. There were reds, whites, and blues used in many of the designs, while green and white was the combination for Joe Dawson's shamrock and stripes covered plane. Reed Chambers sported red, white, and blue on his "Stars and Stripes," Sam Kaye in all probability had red, white, and blue polka dots, and the barber pole design in red and white. Eastman says that the lightning design on Weir Cook's Spad was orange on a black background, others thought the lightning to be yellow. Whatever the precise colors actually were, the overall effect had to have been dazzling and when in the air over Coblenz the 94th surely was seen as the colorful bunch that they really were.

Soon after the III Army Carnival there was deemed to be no further use for the 94th in the Army of Occupation and they were ordered home. In April 1919, the colorful Spads were turned over to the 138th Aero Squadron, the Fifth Pursuit Group who removed the "Hat in the Ring" insignia and replaced them with insignia of their own.

This brought to a close the World War I history of the 94th Aero Squadron, 1st Pursuit Group, A.E.F., and its inestimable contribution to early American combat aviation. The 94th scored the first victories of the war and the last; as the result of 296 combats they ran up a total score of 70 confirmed victories, unmatched by any other American squadron. They indeed put their *Hat in the Ring*.

---

[1] Spiral puttees were long strips of wool wound around the lower leg in lieu of high boots.

[2] This is in reference to the huge explosion in Halifax, Nova Scotia of a munitions ship which practically leveled the town.

[3] U. S. Archives, R. G. 153/Box 6397. Records of the Judge Advocate General 1812-1938.

Rickenbacker and Captain Cooper of the 26th Division. Rembercourt. November 1918.

Captain Eddie in his best uniform and a Hispano-Suiza automobile. Hispano was the builder of the engines which were in the Spad XIIIs, as well as sporty autos.

Rick and number 1 in another well-known photo. Note the Fokker D VII in the left background and behind it the Hannover. It would appear that the 94th had their own German air force.

Major Maxwell Kirby scored the last victory for the 94th on November 10, 1918, in the region of Maucourt at 10h 50. He stands gallantly by SPAD 6546 number 0, which was assigned to Chambers on November 5, 1918. *U. S. Signal Corps photo, E 5727.*

Joe Eastman, Jimmy Meissner, Eddie Rickenbacker, Reed Chambers, and Thorne Taylor. "Ole Number 1" and the Hannover in the background. Rembercourt. October-November 1918. *U. S. National Archives, RG 111, SC 29658.*

November 10, 1918, the day for awarding DSCs to the Air Service at Rembercourt. Seen in this photo before the awards L/R: Captain Dickenson Estee, Captain Eddie Rickenbacker, Captain "Swede" Sellers, Lt. H. Brewster, Lt. Charlie D'Olive, Lt. Bradley Gaylord, Lt. Jimmy Knowles, Lt. H. G. Rath, and Lt. Louis C. Simon, Jr.

Captain Estee is being awarded his DSC and awaiting their turn are Rickenbacker, Sellers, Brewster, D'Olive. Rembercourt. November 10, 1918.

On November 7, 1918, Captain Cedric E. Faunt Le Roy joined the 94th after a long struggle to get to the front. He seems pleased with his success.

Captain Eddie stands by the 94th operations tent after receiving his DSC.

Another picture taken after the awards shows a smiling Rick wearing his best whipcord jodhpurs and regulation uniform jacket. Rembercourt. November 10, 1918. *U. S. Signal Corps photo.*

Faunt Le Roy poses by lucky Spad 7777 number 3 which was his assigned airplane.

Opposite
Top: On October 22, 1918, 1st Lt. J. Gude, ex-94th and then 93rd Aero, while flying Major Huffer's Spad number 1, defected to the Germans. This photograph was taken at the Jasta 65 field at Mars-la-Tour.

Bottom: Another view of Huffer's Spad at the German airfield at Mars-la-Tour.

Below: Spad 16546 number 0 flown by Chambers arrived at the Squadron on November 5, 1918 and was transferred out on April 20, 1919.

Spad 15561 number 30 was flown after the Armistice by Lt. Scroggie. The plane was transferred out on April 20, 1919.

Spad with squadron number 10 taken at an unknown airfield. There were two Spads with number 10: Spad 7675 flown by Lt. Crocker, and Spad 15004 which panned on September 8, 1918.

A Spad named "Nora" and marked with squadron number 15. The serial number is unknown and the photo appears to be taken in November or December 1918.

A post-war photo of Pat Maloney, Joe Dawson, Sam Kaye, and an unidentified pilot. *Joe Dawson album.*

Pat Maloney and his last Spad named "Babe III" in a post-war photograph.

After the Armistice, Sam Kaye, Joe Dawson, Willie Palmer, and Weir Cook. All but Palmer seem to be equipped for flying.

Reed Chambers and a Hannover at Coblenz. Winter 1918-19.

Right: Pat Maloney, Willie Palmer, Joe Dawson, Sam Kaye, and Bob Donaldson. Coblenz, Germany. 1919

Left: Sam Kaye in a formal studio photo. Coblenz, Germany. 1919. Middle: Joe Dawson, Coblenz, Germany. 1919. Right: Willie Palmer. Coblenz, Germany. 1919.

Left: Bob Donaldson. Coblenz, Germany. 1919. Note that in these four photographs, the silver "Hat in the Ring" pin is prominently worn, as is the Third Army shoulder patch. Middle: Pat Maloney. Coblenz, Germany. Spring 1919. Right: A be-medaled Joe Dawson shows off his Distinguished Service Cross with Oak-Leaf and his Croix-de-Guerre with Palm. 1919.

Left: John Jeffers. Germany. 1919. Middle: Weir Cook. Coblenz, Germany. 1919. Right: Reed Chambers. Coblenz, Germany. 1919

Left: Willie Palmer. Coblenz, Germany. 1919. Middle: Joe Dawson. Coblenz, Germany. 1919. Right: John Jeffers. Coblenz, Germany. 1919.

The April 1919 Air Carnival at Coblenz, Germany begins. This line-up shows, nearest the camera, Bob Donaldson's *Checkerboard*, "Red" Outcault's red and white *Barber Pole*, Sam Kaye's red, white, and blue polka dot *Eastah Aigg*, and at the end, Joe Dawson's green and white *Shamrock*.

Another line-up at Coblenz. In the foreground Reed Chambers' red, white, and blue *American Flag*, Sam Kaye's *Eastah Aigg*, John Jeffers' *Japanese Flag*, painted in red, white, and blue, Joe Dawson's *Shamrock*, and, finally, Willie Palmer's *Diamond Dick* also in red, white, and blue.

Bob Donaldson's *Checkerboard*, "Red" Outcault's *Barber Pole*, and Sam Kaye's *Eastah Aigg* from a different view.

Bob Donaldson and his chief mechanic pose by the *Checkerboard*.

Donaldson's mechanic warms up the *Checkerboard*.

Bob Donaldson and his *Checkerboard*. Note how the checker square size diminishes as it goes towards the tail of the Spad.

A view from above of Sam Kaye's *Eastah Aigg* which appears to be light blue all over with red, white, and dark blue polka dots.

Sam Kaye looking pleased with his *Eastah Aigg*. *Joe Dawson album*.

Sam tips Uncle Sam's hat showing his four victory crosses.

Sam Kaye, Sgt. McDonnell his chief mechanic, and the *Eastah Aigg*.

One of the ground officers, who is unidentified, shares the Carnival festivities with the *Aigg*.

Sam Kaye and his creation *Eastah Aigg*.

One of "Red" Outcault's mechanics proudly shows off the *Barber Pole* painted red and white.

Outcault's *Barber Pole* in the hangar at Coblenz. The tail of Reed Chambers' *American Flag* can be seen on the left.

Willie Palmer's *Diamond Dick* with red, white, and blue diamonds. The exhaust stains can be seen on the white fuselage.

Right: Willie Palmer tips the hat on *Diamond Dick*. Palmer's three victory crosses can be seen on the hatband.

Below: Two of Palmer's mechanics and a rear view of *Diamond Dick*.

Palmer and *Diamond Dick*. Coblenz, Germany. April 1919.

Joe Dawson with Irish pride on board the *Shamrock*, painted in green and white.

Dawson's mechanics have their picture taken with the *Shamrock*.

One of Dawson's mechanics swings *Shamrock's* prop prior to a flight at Coblenz. April 1919.

Dawson strikes the favorite 94th pose, tipping Uncle's hat. The four crosses for his confirmed victories are on the hatband.

Dawson in the cockpit of *Shamrock*.

A nice rear view of *Shamrock* showing the wing and tail markings quite clearly.

Weir Cook's *Lightning Bolt* seemed to attract picture taking. William Fowler, Ben Jones, Weir Cook, John Jeffers, Joe Eastman, and Wiley Sparks are pictured.

The caption in Joe Dawson's album said "Talk about hard." Joe Eastman points his Colt .45 while on the upper wing of Cook's plane. Note the small lightning flashes surrounding the radiator.

Left: Wiley Sparks, his best leather flying coat, and Cook's airplane.

William Fowler, who was called Ward, stands by Cook's Spad.

Weir Cook ready to fly, but in a non-military pose, with hands in pockets. Coblenz. 1919

"Red" Outcault takes his turn by *Lightning Bolt*.

Cedric Smith does the old hat trick on Cook's orange and black Spad.

Weir Cook stands by the *Lightning Bolt*.

Cook's seven victory (three planes, four balloons) crosses show clearly on the hatband of Uncle Sam's hat painted on the *Lightning Bolt*.

Below: The orange bolts on a black fuselage show up well in this photo of Cook and his plane.

The *Lightning Bolt*.

John Jeffers taxiing in the *Japanese Flag* on the field at Coblenz.

A good left-side view of Jeffers' Spad. The red, white, and blue rays emanate from a white star with a red center.

A right-side view of Jeffers' special paint scheme which must have been extremely difficult to lay out.

A 3/4 rear view of Jeffers' Spad shows to good advantage the layout of the decoration on the wings and tail area. Jeffers stands by the plane.

Reed Chambers' red, white, and blue *American Flag* Spad. The nose and tail surfaces were pale blue with white stars. The fuselage was red and white strips. The background of the Hat insignia was gold.

There's that pose again! Seven crosses in the hatband stand for six planes and one balloon destroyed. The left side insignia was saved by Chambers and now is in the U. S. Air Force Museum where one can see the gold background to the insignia and the red and white stripes. Chambers is in the photo.

Chambers and his mechanics. Coblenz. April 1919.

The light blue nose with white stars can be seen in this picture, plus the blue paint on the center of the propellor. Chambers stands with his hand on the prop.

Chambers and a view of the blue rudder with white stars.

The 94th Aero Squadron Officers Mess. Coblenz, Germany. 1919. To the victor goes the spoils."

A *Signal Corps* photo (E 6289) of Chambers and the *American Flag*.

A 94th Group shot at Coblenz. Schroeder, three enlisted, Fowler, Smith, Cook, Eastman, Jones, Outcault, Rankin, Sparks.

Jimmy Meissner as a Major. 1919. *U. S. National Archives, RG 18, P-2989-AS.*

Reed Chambers. Germany. 1919. *U. S. National Archives, RG 18, E-6309.*

Homeward bound at last. On board ship, Sam Kaye, Joe Dawson, Reed Chambers, Willie Palmer are all wearing their full decorations. Kaye and Palmer have been promoted to Captain, but Joe Dawson still wears the single silver bar of a 1st Lieutenant.

94th Aero Squadron Aircraft in Color

Nieuport 28 Serial number 6169 Squadron number 1.
Assigned March 18, 1918 to Major John W.F.M. Huffer, Commanding Officer. Flown also by 1st Lt. E.V. Rickenbacker who stripped the upper wing fabric in a combat May 17, 1918. Huffer had the cowling painted with white, blue, and red rings. The rudder serial number was painted over when the markings were changed from French to American.

Nieuport 28 Serial number 6193 Squadron number 2.
Assigned March 3, 1918 to Major Raoul Lufbery who rolled it over on May 1 and again on May 4, 1918. 1st Lt. Phillip Davis was killed in action June 2, 1918 while flying this aircraft which crashed in flames.

Nieuport 28 Serial number 6144 Squadron number 14.
Assigned March 3, 1918 to 1st Lt. James Meissner. This profile shows the aircraft in its first marking configuration early May 1918. Meissner twice lost the upper wing fabric on this same Nieuport on May 4, 1918 and May 30, 1918. The second set of markings changed the number "14" to a white "8" and reversed the direction of the lightning bolts on the cowling.

Nieuport 28 Serial number 6181 Squadron number 15.
Assigned March 18, 1918 and flown by 1st Lt. William F. Loomis initially and later by 1st Lt. John Jeffers and finally by 1st Lt. William Chalmers who was shot down and made a POW on June 7, 1918. The plane was captured intact. This profile shows number 15 as it was decorated and flown by Bill Loomis.

Spad XIII Serial number 15034 Squadron number 22.
Assigned on July 18, 1918 to 1st Lt. Hamilton Coolidge who flew this aircraft in many hard fought combats. The plane became dangerously battle weary and was condemned on October 3, 1918. The actual left-hand squadron insignia and "22" survive today.

This Spad XIII was flown by 1st Lt. Joe Dawson at the III Army Carnival, Army of Occupation, Germany, Spring 1919. As the rudder surfaces of these decorated Spads were all overpainted, it is impossible to positively identify each aircraft. Dawson was assigned serial number 4505 when he joined the 94th on November 19, and which might be this aircraft.

This Spad XIII was flown by 1st Lt. John Jeffers and was nicknamed the "Japanese Flag" because of the rising sun motif. This plane may have been serial number 4589.

1st Lt. Robert W. Donaldson who joined the 94th on November 20, 1918 flew this checker-board design Spad XIII at the Carnival. It is interesting to note how the squares on the fuselage scale down in size as they progress toward the tail.

Maps

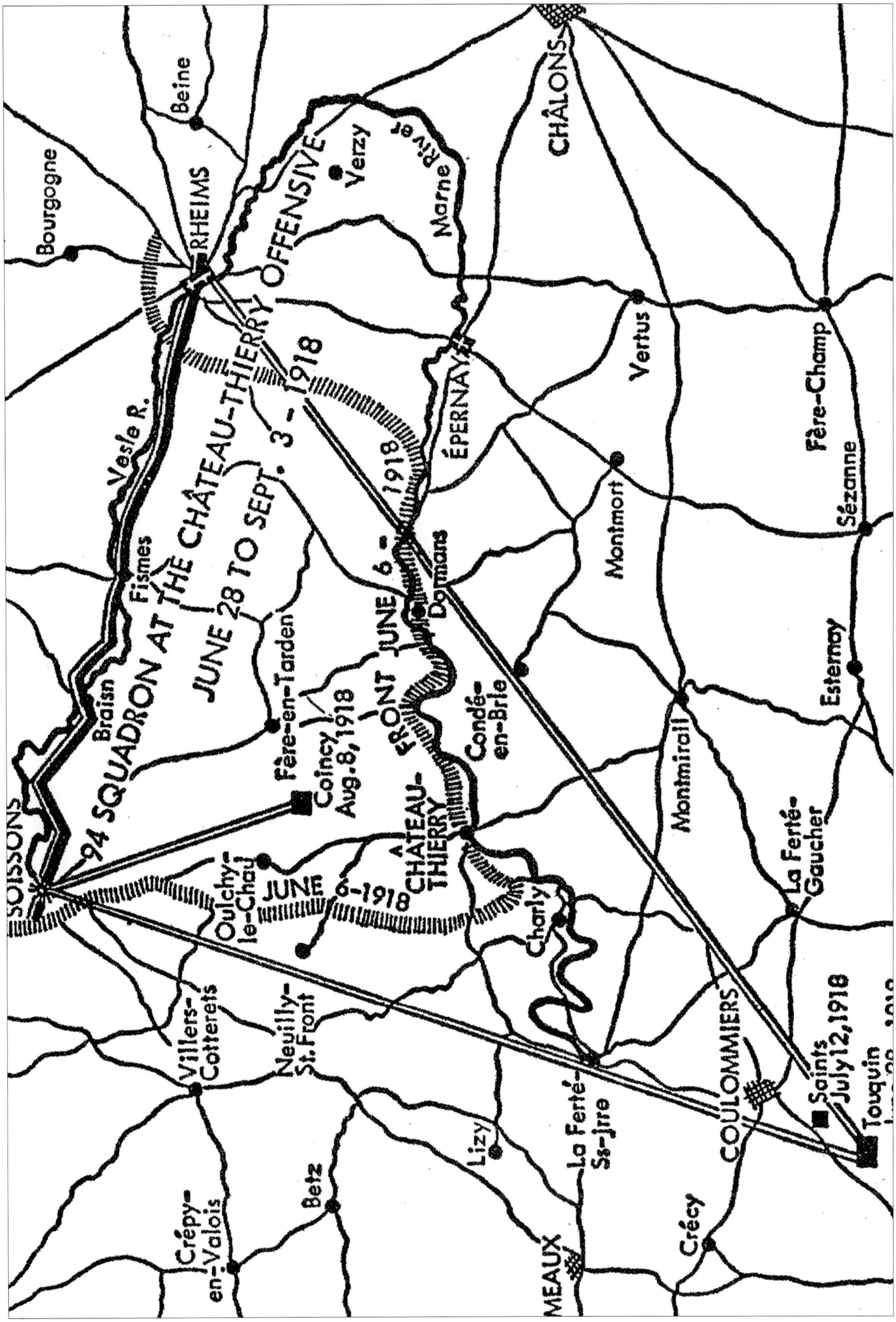

94 Squadron at the Château-Thierry offensive, June 28 to September 3, 1918.

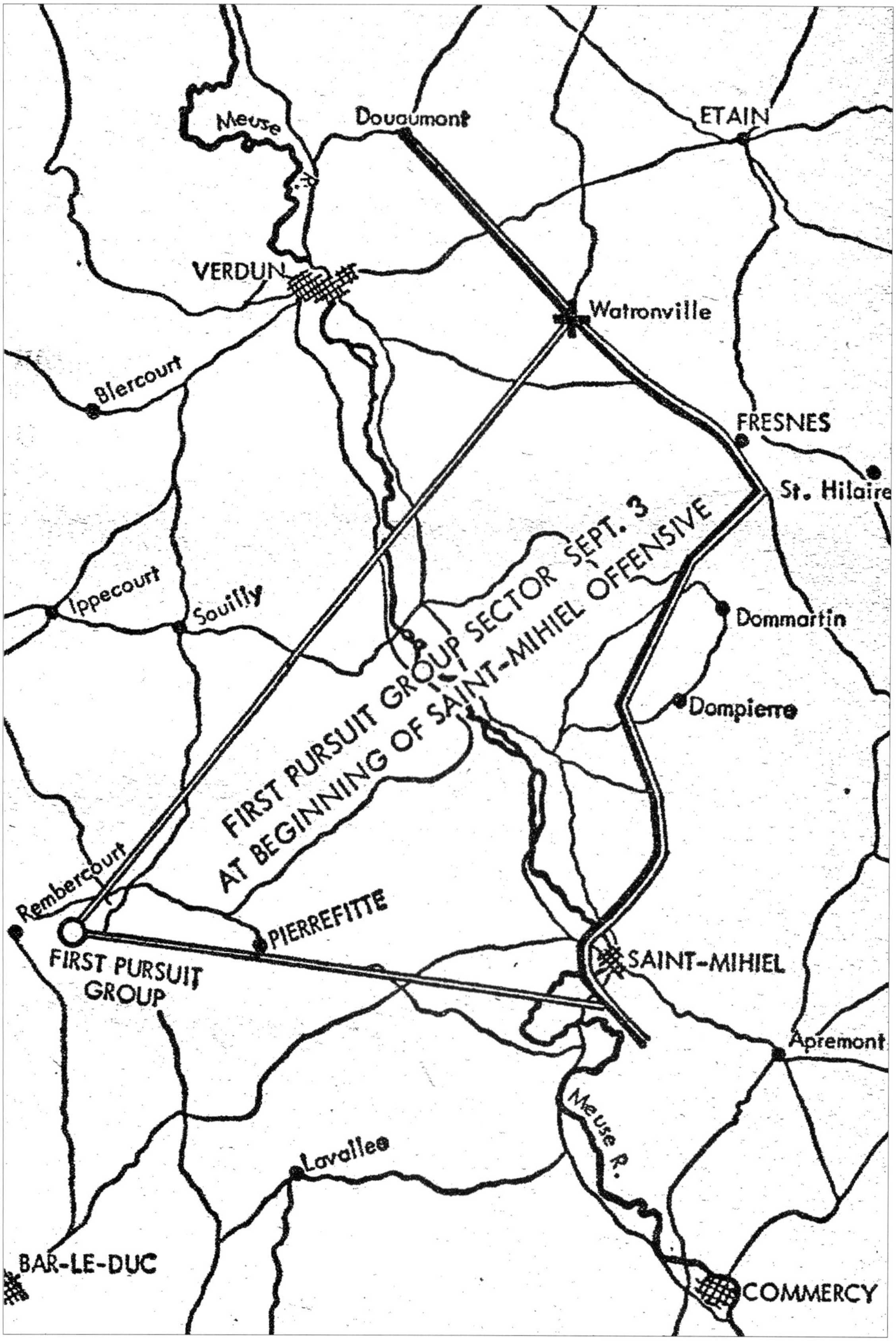

94 Squadron's patrol from Watronville to Saint-Mihiel. September 3-26, 1918.

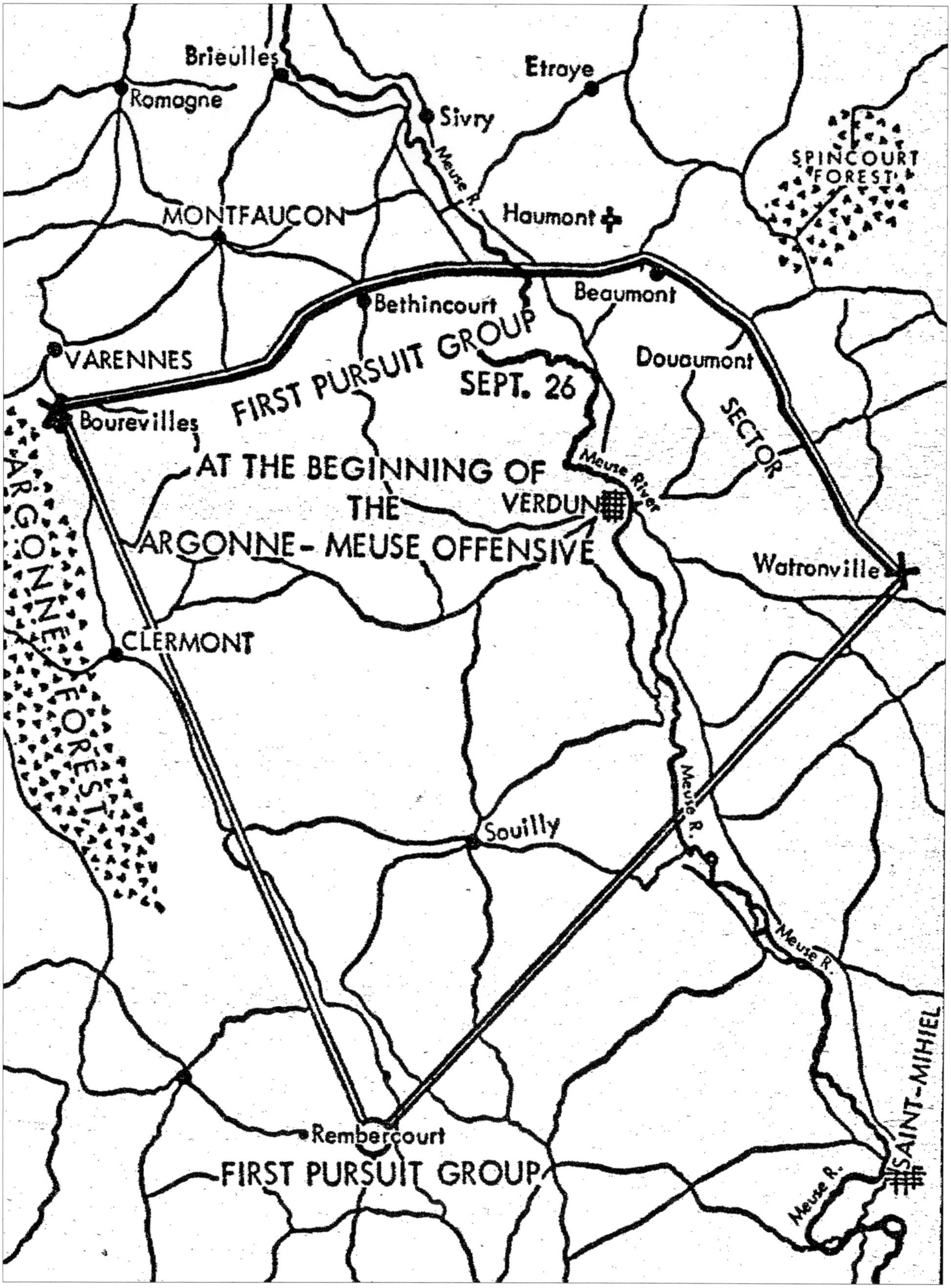

94 Squadron's patrol of the front lines from Bourevilles to Watronville

Appendices

Appendix 1
Citations for the Distinguished Service Cross for pilots of the 94th Aero Squadron

Campbell, Douglas

First lieutenant, 94th Aero Squadron, Air Service.
East of Flirey, France, May 19, 1918
R—Cambridge, Mass.
B—San Francisco, Calif.
G. O. No. 121. W. D., 1918

He attacked an enemy biplace at an altitude of 4,500 meters, east of Flirey, France. He rushed to the attack, but after shooting a few rounds his gun jammed. Undeterred by this accident, he maneuvered so as to protect himself, corrected the jam in mid air, and returned to the assault. After a short, violent action, the enemy plane took fire and crashed to the earth.

Oak-leaf Clusters (4).
One bronze oak leaf is awarded to Lieutenant Campbell for each of the following acts of extraordinary heroism in action: On May 27, 1918, he encountered three enemy monoplanes at an altitude of 3,000 meters over Montsec, France. Despite the superior strength of the enemy, he promptly attacked, and fighting a brilliant battle, shot down one German machine, which fell in three pieces, and drove the other two well within the enemy lines. On May 28, 1918, he saw six German Albatros aeroplanes flying toward him at an altitude of 2,000 meters, near Bois-de-Rate, France. Regardless of personal danger, he immediately attacked, and by skillful maneuvering and accurate operation of his machine gun he brought one plane down in flames and drove the other five back into their own lines. On May 13, 1918, he took the offensive against two German planes at an altitude of 2,500 meters over Lironville, France, shot down one of them, and pursued the other far behind the German lines. On June 5, 1918, accompanied by another pilot, he attacked two enemy battle planes at an altitude of 5,700 meters over Epley, France. After a spirited combat he was shot through the back by a machine-gun bullet, but in spite of his injury he kept on fighting until he had forced one of the enemy planes to the ground, where it was destroyed by artillery fire, and had driven the other plane back into its own territory.

Chambers, Reed M.

First lieutenant, 94th Aero Squadron, Air Service.
Over the region of Epinonville, France,
Sept. 29, 1918.
R—Memphis, Tenn.
B—Onaga, Kans.
G. O. No. 14. W.D., 1920

While on a mission, Lieutenant Chambers, accompanied by another machine piloted by First Lieut. Samuel Kaye, Jr., encountered a formation of six enemy machines (Fokker type) at an altitude of 3,000 feet. Despite numerical superiority of the enemy, Lieutenant Chambers and Lieutenant Kaye immediately attacked and succeeded in destroying one and forced the remaining five to retreat into their own lines.

Oak-leaf clusters (3).
A bronze oak-leaf cluster was awarded to Lieutenant Chambers for each of the following acts of extraordinary heroism in action: First oak-leaf cluster: Near Montfauçon and Vilosnes-sur-Meuse, France. Oct. 2, 1918, Lieutenant Chambers, while on a mission, at an altitude of 2,000 feet, encountered an enemy two-seater (Halberstadt type). He immediately attacked and, after a brief combat, succeeded in shooting it down. Second oak-leaf cluster: Near Montfauçon and Vilosnes-sur-Meuse, France, Oct. 2, 1918, at 7.40 o'clock, Lieutenant Chambers saw four enemy machines (Fokker type) attacking another American machine (Spad type). He immediately went to its rescue, and, after a few minutes of fierce combat, he succeeded in shooting down one. Third oak-leaf cluster: Near the Bois-de-la-Côte-Laimont, France, Oct. 22, 1918, while on a voluntary patrol, Captain Chambers encountered five enemy planes (Fokker type) harassing our infantry at an altitude of 300 meters. Attacking them without hesitation, he shot down two of them and drove the others off.

Jeffers, John N.

First lieutenant, 94th Aero Squadron, Air Service.
Over the region of Romagne, France,
Oct. 5, 1918.
R—Los Angeles, Calif.
B—Los Angeles, Calif.
G. O. No. 138, W.D., 1918

While on patrol he encountered 10 enemy machines (Fokker type) at an altitude of 2,000 feet. Despite numerical superiority and by a display of remarkable courage and skillful maneuvering, he separated one of the planes from the formation and after a brief encounter shot it down in flames.

Kaye, Samuel, Jr

First lieutenant, 94th Aero Squadron, Air Service.
Over the region of Epinonville, France,
Sept. 29, 1918.
R—Columbus, Miss.
B—Columbus, Miss.
G. O. No. 138, W. D., 1918

While on a mission he, accompanied by another machine piloted by Lieut. Reed M. Chambers, encountered a formation of 6 enemy machines (Fokker type) at an altitude of 3,000 feet. Despite numberical superiority of the enemy, Lieutenant Kaye and Lieutenant Chambers immediately attacked and succeeded in destroying 1 and forced the remaining 5 to retire into their own lines.

Oak-leaf cluster.
A bronze oak leaf is awarded to Lieutenant Kaye for the following act of extra-ordinary heroism in action over the region of Montfauçon and Bantheville, France, Oct. 5, 1918: He encountered a formation of 7 enemy machines (Fokker type). Regardless of their numerical superiority he immediately attacked, and by skillful maneuvering succeeded in separating 1 enemy plane from its formation and, after a short combat, shot it down in flames.

Meissner, James A.

First lieutenant, 94th Aero Squadron, Air Service.
In the Toul sector, France,
May 2, 1918.
R—Brooklyn, N.Y.
B—Canada
G.O. No. 138, W. D., 1918

He attacked 3 enemy planes at an altitude of 4,800 meters over the Foret de la Rappe, France. After a short fight he brought down 1 of the machines in flames. During the combat the entering wedge and the covering of the upper wings of his plane were torn away, and after the battle he was subjected to heavy fire from anti-aircraft batteries, but by skillful operation and cool judgment he succeeded in making a landing within the American lines.
Oak-leaf cluster.

A bronze oak leaf is awarded Lieutenant Meissner for the following act of extraordinary heroism in action: On May 30, 1918, he attacked 2 enemy planes at an altitude of 4,500 meters above Jaulny, France, and after a sharp engagement shot 1 down in flames and forced the other back into its own territory.

Rickenbacker, Edward V.

First lieutenant, 94th Aero Squadron, Air Service.
Near Montsec, France,
Apr. 29, 1918.
R—Columbus, Ohio.
B—Columbus, Ohio.
G. O. No. 121, W. D., 1918, and
G. O. No. 32, W. D., 1919.

He attacked an enemy Albatros monoplane, and after a vigorous fight, in which he followed his foe into German territory, he succeesed in shooting it down near Vigneulles-les-Hattonchatel.

Oak-leaf Clusters. (7).
One bronze oak leaf is awarded Lieutenant Rickenbacker for each of the following acts of extraordinary heroism in action: On May 17, 1918, he attacked 3 Albatros enemy planes, shooting 1 down in the vicinity of Richecourt, France, and forcing the others to retreat over their own lines. On May 22, 1918, he attacked 3 Albatros monoplanes 4,000 meters over St. Mihiel, France. He drove them back into German territory, separated 1 from the group, and shot it down near Flirey. On May 28, 1918, he sighted a group of 2 battle planes and 4 monoplanes, German planes, which he at once attacked vigorously, shooting down 1 and dispersing the others. On May 30, 1918, 4,000 meters over Jaulny, France, he attacked a group of 5 enemy planes. After a violent battle, he shot down 1 plane and drove the others away. On September 14, 1918, in the region of Villecey, he attacked 4 Fokker enemy planes at an altitude of 3,000 meters. After a sharp and hot action, he succeeded in shooting 1 down in flames and dispersing the other 3. On Sept. 15, 1918, in the region of Bois-de-Wavrille, he encountered 6 enemy planes, who were in the act of attacking 4 Spads, which were below them. Undeterred by their superior numbers, he unhesitatingly attacked them and succeeded in shooting 1 down in flames and completely breaking the formation of the others. On Sept. 25, 1918, near Billy, France, while on voluntary patrol over the lines he attacked 7 enemy planes (5 type Fokker, protecting 2 type Halberstadt). Disregarding the odds against him, he dived on them and shot down 1 of the Fokkers out of control. He then attacked 1 of the Halberstadts and sent it down also.

Appendix 2
List of Pilots Combats and Official Victories scored while serving with the 94th Aero Squadron

Pilots	Combats	Victories
Capt. E. V. Rickenbacker	50	26
1st Lt. Hamilton Coolidge	17	8
1st Lt. Reed Chambers	27	7
1st Lt. Harvey Weir Cook	16	7
1st Lt. Douglas Campbell	25	6
1st Lt. Samuel Kaye, Jr.	12	4
1st Lt. James Meissner	19	4
Capt. David McK. Peterson	5	3
1st Lt. William W. Palmer	9	3
1st Lt. John Jeffers	6	2
1st Lt. Thorne Taylor	17	2
1st Lt. Alan F. Winslow	13	2
1st Lt. Robert Z. Cates	7	1
1st Lt. Eugene Scroggie	1	1
1st Lt. Alden B. Sherry	5	1
1st Lt. Alan Nutt	1	1
1st Lt. Edwin M. Green	9	1
1st Lt. William F. Loomis	6	1
1st Lt. Wiley S. Sparks	3	1
1st Lt. Edward G. Garnsey	3	1
1st Lt. Charles W. Chapman	1	1
1st Lt. John DeWitt	2	1
Major Maxwell Kirby	1	1
Total		85*

These totals check out with one exception, with those shown in the "Air Service Information Circular," February 9, 1920, Vol. 1, No. 7. Enemy Aircraft Destroyed by U. S. Army Air Service. The exception was Rickenbacker who was credited in the Circular as having 25 confirmed, consisting of 21 planes and 4 balloons.

---

*The total number of 85 is higher than the Squadron total of 70 because many claims were shared by more than one pilot.

Appendix 3
Serving Officers of the 94th Aero Squadron Alphabetically by Rank

Rank	Name	Date Assigned	Remarks
Major	John W. F. M. Huffer	March 7, 1918	Relieved from duty as C. O. June 5, 1918; assigned to H.Q. Air Service as Liaison Officer
Major	Maxwell Kirby	October 15, 1918	Pilot; present November 11, 1918
Major	Raoul Lufbery	April 8, 1918	Killed in action May 19, 1918
Major	Kenneth Marr	April 8, 1918	Relieved as C. O. September 25, 1918; left for U. S.
Major	David McK. Peterson	April 8, 1918	Relieved May 16, 1918 to 95th Aero Squadron
Major	Carl Spatz	September 1, 1918	Relieved September 9, 1918 to 2nd Pursuit Group
Captain	Douglas Campbell	March 1, 1918	Wounded June 6, 1918; returned to 94th from temporary duty in U. S. November 24, 1918
Captain	Reed Chambers	March 1, 1918	Admitted to A. R. C. Hospital 3, November 3, 1918. Returned to Squadron November, 1918.
Captain	Hamilton Coolidge	June 17, 1918	Killed in action October 27, 1918
Captain	Cedric E. Faunt Le Roy	November 7, 1918	Pilot; present November 11, 1918
Captain	James M. Hall	April 8, 1918	Prisoner of War May 17, 1918
Captain	Seth Low	March 7, 1918	Relieved April 2, 1918 to 103rd Aero Squadron
Captain	Henry L. Lyster	March 1, 1918	Relieved March 6, 1918 to 1st Pursuit Group
Captain	James A. Meissner	March 7, 1918	To C. O. 147th Aero Squadron; returned to 94th November 15, 1918. Organization Center, A. E. F.
Captain	Edward V. Rickenbacker	March 7, 1918	Pilot; present and C. O. November 11, 1918
Captain	Bayard H. Smith	September 22, 1918	Adjutant; present November 11, 1918
Captain	Thorne C. Taylor	March 1, 1918	Pilot; present November 11, 1918
1st Lt	O. Eugene Adams	October 8, 1917	Non-flying; relieved of duty November 14, 1918
1st Lt	Charles Alexander	March 1, 1918	Relieved August 17, 1918 to 618th Aero Squadron
1st Lt	Hobart Baker	March 7, 1918	Relieved April 2, 1918 to 103rd Aero Squadron
1st Lt	Alexander B. Bruce	July 23, 1918	Killed in action August 17, 1918
1st Lt	Robert Z. Cates	June 7, 1918	Pilot; present November 11, 1918
1st Lt	William Chalmers	June 7, 1918	Prisoner of war July 7, 1918
1st Lt	Charles W. Chapman, Jr.	March 1, 1918	Killed in action May 3, 1918
1st Lt	Edwin R. Clark	June 6, 1918	Relieved September 13, 1918 to 1st Air Department
1st Lt	Robert L. Collins	October 1, 1918	Relieved November 12, 1918 to 185th Aero Squadron
1st Lt	Harvey Weir Cook	July 17, 1918	Pilot; present November 11, 1918
1st Lt	Lynn P. Cookson	March 1, 1918	Relieved March 14, 1918 to 3rd AIC
1st Lt	A. Cox, Jr.	October 10, 1918	Relieved November 12, 1918 to 185th Aero Squadron
1st Lt	Charles T. Crocker	September 14, 1918	Pilot; present November 11, 1918
1st Lt	Arthur L. Cunningham	March 1, 1918	Pilot, Interpreter, Historian; present November 11, 1918
1st Lt	Phillip W. Davis	March 1, 1918	Killed in action June 2, 1918
1st Lt	James L. Davitt	September 14, 1918	Operations Officer; present November 11, 1918
1st Lt	Leo H. Dawson	November 19, 1918	Pilot; present November 11, 1918
1st Lt	John DeWitt	September 30, 1918	Pilot; present November 11, 1918
1st Lt	Robert W. Donaldson	November 20, 1918	Pilot; present December, 1918

1st Lt	Godfrey K. Dower	October 8, 1917	Non-flying; relieved November 14, 1918
1st Lt	Joseph H. Eastman	March 7, 1918	Pilot; present November 11, 1918
1st Lt	Raymond W. Evitt	October 10, 1918	Pilot; present November 11, 1918
1st Lt	William Fowler	September 10, 1918	Pilot; present November 11, 1918
1st Lt	Edward C. Fisher	October 8, 1917	Relieved November 14, 1918
1st Lt	Edward G. Garnsey	September 16, 1918	Killed in action October 29, 1918
1st Lt	M. Edwin Green	March 7, 1918	Admitted to Evacuation Hospital #7
1st Lt	Oscar J. Gude	March 1, 1918	Relieved July 11, 1918
1st Lt	Charles I. Herrick	May 22, 1918	Relieved May 26, 1918 to 103rd Aero Squadron
1st Lt	Donald G. Herring	September 28, 1917	Ordnance; relieved to 4th Pursuit November 8, 1918
1st Lt	Willard D. Hill	May 11, 1918	Wounded in action May 27, 1918
1st Lt	Mendall E. Hopkins	September 9, 1918	Pilot; present November 11, 1918
1st Lt	Frank O. D. Hunter	May 22, 1918	Relieved May 26, 1918 to 103rd Aero Squadron
1st Lt	Marly R. Jackson	November 18, 1918	Radio Officer
1st Lt	John N. Jeffers	June 5, 1918	Pilot; present November 11, 1918
1st Lt	Ben C. Jones	October 10, 1918	Pilot; present November 11, 1918
1st Lt	Samuel Kaye, Jr.	July 16, 1918	Flight Commander; present November 11, 1918
1st Lt	Paul B. Kurtz	May 18, 1918	Killed in action May 22, 1918
1st Lt	William F. Loomis	March 1, 1918	Relieved August 11, 1918 to 213th Aero Squadron
1st Lt	John A. MacKenzie	October 10, 1918	Pilot; present November 11, 1918
1st Lt	J. Loy Maloney	July 25, 1918	Pilot; present November 11, 1918
1st Lt	Henry B. Marshall	October 10, 1918	Relieved January 14, 1918 to 185th Aero Squadron
1st Lt	William G. Morrison	May 18, 1918	Relieved January 14, 1918; assigned to Gunnery School
1st Lt	Byron B. Norris	November 3, 1918	Relieved November 20, 1918 to 1st Pursuit Group
1st Lt	Alan Nutt	September 16, 1918	Killed in action September 26, 1918
1st Lt	Frederick I. Ordway	June 6, 1918	Relieved June 20, 1918 to 27th Aero Squadron
1st Lt	Dudley M. Outcault	September 29, 1918	Pilot; present November 11, 1918
1st Lt	William W. Palmer	July 16, 1918	Pilot; present November 11, 1918
1st Lt	Charles A. Pankow	October 9, 1917	Non-flying; relieved November 14, 1918
1st Lt	Walter H. Parker	August 17, 1918	Relieved October 2, 1918 to 27th Aero Squadron
1st Lt	LeRoy J. Prinz	June 6, 1918	Relieved July 11, 1918 to 27th Aero Squadron
1st Lt	Charles A. Rankin	March 1, 1918	Engineering Officer; present
1st Lt	Emery A. Samson	September 4, 1918	Pilot; present November 11, 1918
1st Lt	Raymond J. Saunders	September 26, 1918	Killed in action October 22, 1918
1st Lt	Eugene R. Scroggie	September 9, 1918	P.O.W. October 3, 1918
1st Lt	Alden B. Sherry	June 5, 1918	Pilot; present November 11, 1918
1st Lt	Cedric A. Smith	September 20, 1918	Relieved November 19, 1918 to 27th Aero Squadron
1st Lt	Walter W. Smythe	May 11, 1918	Killed in action August 17, 1918
1st Lt	Chester A. Snow, Jr.	June 9, 1918	Pilot; present November 11, 1918
1st Lt	Wiley S. Sparks	July 16, 1918	Pilot; present November 11, 1918
1st Lt	Sigourney Thayer	October 11, 1918	Relieved October 18, 1918 to 95th Aero Squadron
1st Lt	Harold H. Tittmann	June 7, 1918	Wounded in action July 2, 1918
1st Lt	Edgar G. Tobin	March 7, 1918	Relieved April 2, 1918 to 103rd Aero Squadron
1st Lt	John Wentworth	March 1, 1918	Relieved August 4, 1918 to 49th Aero Squadron
1st Lt	Alan F. Winslow	March 1, 1918	Wounded and P.O.W. July 31, 1918
1st Lt	George W. Zacharias	June 5, 1918	Admitted to Hospital 3 October 18, 1918

Appendix 4
94th Aero Squadron Nieuport Aircraft

Serial No.	Side No.	Principal Pilots	Earliest Date	Latest Date	Disposition	Remarks
6137		(Sewall, 95 AS)		03/31/18	Burned	Burned in hangar fire – Villeneuve-les-Vertus
6138	0	(Buckley, 95 AS) Peterson		05/03/18		
6140	0	(McLanahan, 95 AS) Chapman		04/20/18	in flames	Chapman KIA by Ltn. Wenig of Jasta 80b
6141		(Blodgett, 95 AS)		03/31/18	burned	
6142	23	(Taylor, 95 AS) Hill	04/20/18	05/27/18		Hill WIA; wrecked landing behind the lines
6144	8	(Casgrain, 95 AS) Meissner; Cates	04/20/18			Meissner stripped wing fabric 05/02/18 and 05/30/18
6148	13	(Richards, 95 AS) Taylor	03/18/18		147 AS	Damaged in collision with Marr 5/10; rep 05/13/18
6149	21	(Woolley, 95 AS) Campbell/Eastman	04/20/18	05/19/18	wrecked	Eastman wrecked at Menil-la-Tour
6150		(Curtis, 95 AS)		03/31/18	damaged	Damaged in fire at Villeneuve-les-Vertus
6151	14	Cunningham; Eastman;	03/18/18			Chalmers broke landing gear at Dogneville 06/09/18
6153	17	(Buford, 95 AS); Hall	03/21/18	05/07/18	lost over lines	Hall POW between Quellenlager and Vieville
6154	7	(Fisher, 95 AS); Gude; Morrison	03/18/18	06/07/18		Sherry forced landing – written off
6158	0	Peterson; Campbell	04/20/18			Campbell WIA 06/05/18; repaired 06/09/18
6159	12	Rickenbacker; Zacharias	03/18/18			
6163	9	Cunningham; Clark; Coolidge	04/20/18			
6164	10	Campbell	03/18/18	05/04/18	condemned	Campbell first squadron victory 04/14/18
6165		(Rhodes, 95 AS); Eastman		04/12/18	wrecked	Eastman wrecked at Gengoult
6168	5	Wentworth	03/18/18	06/07/18	condemned	Lt. Morlan flew at Colombey-les-Belles after 06/07/18
6169	1	Huffer, Rickenbacker	04/13/18			Rickenbacker stripped wing fabric 05/17/18
6172	6	Marr; Winslow	03/18/18	05/10/18	wrecked	Marr collided with Taylor on field at Gengoult
6178	16	Davis, Lufbery	03/18/18	05/19/18	in flames	Lufbery KIA
6179	11	Chambers	03/18/18			
6180	18	Green; Sherry; Prinz; Jeffers	03/21/18			Prinz forced landing; damaged 06/09/18; rep 06/24/18
6181	15	Loomis; Jeffers; Chalmers	03/18/18	07/07/18	lost over lines	Chalmers POW; plane captured intact
6184	3	Winslow	03/18/18	05/21/18	condemned	Winslow second squadron victory 04/14/18
6185	10	(McKeown, 95 AS) Gude; Kurtz	04/20/18	05/22/18	crash/burn	Plane caught fire in the air; Kurtz killed

6189	6	Marr/Winslow	05/11/18	06/16/18		
6193	2	Lufbery; Davis	03/18/18	06/02/18	in flames	Lufbery rolled over 05/01/18; rep 05/04/18, Davis KIA
6195	8	Meissner	03/18/18	04/20/18	wrecked	Meissner rolled over on field
6201	20	Eastman (?); (Martin, 27 AS)		07/14/18	27 AS (3)	Eastman wrecked 07/02/18 (?); Martin rolled over
6230	4	Smythe; Sherry	05/09/18	08/06/18	salvaged	Smythe forced landing Villers-en-Haye 05/23/18 – OK
6232		(Robertson, 147 AS)		07/14/18	147 AS (5)	Returned from 147 AS 08/14/18
6236	17	Marr	05/09/18			
6243						
6253		(Wells, 147 AS)		07/14/18	147 AS	Wells crashed at Basseville 07/16/18
6254	5	Meissner	06/15/18			
6260	20	Cunningham; Eastman	06/01/18			Probably wrecked by Eastman 06/28/18
6271	7	Tittmann	06/16/18			
6272				07/21/18	147 AS	Salvaged upon receipt from 94 AS
6275	2	Loomis; (Sands, 27 AS)	06/01/18		27 AS	Sands KIA in flames over lines 08/01/18
6283	16	Rickenbacker; Smythe	05/28/18			
6297	3	Green; (Muther, 147 AS)	06/01/18	07/14/18	147 AS (12)	
6349	13	Taylor, (Harmon, 147 AS)	06/01/18	07/14/18	147 AS	Harmon wrecked at Saints 07/20/18

Compiled by Alan D. Toelle

Appendix 5
94th Aero Squadron Spad XIII Airplanes

Serial #	Squadron #	Pilot	Date to Squadron	Disposition
4505	4	Dawson Nutt	07/14/18	09/26/18 Nutt KIA/ A/C Lost
4523	1	Rickenbacker	07/07/18	Returned to Depot 1919
4526	11	Chambers	07/14/18	Condemned 09/25/18
4538	7	Snow	07/18/18	Condemned 09/25/18
4573	20	Palmer	07/15/18	Condemned 09/28/18
4589	3	Taylor, Jeffers	07/14/18	Motor trouble 09/15/18
4605	-	—	09/18/18	09/29/18
4627	21	Maloney	09/01/18	09/17/18
4628	2	Kaye	09/07/18	09/17/18
4629	-	Palmer	09/07/18	09/29/18
7623	17	Spare	09/19//18	09/26/18
7646	5	Spare	09/26/18	09/29/18
7651	26	Spare	09/17/18	Transferred to 95th Aero
7675	10	Crocker	09/17/18	09/19/18
7708	-	Saunders	10/03/18	Saunders KIA 10/22/18 A/C Lost
7743	-	Coolidge	10/04/18	10/27/18 Coolidge KIA A/C Lost
7777	3	Faunt Le Roy		A/C was transferred
8884	-	Garnsey	09/24/18	10/29/18 Garnsey KIA A/C Lost
15003	15	Crocker	07/14/18	09/14/18 A/C Wrecked
15004	10	Spare	07/25/28	09/08/18 Reported panned
15006	19	Eastman	07/14/18	09/26/18 Reported panned
15011	18	Green	07/14/18	09/15/18 Reported panned
15014	17	Marr	07/14/18	09/18/18 Reported panned
15015	-	—	07/14/18	07/19/18 Wrecked
15021	13	Taylor	07/14/18	09/28/18
15022	5	Sparks	07/14/18	09/25/18 Condemned
15027	2	Clark	07/16/18	09/05/18 Experiencing motor trouble
15031	9	Cates	07/18/18	09/25/18 Motor trouble
15034	22	Coolidge	07/18/18	10/03/18 Condemned Combat Damage
15042	12	Zacharias	07/14/18	09/16/18 Continuing Mechanical problems
15052	8	Sherry	07/14/18	08/17/18 Structural & Mechanical problems
15056	23	Spare	07/16/18	08/23/18 Wrecked
15058	14	Sparks	07/16/18	08/19/18 Continued

				Mechanical problems
15067	6 (?)	Winslow	07/18/18	07/31/18 Winslow shot down A/C destroyed
15130	16	Kaye	08/03/18	09/26/18 Panned
15169	24	Cook	07/22/18	08/23/18 Continued Mechanical problems
15225	6	Chambers	09/01/18	09/28/18 Continued Mechanical problems
15234	-	Smythe	08/08/18	08/17/18}Smythe &
15277	-	Bruce	08/08/18	08/17/18} Bruce were killed in a mid-air collision
15561	30	Scroggie	09/24/18	04/20/19 Transferred
16546	0	Chambers	11/05/18	04/20/19 Transferred

There were other Spads which show up briefly in the 94th records, but no actual service with the squadron is indicated. This list, as well as the Nieuport 28 list, was compiled by Alan Toelle and kindly shared with the author.

Bibliography

Air Service Information Circular, Heavier Than Air, Enemy Aircraft Destroyed by U. S. Army Air Service. (Washington, D.C.: The Director of Air Service, February 9, 1920.) Lists all victories of every American in U. S. uniform regardless of number or country of service.

American Battle Monuments Commission. *American Armies and Battlefield in Europe.* (Washington: U. S. Government Printing Office, 1938.)

Aviation Militaire. *Flying School of Tours, Instructions for the American Pupils.* (Tours: E. Arrault et Cie, 1917.)

Aviation Militaire. *Silhouettes d'Avions, Allies et Enemis.* (Paris: Paul Dupont, Mai 1918.)

Aviation Militaire. *Silhouettes d'Avions, Classées par analogie.* (Paris: Adrien Maréchal, Avril 1917.)

Brewer, Leighton. *Riders of the Sky.* (Boston and New York: Houghton Mifflin Company, 1934.)

Bruce, J. M. *Warplanes of the First World War, fighters. Volumes IV and V, France.* (Garden City, NY: Doubleday and Company Inc., 1972.)

Campbell, Douglas. *Let's Go Where The Action Is!* Privately printed by the author. (Cos Cob, Conn. 1968.)

Chinn, George M., Lt. Col. USMC. *The Machine Gun, Volume I.* (Washington: U. S. Government Printing Office, 1951.)

Christienne, Gen. Charles, Lissarrague, Gen. Pierre, et al. *Histoire de l'Aviation Militaire Française.* (Paris and Limoges: Charles-Lavauzelle, 1980.)

Coolidge, Hamilton, Captain. *Letters of an American Airman, Being the War Record of Captain Hamilton Coolidge, USA 1917 – 1918.* (Boston: Privately Printed, 1919.)

Cross & Cockade Journal. The Society of World War I Aero Historians. Various issues.

Davilla, Dr. James J. and Soltan, Arthur M. *French Aircraft of the First World War.* (Stratford, Conn: Flying Machine Press, 1997.)

Decorations United States Army - 1862-1926. (Washington: U. S. Government Printing Office, 1927.

Ellis, Chris. *Military Transport of World War I.* (London: Blandford Press Ltd, 1970.)

Franks, Norman L. R. and Bailey, Frank W. *Over The Front* (London: Grub Street, 1992.)

Franks, Norman L. R., Bailey, Frank W., and Guest, Russell. *Above the Lines.* (London: Grub Street, 1993.)

Franks, Norman L. R., Bailey, Frank W., and Duiven, Rick. *The Jasta Pilots.* (London: Grubb Street, 1996.)

Franks, Norman, Bailey, Frank, and Duiven, Rick. *Casualties of the German Air Service, 1914-1920.* (London: Grub Street, 1999.)

Franks, Norman. *Who Downed the Aces in World War I?* (London: Grubb Street, 1996.)

Gordon, Denis. *The Lafayette Flying Corps. The American Volunteers in the French Air Service in World War One.* (Atglen, PA: Schiffer Military History, 2000.)

Gorrell, Edgar S. Colonel, U. S. A., et al. *History of the U. S. Army Air Service 1917 – 1919.* (National Archives Record Group 120 A. E. F. [World War I] 1917 – 1923.)

Gurney, Gene, Captain, U.S.A.F. *Five Down and Glory.* (New York: G. P. Putnam's Sons, 1958.)

Hall, James Norman and Nordhoff, Charles Bernard. Editors. *The Lafayette Flying Corps.* 2 Volumes. (Boston and New York: Houghton Mifflin Company, 1920.)

Hess, William N. Editor. *American Fighter Aces Album.* (Dallas, TX, Covena, CA: Taylor Publishing, 1979.)

Hicks, James E., Major U.S.A. *French Military Weapons, 1717 to 1938.* (New Milford, Conn: N. Flayderman & Co., 1964.)

Howe, M. A. DeWolfe. *Memories of the Harvard Dead in the War Against Germany, V Volumes.* (Cambridge, Mass: Harvard University Press, 1924.)

Kilduff, Peter. *Over the Battlefronts.* (London: Arms and Armor Press, 1996.)

Lamberton, W. M., Compiler. *Reconnaissance & Bomber Aircraft of the 1914-1918 War.* (Letchworth, Herts., England: Harleyford Publications Ltd., 1962.)

Maurer, Maurer. Editor. *The U. S. Air Service in World War I.* IV Volumes. The Albert F. Simpson Historical Research Center, Maxwell AFB, Alabama. (Washington, DC: Government Printing Office, 1978.)

Moreau-Bérillon, Commandant E. *L'Aviation Française 1914-1940.* (Paris: Chez L'Auteur, 1968.)

Munson, Kenneth. *Bombers Patrol and Reconnaissance Aircraft 1914-1919.* (New York: Macmillan Company, 1968.)

Munson, Kenneth. *Fighters Attack and Training Aircraft 1914-1919.* (New York: The Macmillan Company, 1968.)

Nettleton, George Henry, Editor. *Yale in the World War, 2 Volumes.* (New Haven: Yale University Press, 1925.)

Nowarra, Heinz J., Brown Kimbrough S. *von Richthofen and the Flying Circus.* (Letchworth, Herts, England: The Garden City Press Ltd., 1959.)

Over The Front. Journal of the League of World War I Aviation Historians. Various Issues.

Richards, Henry Howe. Editor. *Groton School in the War.* (Cambridge, Mass: Harvard University Press, 1925.)

Rickenbacker, Edwin V. *Fighting the Flying Circus.* (New York, N.Y: Doubleday 1919, 1963.)

Robertson, Bruce. Editor. *Air Aces of the 1914-1918 War.* (Letchworth, Herts, England: Garden City Press Ltd. 1959.)

Rockwell, Paul Ayers. *American Fighters in the Foreign Legion 1914-1918.* (Boston and New York: Houghton Mifflin Company, 1930.)

Thetford, O. G. and Riding, E. J. Compilers. *Aircraft of the 1914-1918 War.* (Harleyford, Marlow, Bucks, England: The Harborough Publishing Company Ltd., 1954.)

Ticknor, Caroline. Compiler. *New England Aviators, 1914-1918, 2 Volumes.* (Atglen, PA: Schiffer Military History, 1997.)

Treadwell, Terry C. and Wood, Alan C. *German Knights of the Air 1914-1918.* (London, Washington: Brassey's, 1997.)

Weeks, Dr. Raymond, Taylor, Frank J., et al. Compilers. *History of the American Field Service in France, III Vols.* (Boston and New York: Houghton Mifflin Company, 1920.)

Willcox, Cornélis DeWitt. *A French-English Military Technical Dictionary.* (Washington: Government Printing Office, 1917.)

Index

29658